In the past, researchers have treated the development of the emotions and the task of emotional regulation as two separate topics, the former emphasizing normative questions and the latter emphasizing individual differences. An understanding of the first has not been seen as relevant to the second. By bringing them under the perspective of development and emphasizing common core processes, *Emotional Development* illuminates both topics.

All emotions are expressions of arousal, or "tension": Whether a given emotion can or does occur depends on the developed capacity to generate tension and on the meaning of an event in its context, which change with age. *Emotional Development* reveals the common core processes underlying the emergence of specific emotions and the capacity for emotion regulation. It explains the timing of emotional emergence and why emotions function as they do; it also explores individual styles of emotional regulation. Close ties between emotional, cognitive, and social development are discussed as well.

This book will appeal to professors, graduate students, and clinicians who study developmental, cognitive, and social psychology.

Cambridge Studies in Social and Emotional Development

General Editor: Martin L. Hoffman, New York University

*Advisory Board: Robert N. Emde, Willard W. Hartup,
Robert A. Hinde, Lois W. Hoffman, Carroll E. Izard,
Nicholas Blurton Jones, Jerome Kagan, Franz J. Mönks,
Paul Mussen, Ross D. Parke, and Michael Rutter*

Emotional development

Emotional development

The organization of emotional life in the early years

L. ALAN SROUFE
Institute of Child Development
University of Minnesota

PUBLISHED BY THE PRESS SYNDICATE OF THE UNIVERSITY OF CAMBRIDGE
The Pitt Building, Trumpington Street, Cambridge CB2 1RP

CAMBRIDGE UNIVERSITY PRESS
The Edinburgh Building, Cambridge CB2 2RU, United Kingdom
40 West 20th Street, New York, NY 10011-4211, USA
10 Stamford Road, Oakleigh, Melbourne 3166, Australia

First published 1995
Reprinted 1997
First paperback edition 1997

Library of Congress Cataloging-in-Publication Data is available.

A catalog record for this book is available from the British Library.

ISBN 0-521-47486-8 hardback
ISBN 0-521-62992-6 paperback

Transferred to digital printing 2002

For June:
consultant, primary reviewer, inspiration

Contents

vii

Preface

For more than two decades graduate students have come to the University of Minnesota to work on an ongoing longitudinal study of 180 children and their families begun in 1974. The children have been followed year by year from birth to early adulthood. Of course, the special knowledge developed by any particular group of students has tended to center around the ages of the child subjects during the time those students worked on the project. Thus, some students became knowledgeable, and in time even leading experts, on infant emotional development, temperament, and attachment relationships. Others became experts on the emotional functioning of the preschool child and/or the structure and functioning of the preschool peer group and/or parent–child relationships during the preschool period. Later students mastered the intricacies of friendships and peer group functioning, school adjustment and school-related problems, or the development of the sense of self in middle childhood. More recent students have probed identity formation, adolescent family relationships, the challenges of intimacy in adolescence, and child and adolescent psychopathology.

I have come to lament this situation. This is not because development is less interesting with age. Each period of development has been fascinating, and I doubt that the students thought wistfully about how much more interesting an earlier period might have been. Rather, I sensed that the students were becoming further and further removed from the beginning – the beginning of development and the inception of our project itself. To be sure, the students read early reports and did analyses linking each new period with all that had gone before. They could articulate, even better than we could at the beginning, why early attachment quality would be related to later functioning and what would promote or diminish such ties. And they certainly got a feel for development by comparing the current age period with the one before (and by thinking about what lay ahead). But later students didn't have the time to immerse themselves in each preceding period, and when they considered earlier development it was primarily with regard to individual differences. For example, many understood differences in attachment quality, but few were fully informed about normative emotional development.

This situation is somewhat true of the field as a whole. Middle childhood and adolescence, neglected to some extent historically, have come to the fore as foci of study. Moreover, even when infant social and emotional development remains the focus, current research is often concerned only with individual differences – for example, differences in temperament or attachment.

This is not a plea for a return to the good old days. In fact, our earlier students were somewhat short-changed because they weren't able to see long-term outcomes; they were there for the planting but not the harvest. And the field of socioemotional development in general is rightly considering individual differences in some detail. Rather, this is a call to refresh our knowledge of early emotional life.

The study of early emotional development is vital for several reasons. First, it illustrates the fundamental nature of development itself. Even after all these years, it provides unsurpassed examples of the developmental process. Second, it reveals the necessarily close link between the study of normative development and the understanding of individual differences. We forget this link, and it is a lesson to be relearned often. Too many studies of individual differences pay no attention to normative development. Finally, emotional development is the foundation for the study of individual adaptation and psychopathology. Pursuing these fields without being fully grounded in emotional development is analogous to trying to do research in genetics without being grounded in biology.

Even current research in emotional development seems at times to move along without sufficient regard for the solid work of the past. Currently, a major focus is emotional regulation. But this work too rarely makes contact with the descriptive work on the development of the specific emotions, in part because much of this work is now decades old. It is important to bring forward the lessons of the past and at the same time redraw them with an eye on current problems and current understanding.

Thesis

The overall thesis of this book can be summarized in the following seven points:

1. Each specific affect (such as joy or fear) evolves according to the principles of development; that is, it emerges from precursors according to a discernible process, involving transformation and qualitative change, yet maintenance of core aspects.
2. Striking parallels across affect systems exist, in accord with the proposition of "repetitive" processes in development.
3. A key process in affect expression and its change with development concerns the fluctuation of arousal, or what may be better defined as *tension* (but in distinction to the psychoanalytic use of the term).
4. Whether positive or negative affect occurs depends on the degree of tension

engendered, the infant's or child's capacity to modulate that tension, and the context in which the tension is engendered. Increasingly, that context is not purely the physical situation but, rather, the infant's evaluation of the situation.

5. Developmental change centers, therefore, on the capacity for engendering tension, the capacity for modulating tension, and the changing capacity for evaluating threatening or supportive aspects of the context.

6. Similarly, these are three key aspects of individual differences as the child matures.

7. There is a critical role for the infant–caregiver relationship as (a) a critical feature of context (and therefore the infant's evaluation of events) and (b) a basis for developing "procedures" for modulating tension and establishing basic expectations with regard to the disorganizing or growth-promoting potentials of tension.

In considering both normative development and individual differences, a central thesis of this book is that development always builds on what was previously present. Emerging forms of emotion build on precursors, and individual patterns of emotional regulation build on patterns of regulation earlier achieved within the caregiving relationship.

Part I

The nature of emotional development

1   A developmental perspective on emotions

> The premier developmental question is, of course, the nature of the transition
> from one developmental stage to another – the emergence of new forms. How
> does a system retain continuity and yet produce discontinuous manifestations?
>
> Thelen (1989)

The subject of this book is human emotion, with a focus on the early years. The topics include the expression of specific emotions (such as joy, fear, and anger), as well as more complex emotional reactions. Also discussed is the place of emotion in the organization and stream of behavior, ties between emotion and other aspects of functioning such as cognition, and the management or regulation of emotion by individuals. While in the past each of these topics has been approached in a variety of ways, they have often been treated individually. Here they are approached in concert and from a particular perspective, that of development.

A developmental approach offers considerable leverage for understanding behavior. It yields a dynamic view, analogous to seeing films of an animal in motion as opposed to still photographs of the animal at rest. Knowing what led up to something, the network of changes in which it is nested, and its later manifestations provides a critical perspective for understanding. As we will discuss, the smile of the newborn is more meaningful because of what it portends, and the laughter of the 8-month-old is more understandable because of what has preceded it.

To someone considering the expression of joy or other aspects of emotional life in young humans, a developmental perspective means a number of things. For one, it is a particular way of looking at the origins and emergence of behavior, as well as how earlier behavior evolves to later behavior. This includes not only how an emotional reaction at one age differs from that at another age, but also how the later reaction is an outgrowth of the former. A simple interest in the age at which some reaction emerges based on a given criterion does not in itself define a developmental position (e.g., Werner & Kaplan, 1963). Beyond the simple chronology of events, there is an interest in *process* – that is, the

3

nature of the unfolding of these events. In a developmental perspective there is concern with the convergence, coordination, and integration of various threads of behavior change over time, as well as across categories and even domains of behavior. A developmental approach involves looking at the way behavior is organized at a particular point in time and considering both the implications for subsequent behavioral organization and the history of prior organizations.

A developmental perspective also entails a particular way of looking at individual differences. Differences in age of manifesting some particular emotional reaction are only the starting point. One has a special interest in the various ways the normative process of emotional growth goes awry. Therefore, by determining the nature of core features of the normative process one guides the study of individual differences. For example, if a key feature of normative change in emotional expression lies in the tolerance or management of stimulation or arousal, individual differences in regulatory capacities would be examined.

Developmental questions

A unique set of questions emerges when one brings a developmental perspective to bear on the study of early emotion. One asks *when* affects emerge in some form, for example, but, in addition, *how* they emerge; that is, one is concerned with the nature of the unfolding process and the precursors and subsequent transformations of the emotional reaction in question. Moreover, one asks questions about the place of emotional expressions in the overall organization of behavior. How does this change with development? Like other researchers, a developmentalist would want to explain why emotional reactions occur, why they take the form they do, and why they are organized as they are with other behavior. But such questions are approached from an integrative perspective.

Nico Tinbergen (1951), the prominent ethologist, pointed out years ago that the question of why any animal exhibits a particular behavior actually entails four separate questions. These also apply to emotions in the young child and help to define a developmental perspective. The first question, the proximal cause question, is, Why does the animal exhibit the behavior at this particular moment? What caused the reaction now? The second question is, How did the animal grow to respond this way? What were the steps that led to this behavior over the course of the animal's life? Third, why does this *kind* of animal ever behave this way; that is, what is the function of the behavior for the animal (in terms of promoting adaptation or survival of this particular species)? Finally, what are the evolutionary origins of the behavior – that is, how did it evolve phylogenetically?

While it is the second of these questions that is most specifically developmental, a complete developmental viewpoint embraces each of these four levels of explanation. For example, proximal causes of emotional expressions in humans are not static; rather, they too change with development. The same event will prompt one reaction at one age and a totally different reaction at another. Three-month-olds smile at strangers' faces, but later show neutral and then wary expressions. Likewise, the same emotion may be elicited by different events at different ages. Young infants smile when their kicking makes a mobile turn; toddlers smile after solving a problem. Such things are of as much interest to a developmentalist as the age at which a single, given reaction first occurred or the age at which an event first produced a reaction of some kind. Further, the same overt behavior may serve different functions in different contexts, and both functions and context sensitivity change with development. Thus, affective expressions in very young infants may elicit tender feelings or ministrations from adults, and later similar expressions may encourage or discourage interaction; for example, a newborn's sleep smile makes a caregiver feel warmly toward the infant, while later laughter encourages continuation of a game. Both expressions of positive emotion play a role in the infant's adaptation, but in different ways at different ages. Even the place of emotions in the organized functioning of the organism, in comparison with and contrast to somewhat analogous behaviors of other animals, becomes clarified in a developmental analysis (such as comparing threat and appeasement gestures in various species).

To illustrate the scope of a developmental approach, consider the following example:

A 12-month-old infant plays with a variety of toys on the floor of a laboratory playroom. Her mother sits a short distance away. As the child examines various objects in front of her, a large puzzle piece (a brightly colored orange carrot) briefly captures her attention. She then grasps the piece with widened eyes and in a smooth motion turns and extends it in the direction of her mother, smiling broadly and vocalizing. Her mother returns her smile and comments about the carrot.

Given the presence of the smile in this everyday scenario, all observers would agree that an emotional reaction has occurred. But what the smile means, *why* it occurred, could be given a number of interpretations. From a developmental perspective, full understanding of this seemingly simple affective reaction requires consideration of the several levels of explanation proposed by Tinbergen.

In explaining why the infant exhibited the observed positive affect at this moment, Tinbergen's proximal cause question, at least three things might be considered. First, it is clear that a somewhat advanced recognition process occurred and that there was some special meaning of the carrot piece for the infant.

Explaining this meaning, of course, would entail a great deal, including cognitive and experiential (feelings) considerations, as well as the history of experience with such an object. Still, we can say that the affect was "caused" by the infant's recognition of the carrot. Second, we also would note the place of the affective expression in the stream of behavior. We would consider the systematic deployment of attention and the strong orienting reaction that preceded the recognition process and affective expression. This would include the role of maturing physiological and neurophysiological changes. We could say that the smile was caused by this psychophysiological reaction (though we may want to define the total emotional reaction as including it). Finally, we would attend to the surrounding context that supports the affective behavior, most notably the presence of the caregiver. Without the caregiver as the object of sharing, it is doubtful that the affective reaction would have been of the same magnitude, and it may not have occurred at all. Thus, even the question of why the infant smiled in this instance involves considerable complexity.

In approaching the question of how the infant grew to show this behavior – that is, the developmental course of such an observed reaction – we would again be concerned with a number of issues. What does the 12-month-old's reaction draw on and build on from the early months of life, yet how is it qualitatively different from what was present before? How is this reaction the same and different from the reaction of younger infants? In the first half year infants clearly show smiles of recognition. Is there then no development reflected in this 12-month-old's behavior? Surely this cannot be. We would note changes in the timing (immediacy), magnitude, and specificity of the reaction, which Thompson (1990) refers to as the "dynamics" of emotion. When smiles of recognition first emerge in the early months of life, considerable inspection by the infant (and often gradually building excitement) precedes the smile. Here the reaction is immediate, on sight. This suggests a qualitative advance toward categorical, memory-based meaning, where concepts are affectively colored. All of this is supported by neurophysiological development. Further, we would note the place of the affective reaction in the stream of behavior and its organization with the other behaviors that co-occur and follow it. There are notable developmental changes in the control and modulation of affect, as well as in the way affect punctuates the behavioral stream. Such an integrated behavioral organization – observe, recognize, then with automaticity turn, smile, show, and vocalize *simultaneously* – would not be seen in the first half year; yet careful study would show that this complex reaction is based on an integration of building blocks that were present months before. What such an integrated pattern of behavior portends for subsequent development would also be of interest. The child's behavior points toward the emergence of self-generated emotion and emotional self-regulation. Finally, as implied, we would be concerned with how this integrated affective response is coordinated with other developments in the cognitive and social domains, including the development of awareness, anticipation, intentionality, object concept, self–other discrimination, and the formation of specific attachments.

The issue of function, that is, how this reaction serves the adaptation and development of the infant, is also multifaceted. There is a widely discussed function with respect to the world outside of the infant; specifically, the communicative value of such behavior. Well-being, a desire for interaction, and so forth are communicated to the caregiver, who reads and responds to this "signal." Beyond this, one must consider functions *for the infant*. In particular, what is the role of the affective, expressive behavior in promoting engagement of the stimulating and novel surround? A full understanding of function will include consideration of both the infant's pleasure (which is experienced and communicated) and the process by which novelty-engendered arousal is managed. It is notable that the affective/motoric reaction terminated the brief period of behavioral stilling. Affective reactions commonly follow strong orienting reactions to novel events and co-occur or are followed by the freeing of further behavioral expression. The infant must be able to go forth, as well as encourage social partners to continue their part in novel stimulation. The capacity to engage novel aspects of the environment is a critical aspect of human adaptation, as is the capacity to elicit care. Emotion can support as well as inhibit such engagement; it is organizing as well as disorganizing (Campos, Campos, & Barrett, 1989; Schore, 1994; Thompson, 1990).

How human emotional expression compares with that of other animals (including unique aspects and functions of human emotion) would also shed light on the meaning of the infant's smile. For example, the tail wagging of the dog on encountering a new person may have some of these same functions. Others have written about parallels in the facial communication gestures of nonhuman primates (Chevalier-Skolinkoff, 1973).

This brief glimpse of a developmental perspective will be elaborated in subsequent chapters and clarified continually through illustration. Indeed, one overarching goal of this book is to define and illustrate a developmental perspective by bringing it to bear on the complex topic of emotional development. In the remainder of this chapter the assumptions or principles guiding our study of emotional development will be presented, followed by a brief outline of the plan of the book.

Guiding assumptions

Four major propositions guide the examination of emotional development in this book. They may be briefly outlined as follows.

There is order in development (the ontogenetic principle)

That which comes to be emerges in a lawful way from that which was there
before. Things are not simply always there, nor do they arise from nothing.
Even behavior postulated to be innate, or "genetic," develops. A satisfactory
developmental explanation traces a process wherein initial conditions represent
prototypes (i.e., essential, core features) for what will arise through developmental transformation. While a knowledge of initial conditions does not allow
the specific prediction of an outcome, outcomes are always lawfully related to
origins. Uncovering and describing the order in emotional development is the
primary goal, as in any science (Gould, 1989; Schore, 1994; Waldrop, 1992;
Werner & Kaplan, 1963).

Emotion is tied to development in other domains

Emotional development must be studied in concert with cognitive and social
development. This is partly the proposition of holism – that the individual functions as a totality, and no part can be understood in isolation (Gottlieb, 1991;
Magnusson, 1988; Werner & Kaplan, 1963). As Kuo (1967) has put it, "In any
given response of the animal to its environment, internal or external, and in any
given stage of development, the whole organism is involved" (p. 92). Without
considering the growth of anticipation, awareness, and intentionality, and without considering the social matrix in which development unfolds, an understanding of emotional development would be extremely limited. Development is an
integrated process, so that other domains of development have profound implications for emotional development, and studying emotional development sheds
light on cognitive and social development (Fogel, 1982; Frijda, 1988; Schore,
1994; Thompson, 1990). The study of emotional development is necessarily
integrative. As Gerald Edelman (1992) has put it, "Emotions may be considered
the most complex of mental states or processes insofar as they mix with all
other processes" (p. 176).

The major domains of emotional development (emergence of the affects and emotional regulation) are part of the same whole

In the ontogenesis and expression of the specific emotions or affects, there are
clues for understanding the process of emotional regulation. In explaining why
one affect rather than another is expressed and the changing basis for affect
expression with age, core issues for understanding emotional regulation will be
identified. Emergence of the affects is largely a normative issue, although individual differences in age changes are found. Emotional regulation, on the other

hand, is often an arena for the study of individual differences, although there are normative changes in regulatory capacities. The fruitful study of individual differences is based on the consideration of normative processes, and the study of normative processes is informed by consideration of individual differences (Sroufe, 1991).

The adequacy of a developmental account depends on unification

The adequacy of a developmental account depends on the overall order and coherence it brings to the domain. It cannot be supported by isolated facts but is based on converging lines of evidence across both domains and developmental periods. The process as well as the fact of change must be brought to light, and parallels in change across domains should be seen. The adequacy of explanation is judged by how well precursors and subsequent transformations of a given behavior are understood, in terms of sequence and process. An adequate description should apply across subdomains – for example, be parallel for the major affects (e.g., joy, anger, fear). Further, the general explanation would be deemed more valid to the degree that the described process has implications for other major domains of development (i.e., cognition and social behavior) and is in harmony with the current understanding of development in those domains. One would also gain confidence in the validity of the description when major aspects within the domain of emotional development itself are brought into harmony – that is, when the explanation of the unfolding of the specific affects and the development of the capacity for emotional regulation is based on the same core process. Rather than being totally disparate aspects of study, the emergence of the affects and emotional regulation, normative change and developing individual differences, should be unified by an adequate developmental description.

The plan of the book

In the introductory chapters that follow, we will first consider theoretical issues that have been dominant in the field. This will provide a framework for discussing the thorny problems of definition that plague this area. The resolution suggested will rely on the idea of emotions as developmental constructs. This will be followed by further elaboration of what is meant by the nature and organization of development itself.

In the next major section we will explore the unfolding of the emotions – that is, the developmental process by which the specific affects such as joy and fear emerge. Each specific affect emerges from precursor processes present in the earliest months of life, according to a describable process involving transformation and qualitative change, yet with maintenance of essential core features. Moreover, striking parallels across the affects will be seen. At the same time, systematic changes in the conditions that produce affective reactions in the infant occur, with a transition from physical parameters of stimulation at first being effective toward a central role for the meaning of the event for the infant.

The importance and changing nature of the meaning of events for infants will bring us to a consideration of the reciprocal influence of affect and cognition. Emotions will be seen to arise through an active process by which infants find meaning in environmental events. Over the course of development, such meaning is increasingly based on both the infant's past experience and sensitivity to the context in which events occur. By the second half of the first year, not external events per se, but the infant's "evaluation" of events in context, are the determinants of affective arousal and expression.

These considerations lead to a broader discussion of emotional development, including the topics of emotional regulation and individual differences. An arousal regulation process, uncovered in the study of each affect system, is a key feature of individual differences. Developmental changes in arousal regulation are central in governing changes from precursor affects such as pleasure to more mature affects such as joy, and arousal modulation also underlies whether positive (e.g., joy) or negative (e.g., fear) emotional reactions occur in a particular circumstance. Whether an event, even in a particular circumstance, leads to joy or fear depends on processes within the infant. Therefore, individual differences with regard to meaning analysis and arousal modulation are deemed to be critical.

Social aspects of development, which are always critical, are discussed specifically in subsequent chapters. The infant is seen as embedded in social relationships, and the caregiving relationship is seen to be critical for two reasons. First, the security of context is a pivotal feature in governing emotional reactions, and the familiar caregiver is a prominent basis for infant security in novel circumstances. Moreover, in time, the infant comes specifically to utilize the caregiver through his or her own directed actions in order to achieve reassurance. Second, feats of emotional regulation can often first be accomplished in partnership with the caregiver, prior to being within the individual capabilities of the child. So important are these considerations that the evolving attachment relationship is conceptualized in terms of progressive changes in the dyadic regulation of emotion, with an increasingly active role for the infant at each phase.

In the final chapters of the book, the development of the affects and individual emotional regulation are projected forward into the toddler and preschool periods. A special topic is the growth of emotional self-control.

2 Conceptual issues underlying the study of emotion

> Without some version of a motivational principle, emotion makes little sense, in as much as what is important or unimportant to us determines what we define as harmful or beneficial, hence emotional.
>
> Lazarus (1991)

The concern in this book is both with emotions as events and with emotional regulation as a core feature of normative and individual development. Theoretical treatments have rarely been this broad. Generally, they emphasize one aspect or the other. Therefore, it will be necessary to draw on insights from a variety of perspectives. There are excellent works on the emergence of the affects (e.g., Izard, 1978, 1990), the instigation of emotion (Frijda, 1988; Lazarus, 1991; Mandler, 1984), and emotional regulation (Fogel, 1993; Schore, 1994; Thompson, 1990).

According to Arnold (1960), a "balanced" theory of emotion differentiates emotional experience from other experience, accounts for the arousal of emotion and bodily change, and specifies the place of emotion in goal-directed action. A "complete" theory also distinguishes emotions from feelings and one emotion from the other, and it specifies neurophysiological mechanisms and the significance of emotion in personality integration. Thus, emotions and emotional life are multifaceted, entailing a consideration of physiological, cognitive, and social factors, and expressive as well as internal components (Schore, 1994). Major works have been written on each of these topics. A developmental point of view requires some acquaintance with each of these aspects, for none, in isolation, is adequate to the task at hand. We will touch on all of them in this chapter, and they will receive more expanded treatment in later chapters. First, a beginning definition of emotion itself will be presented.

Defining emotion

Any conceptualization of emotion must begin with the question of what an emotion is. Beyond that, any theoretical position must at least deal with some of the following: When do emotions occur? How do they occur? Why do they

11

occur? Some positions have dealt principally with one or another of these, yet still have made valuable contributions to the literature. An adequate developmental position, however, must ultimately deal with all of these. In addition, it must reflect the central place of emotion in human life. Emotion is part of all critical transactions with the environment. It guides, directs, and sometimes disrupts action (Campos et al., 1989; Izard, 1991; Schore, 1994; Thompson, 1990). And it is the currency of personal relationships. As Magda Arnold has written, "From common experience we know that emotion moves us, fills our days with light and shade, makes us actors rather than spectators in the drama of life" (1960, p. 91).

A major goal of this book is to define emotion from a developmental perspective. Given the number of monographs written on emotion, it should be clear that no simple, one-line definition can suffice. In fact, as will be clear when previous efforts are examined, such one-line definitions (e.g., "the felt action tendency toward anything intuitively appraised as good and away from anything bad" or "the person's cognitive label for an arousing event") are always insufficient – incomplete or vague at crucial points.

Still, we must begin the definitional process somewhere. There is some consensus among investigators, and examining this consensus can help point to the pressing definitional issues that remain.

The emotional complex

Regardless of focus or theoretical orientation, virtually all investigators of emotion emphasize that emotions must be viewed as complex transactions with the environment (see Frijda, 1988, and Schore, 1994, for reviews). Most theorists recognize a role for a cognitive process (appraisal, meaning analysis, etc.), and all point to associated physiological changes. Most describe emotional behavior in terms of a chain of events, such as the following:

Stimulus-in-context → cognitive process → experienced feeling → behavior

It is, of course, possible for behavior or feelings to loop back and influence the ongoing cognitive process (or even the "effective stimulus") and so forth. Many theorists speak of a continued tuning or modulation of emotions, rather than a simple discrete response (e.g., Fogel, 1993). Still, there is agreement that emotion can be conceptualized only as some kind of complex process. Few define emotion as simply the experienced feelings, and few leave out cognitive factors. Mechanisms such as perception, recognition, appraisal, judgment, or meaning analysis are part of virtually every theory.

This simple scheme leaves much room for different emphases and disagreement among theorists. For example, some have emphasized the instigation of emotion, generally focusing on cognitive processes (e.g., Mandler, 1975, 1984). Others have emphasized physiological processes (Hebb, 1946; Tomkins, 1962), which are sometimes viewed as preceding (the James–Lange position) and sometimes as following (the Cannon–Bard position) the cognitive process. Still others have emphasized the function or adaptive value of emotion (Arnold, 1960; Campos et al., 1989; Darwin, 1859; Izard, 1991; Plutchik, 1980).

The emphasis, of course, influences the definition. Izard (1978, 1990), for example, emphasizes the communicative function of human emotion and, following Darwin (1872/1965), its role in adaptation. Not surprisingly, his definition of emotion rests heavily on facial expression, and his sequential chain would emphasize the feedback (subsequent feelings) from changes in facial musculature:

Event → simple perception (or cognition) → facial change → feelings/behavior

Technically Izard sees the facial change and feelings as being concurrent, part of a total response. In early infancy he believes there need be no cognition.

By contrast, Arnold (1960), who believes that emotion has an important role in guiding and directing behavior, defines the core of emotion as a felt action tendency (see also Frijda, 1988); it is neither the feelings, nor the physiological change, nor the cognitive appraisal. Her chain might appear as follows:

Event → immediate intuitive appraisal (felt action tendency) → physiological/behavioral reaction → continuing cognitive appraisal

While emphasizing the immediate, subjective reaction to the event, in her process view, subsequent physiological reactions enter into ongoing appraisal.

As a final example, Mandler emphasizes "meaning analysis" in the instigation of emotion. In accord with the James–Lange theory and with Schacter (1966), he views emotion as a cognitive interpretation of physiological arousal. His chain would be as follows:

Event → arousal (due to interruption of a plan) → meaning analysis → labeled feeling

Plutchik (e.g., 1983), who argues specifically that emotions can be properly defined only as complex chains of events, has presented a somewhat more elaborate scheme than the chains just sketched. His general model and illustrations for fear and sadness are presented in Figure 2.1. As with most others, in his scheme cognitive activity precedes the arousal of feelings and physiological change.

The issue is not to decide which of these positions is correct and which are wrong. Each draws attention to an important part of the larger picture and may

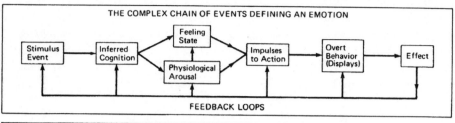

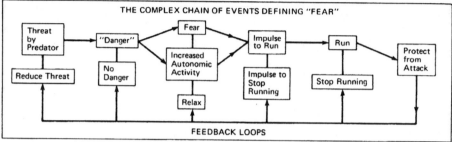

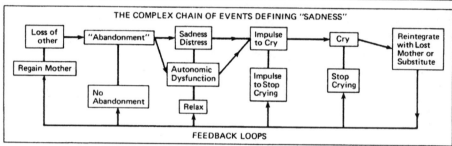

Figure 2.1. Plutchik's (1983) causal model for emotion in general and for fear and sadness.

be drawn on in the search for a comprehensive developmental account of emotion. As we shall see, developmental data are quite germaine to the issues raised by these various perspectives. For example, during the infancy period, a changing role for cognitive factors is apparent. And from this perspective, the question of whether physiological arousal precedes or follows other indicators of emotion may be given various answers, depending on the young child's developmental level and the nature of the event. In young infants, heart rate (HR) acceleration can be shown to precede changes in facial or postural expression in aversive situations (Vaughn & Sroufe, 1979). Here the physiological change precedes the behavioral reaction, but in older infants this is often not so. Most commonly, behavioral and physiological changes spiral cyclically upward as the infant becomes upset.

A working definition

Regardless of emphasis, all observers agree that emotions generally entail physiological changes and facial, postural, or other behavioral change. Most investigators also include an experiential component. Consistent with these considerations, *Webster's International Dictionary* defines emotion as "a physiological departure from homeostasis that is *subjectively* experienced in strong feelings and manifests itself in neuromuscular, respiratory, cardiovascular, hormonal, and other bodily changes preparatory to overt acts which may or may not be performed" (emphasis added). Thus, this definition includes physiological change and experience, but in the manner of the James–Lange theory sees the experience as in response to the physiological change.

Emotion will be tentatively defined in this book as *a subjective reaction to a salient event, characterized by physiological, experiential, and overt behavioral change.* This definition leaves open the question of whether physiological reactions are concurrent with, antecedent to, or follow experiential components. Also, in agreement with Arnold (1960), Frijda (1988), Horowitz (1987), and others, emotion in this definition is viewed as subjective, connoting a relationship between person and event. This concept is required because the same event may elicit different emotional reactions (or none) in different people or even in the same person across time or contexts. Thus, it is not the event but the person's *evaluation* of the event that leads to the particular emotion (see also Lazarus, 1991). The terms *subjective, salient,* and *evaluation* all imply a cognitive emphasis in this position, although in early infancy such cognitive activities may be quite primitive. Indeed, the changing nature of the cognition–affect connection is one key element in a developmental analysis.

The definition does not specify whether the emotion includes the cognitive appraisal or follows it, or whether it includes the behavioral response or precedes it. The word *emotion* itself can be interpreted to mean "away from motion," suggesting that it might not include the subsequent overt motor reaction. However defined, when emotional reactions are observed, there commonly is a notable arrest of behavior, regardless of whether this is followed by some motoric reaction. This is probably the more important point.

Emotion and affect

Emotion and *affect* are often used interchangeably. At other times *affect* is used to denote the expressive component (*Oxford English Dictionary*) or the subjective feeling component (*Webster's International Dictionary*) of emotion. Here the use of the term *emotion* will be restricted to the complex reaction discussed earlier, which includes cognitive, affective, physiological, and other behavioral components. *Affect* will be used to refer to both the feeling component and the facial and postural expressive components of emotion.

Theoretical issues

Functions of emotions

Evolutionary theory provides an important background for studying the development of emotion, especially its emphasis on function. Certain aspects of this position seem so firmly established that they are bedrock, either the starting point for further theorizing or the reference for evaluating theoretical efforts (e.g., Plutchik, 1983). Any useful theory of emotion must square with human evolutionary history.

Two cornerstones of the evolutionary perspective are that core emotional reactions are species general and that they have evolved from simpler forms in other animals (distress signals, bared fangs, nurturant care directed at offspring, etc.). Thus, emotions are assumed to be deeply built into the species repertoire and to have "old brain" connections. Many basic emotions are well established as being culturally universal and as emerging early in childhood (Ekman & Friesen, 1971; Ekman & Oster, 1979; Izard, 1978, 1990; Izard & Malatesta, 1987). Izard lists these core emotions as interest-excitement, enjoyment-joy, startle-surprise, distress-anguish, rage-anger, disgust-revulsion, contempt-scorn, fear-terror, shame-shyness-humiliation, and guilt-remorse. While there are blends of emotions, these 10 also occur in pure form and will be exhibited in characteristic facial expressions.

This universal language of emotion bears testimony to the power of Darwinian theory. When such behavior is noted it is assumed that it is part of the repertoire because it has critical survival value and is of basic importance in development. That is, emotional reactions must be functional with respect to promoting the safety, environmental mastery, and, ultimately, reproductive success of the animal: "Emotions are attempts of the organism to achieve control over these kinds of events that relate to survival. Emotions are the ultraconservative evolutionary behavioral adaptations, based on genetic codings that have been successful . . . in increasing the chances of survival of organisms" (Plutchik, 1983, p. 223).

Prominent functions of human emotions are (1) to communicate inner states to important others, (2) to promote exploratory competence in the environment, and (3) to promote adequate responses to emergency situations. Emergency reactions (e.g., vasodilation of the skeletal muscles to increase their glycogen supply) often occur as first responses to new stimuli in previously quiet organisms. The function of this pattern is to prepare for sustained or strong muscle action (Arnold, 1960; Plutchik, 1983). But not all emotional reactions are of the emergency sort. Many "positive" emotions (pleasure, joy, interest) serve to encourage ongoing transactions with the environment (e.g., Thompson, 1990). As will be discussed in later chapters, such mechanisms are vital for our opportunistic species, since what is learned through curious exploration or play may later promote protection or sustenance.

Emotional reactions communicate the needs, intent, or desires of the organism and thus are vital to our group-living, socially dependent species. The case is especially striking for human infants who must survive a prolonged period of relative helplessness. "If young organisms had to wait until the infant learned how to attract its mother's attention and support, and if the mother had to learn how to provide it, the chances of survival would be small" (Plutchik, 1983, p. 237). The infant's emotional reactions communicate need to the caregiver, whose reciprocal emotional reactions prompt effective care (Field, 1985; Fogel, 1993). Human emotions evolved in large part to promote social connectedness (feelings of attraction, love, grief at loss, etc.), and divorcing emotion from social context leads to gross oversimplification. Shared emotion is the fabric of human social relationships. It provides the rhythm or punctuation in human interaction and communication (e.g., Fogel, 1993; Stern, 1974). As David Hamburg (1963) has put it, "Society is not composed of neutral actors but of emotional beings – whether we speak of baboons, chimpanzees or man, emotion lies at the core of the social process . . . the physiology of emotion ensures the fundamental acts for survival" (p. 316).

In humans, emotions have taken over much of the role played by instincts in lower animals; yet there is a difference between instincts and emotion, though both are rooted in biology (Breger, 1974). Instinctive behavior is more narrowly programmed, more automatic, and less flexible. Emotionally guided behavior is more flexible and modifiable. One may inhibit an attack even in the face of anger or tolerate separation feelings on reassurance that the partner will return, and one may select from numerous options in acting in response to emotion. This flexibility is a major advantage of the human species and, at the same time, represents a major vulnerability. The complexity of human emotional/behavioral organization makes it susceptible to enumerable patterns of distortion.

Especially as we turn our attention to individual differences in adaptation in Part III, we also emphasize another function of emotion, namely, its ongoing role in behavioral regulation. Emotions not only guide and direct action toward or away from aspects of the environment, they also serve to amplify, color, and shape action. They inform the child concerning inner states, outer potentials, and the consequences of actions taken (see also Emde, 1980; Izard, 1991; Plutchik, 1983; Schore, 1994; Thompson, 1990).

The neurophysiology of emotion

There is a vast literature on the neurophysiology of emotion. Historically, much of this work was concerned with physiological aspects of emotional reactions themselves – that is, the psychophysiology of emotion. In most recent treatments the principal foci have been the role of physiological factors in the instigation of emotion and neurophysiological maturation as a context of emotional development. Both endeavors are of concern to us.

Physiological aspects of emotions are important in part because some of the most profound developmental changes occur in the patterning of emotional responses – that is, in the organization of cognitive, physiological, and expressive components. For example, HR changes can precede or follow other components of the reaction, and this changes with age. Also, with development, the universal facial expressions of emotions, a deeply neurophysiological aspect of the response (Izard & Malatesta, 1987; Tucker, 1992), become more coordinated with other aspects of the reaction.

The emerging work on the developing neurophysiological context of emotion is also of interest, not because of a search for a final, ultimate cause of emotion, but because of the basic assumption of the unity of development. The development of emotions and emotional regulation must be congruent with brain development, and the nature of brain development will reveal general developmental principles – just as will the study of emotion.

Physiological concomitants of emotion. There never has been any question about the involvement of physiological processes in emotional reactions. Heart palpitations, flushing, and stereotyped facial expressions have been part of every researcher's definition. There has been controversy about how to define the role of such changes in the emotional complex. Two early views were (1) that physiological changes initiate a sequential emotional response (James, 1890) and (2) that such changes are part of a total reaction, with all components initiated essentially concurrently (Cannon, 1927).

The first viewpoint led to positions emphasizing the cognitive appraisal of physiological changes in arousal (e.g., Mandler, 1984) and to research questions about the patterning of autonomic responses in emotional reactions. James's original idea was that each emotion is associated with a distinctive patterning of HR, blood pressure, and other indicators of autonomic change. Such a pattern, felt by the individual, is then interpreted (experienced) as the particular emotion. Demonstrating such a specificity of autonomic response has been difficult, perhaps because emotions often occur in complex mixtures and vary in intensity as well as kind. Following a thorough review, Levenson (1988) concluded that the idea remains worth pursuing, although he also felt that an intensity dimension to emotion should be considered as well.

Cannon's (1927) position and the many that have followed it were developed in part to account for the speed of emotional reactions in many instances. Emotional experiences frequently occur much too rapidly to be in response to slowly occurring visceral changes, and emotional experience still occurs when visceral reactions are excluded, as in certain clinical conditions or in experimentally prepared animals (e.g., Arnold, 1960).

As disparate as these two positions may seem at first, they can be reconciled given modern views of emotions as dynamic reactions (Schore, 1994; Thompson, 1990). It seems most sound at this time to take the position that autonomic changes are activated as part of the emotional reaction, rather than as leading to it. Any subsequent sensing and/or interpretation of such changes would, of course, greatly add to the emotional experience. The James position could still be correct in assuming that there was a specific pattern of autonomic reaction associated with particular emotions, even if the emotion is viewed as being initiated before autonomic reactions have progressed. The Cannon position could be correct in assuming that certain sensations (perceptions, cognitions) arouse emotional experience rather immediately and at the same time set other changes in motion.

Our current understanding of brain organization and functioning provides a way of harmonizing a key role for subcorticolimbic structures, along with associated autonomic reactions, with the fact that emotions can occur quite quickly upon recognition of some event (Gellhorn, 1968; Kelley & Stinus, 1984; MacLean, 1973, 1993; Schore, 1994). First, the hypothalamus and limbic structures such as the amygdala and hippocampus are well known to be implicated in emotional reactions, based on brain stimulation, microelectrode recording, and brain imaging studies (e.g., Collins & DePue, 1992; Isaacson, 1982; MacLean, 1993; Nelson, in press). Second, the limbic system is richly connected via major pathways to the frontal cortex and the sensorium, as well as to major motor pathways. All sensory modes are processed through the limbic system (Kelley & Stinus, 1984; Schore, 1994).

Thus, as suggested by Gelhorn (1968) and more recently by numerous others (Nelson, in press; Schore, 1994; Thompson, 1990; Tucker, 1992), the two-way connections between the frontal cortex and limbic system seem to hold the key for the rapid experience of emotion in many cases. Cortical impulses can "tune" limbic structures, and at the same time impulses from the hypothalamus and limbic system can feed back to the cortex, while concomitant signals proceed out to the viscera. The focusing function of the thalamus may also play a role, the result being that as stimulation continues it can be increasingly arousing, or arousal can continue even when external stimulation has ceased. This is a considerable elaboration of Cannon's notion that the psychological experience and the initiation of the autonomic reaction can occur simultaneously. And, of course, autonomic changes can be further analyzed by the cortex in an interactive manner.

Not all sensations will arouse emotion because not all sensations will prompt the same cortical stimulation of limbic structures or be processed by limbic structures previously tuned to respond to them. Full-blown emotional reactions may sometimes be immediate because they resonate with well-worn cortico-limbic pathways or loops. This may be especially true with the emergence of categorical perception and categorical memory. Perhaps emotions may sometimes be aroused with minimal cortical involvement, where certain kinds of stimulation are prepotent for emotion due to evolutionary history. Such may be the case, for example, for the disgust reaction to a bitter taste (Izard & Malatesta, 1987), which may be based in the old olfactory brain (Schore, 1994).

The major conclusion that emerges from considering the physiology of emotion is, again, the notion of emotion as a complex process. Emotional experience results from a complex interplay among brain structures that mutually influence each other in an ongoing way. Lazarus (1991) argues that this must always be the case. When it appears to be the case that some stimulus directly produces an emotional reaction (as in the disgust case earlier), he argues that this should be thought of as a reflex (like startle) and not as a genuine emotion. In any case, such reactions are clearly the exception and not the rule in emotional life.

The neurophysiological context of emotional development. The primary concern in this section is with developmental changes in brain anatomy/neurophysiology and concurrent changes in emotion and emotional regulation. Both the general nature of postnatal brain development and the emerging details regarding the maturation and integration of various structures and pathways have notable implications for emotional development.

The postnatal growth of the human brain reveals important principles of development that will be elaborated in Chapter 3. The first of these is the distinction between *epigenesis* and simple linear expansion. Brain growth has been described in terms of stagelike processes and qualitative change (Edelman, 1987; Schore, 1994; Tucker, 1992). It does not develop through the simple addition of new structures, but primarily in terms of changes in the complexity of organization, with increasing integration among components. (In fact, much of the functional change during brain maturation is the result of "parceling" or "pruning" of overproduced synaptic connections, a process Tucker refers to as "sculpting.") Not the formation of new structures, but the emergence of new, more elaborated, and differentiated pathways characterizes much of postnatal brain development. Computer models of the brain are giving way to systems models (Edelman, 1992), with a growing appreciation of the mutual interactions between cortical and subcortical components and the complex balancing of systems, such as the sympathetic and parasympathetic. Organization is both "top down" and "bottom up" (Tucker, 1992).

These general considerations and the documented details regarding brain development lead us to expect qualitative changes in emotional life at several points in early development (Schore, 1994; Thompson, 1990; Tucker, 1992). Such a qualitative change would occur in the initial months of life as the cortex first becomes functional. Another is posited at around 9 or 10 months as the frontal lobes mature and the corticolimbic pathways elaborate. Others are posited in the second year as interactive systems come into balance (Schore, 1994). Such coordination between brain development and emotion is not simply because the brain is the physiological substrate for emotion, but because changes in emotional experience in fact affect brain development (Schore, 1994).

Qualitative changes in brain maturation have implications both for the emergence of specific emotions (e.g., those requiring recall memory and the rapid categorization of events) and for processes that govern emotional life. For example, the diffuse arousal and limited capacity to tolerate stimulation in the first months, and the more modulated reactions that emerge later, are in complete accord with knowledge of central nervous system (CNS) development (Schore, 1994; Thompson, 1990). Such correspondences will be elaborated in Chapter 4.

The role of cognitive factors

There have been many clear demonstrations of the role of cognitive factors in emotion. These include studies to be discussed later, in which infant emotional and cognitive development are shown to proceed in parallel (see especially Chapters 5 and 7), studies in which the influence of context on infant affective reactions to the same event are demonstrated (Chapter 8), and studies showing a role for cognition in the development and instigation of specific emotions. For example, expectation has been demonstrated to play a prominent role in the instigation of emotion by as early as 6 months of age (e.g., Parrot & Gleitman, 1989).

Probably the most compelling adult data come from the classic studies of Schacter (1966) and Lazarus (1966). Schacter demonstrated that following epinephrine injection, with the consequent physiological changes, subjects reported feeling either anger or euphoria depending on the cognitive set provided for the subject through the behavior of stooges. The effect was stronger in drug than in placebo conditions; that is, the cognitive set alone was not sufficient to produce a strong emotional reaction. Rather, the physiological changes provided an important base for the action of the cognitive set. In Schacter's view the subject experiences the physiological change and interprets it in terms of the cognitive set provided. Though in this instance the physiological reaction precedes the emotion, these data do not confirm the James–Lange position; rather, Schacter's interpretation that the same physiological reaction produces different affective reactions would be a clear refutation of James. While there are a number of problems with this study (e.g., physiological reactions were not actually measured and may have been different in the two set conditions), these data support the idea that cognition can play an important role in affective experience.

Lazarus's work (e.g., 1966) was even more compelling since it did not involve the artificiality of drug induction and since both tonic and phasic autonomic reactions, as well as verbal report, were recorded. Lazarus showed that reactions to emotionally arousing films could be dramatically altered by the experimenter-provided or (with some subjects) subject-provided cognitive set. For example, in one condition, the subjects were led to believe that the rather odious subincision operations performed on the male organs of adolescent tribal members were a routine part of adolescent development, a procedure eagerly awaited by the participant. The narrative accompanying the film was dry and matter of fact. In another condition the excruciating pain was dramatized in the narrative. Emotional reactions, in terms of both autonomic changes and verbal report, were dramatically greater in the latter condition. Clearly, cognitive factors altered the reaction.

Cognitive factors are not difficult to incorporate into modern physiological theories. Cognition is important for corticolimbic interactive theories in that it would provide the mechanism whereby differential cortical impulses to the diencephalon would arise and differential corticolimbic patterns be initiated. Similarly, in a nonlocalized theory such as Hebb's (1949), the violation of expectancy is a psychological process parallel to the disruption of "phase sequences" (Hebb's physiological construct). Similarly, Tomkin's (1981) density of neural firing construct (used to explain different emotions) presumably begins with cognitive processes.

The nature of cognitive constructs. The cognitive constructs invoked by different theorists have varied considerably. Some theorists center their position on what may be considered "cold cognition," a process that arises automatically and is focused primarily on interpreting information in the external environment; others invoke "hot cognition," which includes a subjective consideration of events in context, as well as feeling states and past experiences (Lazarus, 1991).

Mandler (1975, 1984) is representative of the former. His "meaning analysis" is activated when an interruption in the execution of a plan produces physiological arousal. The interpretation given to the source of the disruption leads one to label the arousal in different ways, and this label *is* the emotion. Thus, in anger, there is arousal due to the interruption of some plan in operation. The arousal is perceived as due to an obstacle and the anger reaction ensues. Fear occurs when an unexpected or aversive event interrupts or disrupts cognitive or behavioral flow and is "interpreted as fearful." Emotion is largely superfluous in this position, largely because it is concerned only with the instigation of emotion and not with its functions.

Other researchers have emphasized the individual's more *subjective appraisal* (e.g., Arnold, 1960; Frijda, 1988; Lazarus, 1991). Not simply the arousal or features of the external stimulus are appraised, but the event in its total context, based on the personal meaning of the event for the subject. Such an emphasis on subjective factors seems necessary to account for the great variation between individuals and even within the same individuals across time or contexts. It also is more serviceable in accounting for positive affect. When 10-month-old infants smile or laugh when pulling a dangling cloth from their caregiver's mouth, then laugh uproariously as they try to stuff the cloth back in, little role may be seen for disruption of plans or an automatic interpretation of external information. Cognition is critical certainly, because one would not see this reaction with an unfamiliar partner or even with the mother in some situations or following certain experiences. The strong affect is not based simply on the appearance of the caregiver or the motor acts of the infant, but on the infant's evaluation of the total context, which includes previous as well as present experience.

Cognitive development. These considerations of cognitive factors are important because they point to the close ties between emotional and cognitive development. Mandler's concept of the disruption of plans points to a key role for the development of intentionality and the developing structure of cognitive schemes. Likewise, an emphasis on appraisal points to the importance of developments in memory, categorization, and the ability to coordinate multiple features of a situation, as well as actions and percepts and past and present experience. The development of relational abilities is critical. The child not only interprets arousal differently in different contexts, but because of a growing ability to take context into account can tolerate even very high levels of arousal in certain circumstances, the result being positive rather than negative affect. Moreover, with development the process of emotional arousal would change. Analogous to the developing ability to recognize particular objects (which do not need to be constructed each time from perceived parts), by late in the first year an event can be immediately recognized as threatening or benign. Thus, by this age emotion no longer must involve a sustained process of engagement and a gradual buildup of tension. Arnold (1960) therefore distinguishes between early affective reactions (which she calls "feelings") and later emotions, which involve "objects."

The debate over cognitionless emotion. The debate over whether emotion always requires cognition continues (Izard, 1990; Lazarus, 1991; Zajonc, 1984). Those who posit that cognition is not required point both to the immediacy of affective responses in some circumstances and to the very early expression of emotion in infants to argue that terms like *appraisal* and *meaning analysis* cannot always be appropriate, or that cognition must be defined too broadly (e.g., any information processing) to account for all instances of emotion (Hoffman, 1985). Those who take the position that cognition must always be present argue that counterinstances are often merely reflexive (which is clearly true in the case of a reaction such as startle), that with experience and priming appraisals may be quite rapid, and that persons need not be aware of the process when the meaning is deeply established.

This debate, however, obscures the more important issue; namely, what is the changing role for cognition in emotion as development proceeds. Moreover, if there are early emotional experiences, wherein applying the term *cognition* seems stretched, how are such early emotional experiences related to later, cognitively mediated experiences. These are the issues that will receive extensive attention in this book.

Social factors

The social context of emotion and emotional development will be a major theme as well. Therefore, the introduction here will be brief. As discussed earlier, shared emotion is the currency of close relationships. Reciprocally, emotions are influenced by and primarily occur in social contexts, and they evolved in humans largely due to their communicative significance. They are often socially created in the course of dyadic interaction. Fogel (1993) argues, for example, that joyful responses (as witnessed by the broad smile) only *seem* to be expressed in a discrete fashion; actually, they build in the process of interaction.

One major theme in later chapters is the importance of social context for the activation and expression of emotion. This includes the fact that emotions such as joy and rage are often expressed in their strongest form in interaction with caregivers. Caregivers often strive to elicit pleasure and joy, and this goal has been noted to structure the pace and quality of interaction (e.g., Stern, 1974). Other emotions are also socialized in explicit and implicit ways (Fogel, 1993; Kochanska, 1993; Lewis, 1992). Beyond this, caregiver presence and availability represent a salient context for the evaluation of events and thereby the experience of affect. In Chapter 8 we will discuss the critical finding that the very same event can produce strong negative or strong positive affect depending on the social context.

Caregiving relationships also play a vital role in the normative development of the capacity to regulate emotions and in individual differences in emotional regulation. In accord with the writings of numerous investigators, working primarily within a neopsychoanalytic perspective, we will develop the thesis that emotional regulation is first a largely dyadic process and only later becomes an individual capacity (see, e.g., Beebe & Lachman, 1988; Emde, 1980; Field, 1985; Fogel, 1993; Schore, 1994; Tronick, 1989). Moreover, the patterning and quality of the earlier dyadic regulation represents the *anlage* or *prototype* for the emerging self-regulation of emotion.

Recently, an outpouring of work on the neurophysiology of emotion has dramatically underscored the importance of social context. Some has documented the way in which caregiving stimulation and regulation alters the hormonal and neurophysiological activity of infant animals (e.g., Hofer, 1990; Kraemer, 1992). Repeated patterns of moderate arousal and regulation (or overarousal and dysregulation) shape and entrain the neuroendocrine response characteristics of the infant, even when later separated from the mother. Moreover, substantial research suggests that the maturation of the brain, including pathways for emotion and emotional regulation, is "experience dependent" (Greenough & Black, 1992); that is, social interaction directly influences central nervous system development (Schore, 1994; Tucker, 1992).

Principles of emotion and emotional life

Despite the definitional variety and the complex, multifaceted nature of emotion, certain general principles may be outlined that will guide our ongoing consideration. These are embodied in the work of numerous theorists, but we will center our presentation on those found in Lazarus's (1991) cognitive-motivational-relational theory.

A first principle is that the emotional process must be thought of in systems terms, an organized configuration of antecedent, mediating, and outcome variables, which are interdependent. No single aspect – cognition, facial expression, or so forth – can be considered dominant (see also Fogel & Thelen, 1987).

The second principle concerns emotional development. It is posited that not only do new emotions become available in the repertoire over the first months and years of life, but there are fundamental changes in the emotional process as well. Emotion arises in different ways and is influenced by different factors with development. Furthermore, increasingly with development, individuals evolve distinctive and characteristic ways of reacting to stimulation, modulating arousal, and expressing emotion.

Lazarus cites a third "specificity" principle, which posits that the emotional process is distinctive for each particular emotion. While emotions often are complex blends, there also are "differential affects" (Izard, 1991). Different emotions are aroused in different ways and have distinctive functions.

Fourth, emotions are dynamic processes (Thompson, 1990). As Frijda (1988) states, "Emotions are elicited not so much by the presence of favorable or unfavorable conditions, but by actual or expected changes in favorable conditions" (p. 353). Thus, emotions are influenced by preceding, current, and anticipated experience (at least by the end of infancy), because these influence the ongoing appraisal of events.

Fifth, a key relational principle "states that each emotion is defined by a unique and specifiable relational meaning" (p. 39). Such relational meanings vary for the emotion, the person, and the person's experience-guided *appraisal* of the event. Lazarus's relational meaning concept is similar to Frijda's law of situational meaning and law of concern. The former posits that "different emotions arise in response to different meaning structures" of different situations (p. 349). The latter states that "emotions arise in response to events that are important to the individual's goals, motives, and concerns" (p. 351). This is a critical principle for examining emotional development.

These principles, along with propositions concerning the general nature of development to be presented in Chapter 3, will guide our consideration of the unfolding of early emotional life.

Conceptual and methodological issues for studying emotional development

Perhaps the major problem underlying theoretical and research efforts in the study of early emotion centers on issues of the definition and criteria of emotion. How emotion is defined and what are taken to be signs of emotional expression greatly influence findings concerning the causes, consequences, and correlates of emotion and, thus, the validation of theoretical propositions. In the field of early emotional development, the problem of criteria is especially vexing because of the impossibility of using verbal report for the corroboration of other indices of emotion. Much of the debate has centered on the use of facial expressions as the singular criterion of emotion.

Criteria for emotion

How can we determine that an infant has a particular emotion in his or her repertoire? As discussed earlier, emotions often are viewed as complex phenomena, involving overt behavior, subjective experience, and bodily change. For example, definitions of fear and anger have often emphasized motor behavior (withdrawal or attack; e.g., Cannon, 1927; Hebb, 1946), as well as an important role for facial and physiological reactions (e.g., Arnold, 1960; Funkenstein, King, & Drolette, 1957; Izard, 1978) and cognitive factors such as appraisal and judgment (e.g., Lazarus, 1991). Infants have been inferred to be fearful if they move away, turn away, or gaze away from a presumably aversive event, or if they cry, pucker, or exhibit a fear face, or if they show prolonged heart rate accelerations (Bronson, 1972; Izard, 1978; Rheingold & Eckerman, 1973; Schaffer, 1974; Waters, Matas, & Sroufe, 1975). Depending on which of these one uses to indicate fear, different ages of onset will be suggested.

One key problem is that various indices often do not agree (e.g., Plutchik, 1983). For example, avoidance (turning away) is considered to be a clear-cut behavioral indicator of fear, especially within certain contexts (e.g., Hebb, 1946; Rheingold & Eckerman, 1973). But in a detailed study of infants' reactions to approaching strangers, it was found that behavioral avoidance was not associated with HR acceleration (Waters et al., 1975). The authors concluded that the autonomic "fear" reaction was actually prevented by the behavioral response when the infant turned away; that is, in a certain sense these infants were not afraid, even though by overt behavioral criteria they showed a clear-cut fear response. (Hiatt, Campos, and Emde [1979] also present a similar conclusion based on another study.) More subtle gaze aversion, which might not be considered a clear indicator of fear (cf. Rheingold & Eckerman, 1973), was accompanied by HR acceleration in the Waters et al. study. Thus, using an autonomic response as a validating criterion, gaze aversion appeared to be an index of fear, while turning away did not, a clearly paradoxical conclusion.

These findings illustrate the complexity of the criterion problem. Given such complexities how shall we proceed to determine the presence or emergence of an emotion in the infant's repertoire? Several approaches have been taken.

Response-based and stimulus-based definitions of emotion. Equating fear with behavioral avoidance is an example of a response-based definition. If behavioral avoidance has occurred, there is fear; if not, then there is no fear. Crying is another example. Since crying is often the infant's last resort, occurring when organized behavior breaks down, it represents an even more restrictive criterion than avoidance and can be used to illustrate the problems of a response-based definition. That is, by the second half year if infants have any available coping options they will not cry, and only in the most extreme conditions will this response be observed. Frequently, infants do not cry when faced with the mild stresses used in psychological experiments. Therefore, one could well conclude, using this criterion, that strangers are no more aversive ("frightening") to infants than their own mothers, as did Rheingold and Eckerman (1973). This could be concluded even if these two "stimulus conditions" were associated with strikingly different patterns of behavioral organization and even if abundant evidence for active coping was seen in the case of strangers. Infants may sober, withdraw, actively avoid, refuse to engage again, and so forth and still not cry. Crying, thus, would be a rather limiting criterion of negative emotion. (This will be discussed further in Chapter 6.)

Response-based definitions may, of course, lead to instances of overinclusion as well. It could be concluded, for example, that infants experiencing the Le Boyer method of childbirth are in a state of pleasure because of the occurrence of smile faces. But such a conclusion overlooks entirely the following facts: (1) that virtually all neonatal smiling occurs during sleep, (2) that premature newborns smile more frequently than full-term infants, and (3) that even microcephalic newborns (with no functioning cortex) show these smiles (see Chapter 5). These neonatal smiles, therefore, obviously cannot indicate pleasure. Similarly, the presence of "fear faces" during birth (Stirnimann, 1940) really cannot be taken to index fear as implying an awareness of threat. As Fogel and Thelen (1987) have argued, components of a system (such as facial change) may be present long before the total system is organized and grants components their mature meaning. Central to the definition of emotion in this book is the subjective relationship between infant and event. Thus, response-based definitions can lead to overinclusion as well as underinclusion.

In proposing that response-based definitions must be anchored to context and stimulus conditions, it is not being argued that overt behavior is of little importance. Observable behavior is the final arbiter of any question in scientific psychology. But behavior must be viewed in context and with the understanding that various behavioral reactions may have the same meaning, while the "same" behavior may have different meanings (see Chapter 3).

Facial expressions as indicators of emotion

One response-based position articulated by Izard (1991) and others is that centering on the facial expression of affect. The position of these evolutionists is basically that emotion is intimately tied to its communicative function. Just as one octopus will turn a dark red as a threat to an intruder, who in turn signals its nonhostile intent by becoming a light pink, humankind with its infinitely more complex signal system communicates with members of its own species. Smiles communicate affiliative intent, appeasement, pleasure, a desire for continuance, and so forth (see Chapter 5). Frowns communicate displeasure. Distress and fear warn others and indicate the need for assistance. There can be no question of the importance of such communicative functions.

When fully embraced this position is the ultimate response-based position. When a certain facial expression can be observed, then, and only then, do infants have that emotion in their repertoire (Izard, 1978, 1990, 1991; Izard & Mala-testa, 1987). Other behaviors cannot substitute. If infants sober, show strong HR acceleration, glance away, look again, and again show HR acceleration, it may still be argued that this is not a fear reaction if unaccompanied by a fear face, even if this reaction pattern is repeatedly associated with a particular stimulus event. Even crying would not indicate fear, but rather distress. And if infants show a fear face somewhere within thousands of feet of film, they are presumed to have fear within their repertoire regardless of the context in which the facial expression occurred and regardless of the replicability of the response in this context.

The facial expression position has strengths. Great progress has been made in objectifying the coding of facial expressions (Ekman & Friesen, 1975, 1976; Izard, 1978, 1990; Oster & Ekman, 1978). Either from facial gestalts or from the action of specific facial muscles, a high reliability among coders is possible. Such analytic advances may offer much to the study of the emergence of the various emotions (or the infant's developing control over them), since partial facial expressions or particular muscular responses may developmentally pre-cede (or follow) the appearance of the complete facial response or vice versa. With the development of reliable coding techniques, it also is possible to ex-amine the antecedents and correlates of facial affect responses. It may be de-termined whether changes in various facial responses are associated with particular patterns of autonomic response (e.g., surprise and HR deceleration, fear and HR acceleration), and whether autonomic changes precede or follow changes in facial expression (e.g., Barrett & Campos, 1987). The study of facial affect may well provide an important entrée into the study of emotion more generally.

Moreover, although some classic facial expressions of emotion are quite rare in infancy, there is some evidence that when these (or their elements) do occur, they tend to be observed at ages that make sense given other aspects of devel-opment (Hiatt et al., 1979; Izard & Malatesta, 1987; Vaughn & Sroufe, 1979). Elements of the surprise face, for example, are reported in the second half year of life, consistent both with the literature on cognitive development and with other criteria for this emotion (see Chapters 6 and 7).

There are, however, problems associated with a complete reliance on facial expressions as the criteria of emotion. These problems are both theoretical and pragmatic. Theoretically, the emphasis on the communicative function, while having obvious validity, obscures probable functions of emotions for the indi-vidual. Emotional reactions must play some role in guiding, directing, ampli-fying, and tuning the behavior of the individual. Beyond the question of why facial expressions of emotion occur (communication), there is the question, why do emotions occur? Once one conceptually separates the functions of communication from other functions (e.g., preparation for flight or fight, releasing tension and freeing behavior), it would seem clear that the emergence and development of the emotions could be at least partially independent of facial expression. Moreover, beyond the question of why emotions occur, within a developmental perspective one is also concerned with how and in what circumstances they occur, especially as these change with age. Such questions fall by the wayside with a singular focus on the emergence of facial expressions.

The biggest pragmatic problem with a heavy reliance on facial expressions concerns the rarity of some classic facial expressions, especially in infancy. By any other criterion there certainly are a range of emotions in infancy, at least by the second half year of life (Matsumoto, 1987). Plutchik (1983) discusses over "100 different behaviors or expressions or patterns of movements" (p. 233) linked to emotional expression in infants, including hand movements described by Papousek and Papousek (1977).

An undue emphasis on a single aspect of emotion, namely, facial expression, is unfortunate. Many others, including scholars of facial expression, have urged the use of convergent measures for describing emotion (Campos et al., 1989; Ekman & Oster, 1979). Disallowing an emotion before the emergence of the characteristic facial expression in the repertoire (as well as disallowing changes in the emotion at ages after the expression appears) removes much of development as a consideration for study. What remains for study are age changes in the facial expressions themselves and changes in the capacity to mask affect expressions. Neglected are the links between earlier and later emotional reactions and, especially, the changing organization of emotion and cognition. Further, different mechanisms may underlie the same emotional expression across ages, and such information is unlikely to be sought when the developmental question is reduced to when a particular facial expression first appears. Izard, for example, makes no distinction between early, reflexive affective expressions and later emotions based on meaning, a key distinction in this book.

A key goal for developmental understanding would be to trace various emotions from different (or common) precursors, yet the facial affect position assumes that there are no important developments within an affect system prior to the emergence of the associated facial expression. Similarly, relying on facial responses, it is difficult to pursue developmental relationships among phenotypically different emotions. If two emotions (e.g., anger and fear) involve different facial musculature, it would be difficult to ascertain common precursors. One simply assumes that they do not exist. Ontogenetic links between emotions, and even within the same emotional system, may lie within commonalities of the instigating circumstances rather than commonalities in the components of facial response. With an emphasis on facial response, ties with other aspects of development must remain unidirectional – find the age of emergence of the given facial expression; then seek its correlates.

Facial expressions evaluated with other criteria

Two studies may be used to illustrate the problems of relying on facial expression as the sole criterion in defining emotion (Hiatt et al., 1979; Vaughn & Sroufe, 1979). In each study infants older than 8 months and under 17 months were the subjects. Both studies used trained coders, high-fidelity videotape recordings, and well-established schemes for coding facial expression. In each study situations likely to elicit the emotions in question were used, and independent evidence for the validity of the procedures was provided. On the basis of both developmental theory and alternative criteria, infants observed should have manifested surprise and fear (two key emotions studied). And indeed, by some criteria they did. Yet there was virtually no evidence for the classic fear face expression or surprise face expression, despite the fact that more than 200 observations were made.

There were both similarities and differences in the two studies. Both had concurrent validation data (HR for Vaughn & Sroufe; behavioral change for Hiatt et al.). Vaughn and Sroufe emphasized the presence of the total facial response, while Hiatt and colleagues used forced choice judgments; that is, their judges had to say whether the expression witnessed was one of the following: happiness, surprise, anger, fear, disgust, sadness, or neutral. Coders in the Vaughn and Sroufe study could consider the expression to be any of these or, in addition, interest, distress, shame, or any other expression; only if the expression was a classic surprise or fear face was that coded. In both studies, however, coders checked for the presence of components of the particular facial expression.

In the study by Hiatt et al. (1979), there were two surprise conditions (vanishing object and switching toy), two fear conditions (stranger approach and "visual cliff"; see Chapter 6), and two happy conditions.

Results for the surprise condition were mixed in both studies. Very little evidence for the complete facial expression was found. Hiatt and colleagues do not report whether any (of 27) infants showed a classic surprise face, but only 20% showed a mouth-opening reaction consistent with such a face even once. This is a critical criterion for surprise, though it also occurs in interest, a likely reaction to their procedures (and a reaction that was not coded). Many more smiled in the conditions expected to generate surprise, showing both that the situations were salient for the infants (as was confirmed by observed search behavior) and the difficulty of producing a pure surprise reaction in infants.

Judges were able to discriminate the surprise expression from happiness in one of the surprise conditions. But such a distinction is forced. The classic surprise face need not occur for a judge to rule out happiness. It is doubtful that in these taped examples the judges could have distinguished surprise from interest, which also involves widening the eyes and opening the mouth.

Consistent with the Hiatt et al. data, Vaughn and Sroufe found only two surprise faces in the observation of more than a hundred 8- to 16-month-old infants, although a few more showed classic components of the surprise face. In their procedure, the infant's mother played peekaboo from behind a screen until the infant was fully engaged in the game (and affectively positive). Then, the mother appeared wearing a mask for two trials. Finally, when the expectation of one's mother with the mask was established, a stranger appeared with the mask. The stranger then talked to the infant from behind the mask, creating another incongruity. Finally, the stranger removed the mask and loomed close to the infant's face. It was expected (and confirmed by HR data and observations of attention) that the early phases of this situation would be highly salient, arousing, and surprising, yet little evidence of surprise faces was found.

Similarly, Charlesworth and Sroufe (unpublished data) saw only rare instances of the surprise face or its components in a large number of observations with infants in the second half year, using a vanishing toy paradigm. This was despite the fact that a great deal of sustained attention (with concomitant HR deceleration) and search behavior (looking for the object in the experimenter's hand or on the floor) was generated by these procedures. That is, by other acceptable behavioral criteria, many of the infants were surprised.

With respect to the fear face, the data are even more uniformly negative. Hiatt and colleagues apparently observed no classic fear faces, and even the eyelid and eyebrow components were not differentiated. Moreover, judges were not confident in their global categorizations of fear, being just as likely to code sadness, anger, or disgust. "Such a lack of patterning suggests that a general category of 'distress' may be a more parsimonious means of categorizing the negative expressions displayed in the two fear eliciting conditions" (p. 1033). This is in agreement with the observations of Vaughn and Sroufe. Even when the stranger loomed close to the infant's face, no fear faces were observed, despite the frequent presence of cry faces, crying, and sustained HR acceleration. This procedure clearly upset many infants; yet "fear" faces were not observed.

Many of the subjects of Hiatt and colleagues refused to cross the "visual cliff" (where a glass table top creates an illusion of a drop-off) or crossed in an oblique manner, clearly demonstrating their aversion to this event. Some of these maneuvers (such as gaze aversion or turning away as the stranger approached) may have actually prevented full-blown fear responses. Still, such behaviors show a differentiated emotional response, complete with HR change, which is not available to younger subjects. Without doubt, evidence for emotional development is indicated in these studies, despite the absence of clear findings concerning facial expression. One would not wish to disregard such developmental changes simply because they occur before the emergence of regularly occurring fear faces.

The main conclusion from these studies is not that facial expressions are invalid indices of emotion. It is not even that 8- to 16-month-old infants will never show such facial expressions. Such expressions have been filmed (Izard, 1978, 1990), though they have only rarely been shown to be associated predictably with specified contexts. Rather, fear faces seem to occur in situations that generate distress of great intensity (e.g., inoculation), and there they are not anticipatory but occur in the stream of the overall distress reaction. They certainly would become more common in psychologically aversive contexts with older toddlers, perhaps because of a maturation of the facial musculature and even more likely because of more rapid cognitive processing – probably a prerequisite for this indicator of fear.

A descriptive system of facial expressive behavior, such as Izard's Max or Affex systems, can be used to categorize expressions, with apparently a vast percentage of responses "fitting" categories or representing blends, especially when categories such as "interest" are used (e.g., Izard, 1991). Two major problems, however, are whether closely related expressions can be distinguished in early infancy and what is the meaningfulness of such expressions when they do occur. For example, Oster, Hegley, and Nogel (1992) report that expressions of anger and sadness cannot be reliably distinguished from global distress. Claims that such distinctions can be made confound an intensity of negativity dimension. In Huebner and Izard's (1988) study, for example, mothers reported that they would pick up babies showing preselected expressions – distress, anger, sadness, interest – to a different degree. Such distinctions do not really confirm a discrete affect theory because the four conditions, which rank from hard crying to no crying, were almost perfectly linearly ordered. Moreover, at times, expressions of some emotions are found paradoxically early (e.g., sadness, a mood concept, in 2-month-olds), with no tendency to become more frequent with development (Izard, Hembree, & Huebner, 1987).

The issue is not whether emotions in general, or facial expressions in particular, are innate. This can be granted. The conclusion from all this research is simply that facial expression is not the only or always the best criterion for inferring emotional reactions in infants (Campos et al., 1989; Ekman & Oster, 1979; Plutchik, 1983). Izard is most likely correct that there is a tendency for the activation of a total response unit (facial expression, physiological change, feelings). However, development and experience play key roles in activating such responses. He certainly is correct in pointing to the importance of facial expressions of emotion in infancy, but their greatest importance comes from how they are organized and integrated with other aspects of emotion and with development in general. As Plutchik (1983) has concluded, "It is extremely unlikely that there is a one-to-one isomorphic relation between the facial expression of the infant and a unique corresponding subjective experience" (p. 245).

Moving toward a synthesis

It is not so much that a new theory of emotion or new methods of study are needed. Rather, existing positions need to be woven together in the light of classic and newly emerging developmental data. A combination of existing research procedures and an elaboration of existing theoretical positions, such as those of Arnold, Campos, Frijda, Izard, and Lazarus, would provide a sufficient framework for examining emotional development. For the most part, prominent work in the past has focused on one part or another of the total domain. Some researchers, like Izard, focused on affective expression; others, such as Mandler, on the instigation of emotion. Still others have provided important integrations of the literature on emotional regulation (Bridges & Grolnick, 1995; Schore, 1994; Thompson, 1990) but have not connected this work with findings on the development of the specific emotions.

Other more comprehensive theories are vague at crucial points and are weak exactly at the points of others' strengths; for example, Arnold says little about the communicative function of emotion, which is the particular strength of Izard's position. More serious is her failure to treat cognitive processes adequately – that is, to specify the manner in which intuitive appraisal operates and how the organism is alerted to the need for such an appraisal (in contrast to Mandler's use of interruption). Her solution to this problem is to make appraisal always present. What is needed are propositions concerning the way contextual and personal factors sensitize the individual to perceive and evaluate events in varying ways. For example, an infant who is ill is much more likely to show distress at maternal leave-taking than is a healthy infant. Immediate intuitive appraisal of the same event is altered by context. This is a strength of Frijda's and Lazarus's positions.

Lazurus's theory, by contrast, is primarily about *how* emotions are activated (when and what emotion), with rather little emphasis on *why*, quite the opposite of Izard's theory. Adaptation, as discussed by Lazarus, primarily refers to individual differences in psychological health and rarely touches on the topic of functions of emotional experience and expression in the ongoing life of the individual, which are strengths of Arnold's theory.

New developments in psychoanalytic theory are quite important to the synthesis we seek. Psychoanalytic theory, even at its inception, was a strongly developmental, general theory of behavior, with emotion at its core. However, until recently it was not central to theories of emotion because of its historical ties with drive reduction and energy conservation concepts. Such concepts are now seen as inadequate in accounting for behavior. Much important human and animal behavior, such as exploration and play, may be explained without drive reduction concepts (White, 1959). Interesting stimuli will cause an infant to interrupt feeding, will prolong wakefulness, and will even cause an interruption of crying (Wolff, in Emde, 1980). Harlow's (1958) classic studies with cloth and wire surrogate mothers and Bowlby's (1969/1982) work on human infant–mother attachment suggest that even attachment behavior (a cornerstone in psychoanalytic theory) is better explained by unfolding, evolution-based capacities than by the mother's association with the reduction of drive.

Because of the inadequacy of drive positions, many theories discarded motivation as well. The problem with discarding all motivational concepts is that one winds up with autonomous cognition – for example, plans arranging and carrying out themselves. Clearly, the task is to evolve a theoretical position that discards drive reduction as a master force in behavior, while retaining motivational concepts. This is precisely what has happened in the evolution of psychoanalytic theory (e.g., Loevinger, 1976).

Numerous investigators of emotion from a neopsychoanalytic perspective have dispensed with the notion that infants are motivated solely to keep tension at its lowest level. In its place is a view emphasizing the *goals* of emotional regulation and interactive synchrony, harmony, or mutuality (e.g., Beebe & Lachman, 1988; Emde, 1980; Lichtenberg, 1989; Schore, 1994; Stern, 1985). Such "goals" need not imply specific intentions (Fogel, 1993); nonetheless, infants are viewed as motivated to maintain both engagement with the social and object world and a degree of internal harmony. Within such views, motivation is not viewed as incompatible with high levels of excitation or tension, which may even be sought. We will elaborate on these ideas throughout the book.

This more modern view can be readily integrated with a contemporary "epigenetic systems" position, in which all levels of functioning are seen as mutually influencing (e.g., Gottlieb, 1991; Schore, 1994; Fogel & Thelen, 1987). Emotions are not seen simply as negative, disruptive outcomes, but as positively motivating and organizing as well. They are integrated with perception and cognition in the service of social and other adaptive behavior. Such considerations lead to appropriately complex developmental questions such as, How do components of emotional responses become integrated with experience or internal states involving feeling and cognition? and How are complexly patterned affects like guilt and depression related to simpler discrete emotions that arise earlier? (Emde, 1980, p. 79). Qualitative changes in emotional life are seen in infancy based on changes in anticipation, intentionality, and, in general, the growth of meaning. In the second half year, affect comes to provide a signal to oneself, not just to social others; "in other words, *social* signals become *psychological* signals as well" (Emde, 1980, p. 101). Such ideas represent the core of a truly developmental position.

Conclusion: a developmental perspective on the classic issues

In elaborating a developmental position in subsequent chapters, classic questions in the field of emotion will be addressed. First, what instigates an emotion? In addition to such factors as novelty, incongruity, and interruption, underscored by others, the notions of changing causal factors associated with development, the changing saliency of various events, and an increasing role for the young child in determining the saliency of events will be emphasized. For example, the interruption of plans seems a quite viable concept with 9-month-olds and may be related to qualitative changes in emotion at about that age. But it is not a very persuasive factor for 4-month-olds, who may have motor "plans" but are really not properly viewed as able to interpret the meaning of "violation" concerning such plans. In these developmental differences lie clues to the different ways in which emotion may be aroused at any age.

Second, how are differences in emotions to be characterized? Emotions have previously been characterized in terms of behavioral differences (e.g., Cannon's flight or fight), presumed differences in physiological changes, subjective experience or label, and intensity. Infantile distress, for example, may be viewed as similar to anger, but more intense (Plutchik, 1980). Developmental concepts of precursors (prototypes) and differentiation may be used to draw quite different distinctions and to explain how more complex emotions (e.g., guilt) derive from developmentally more fundamental emotions (e.g., anger and/or fear). In this view, for example, infantile distress is not merely more intense than later anger; it is also viewed as less differentiated (more global and diffuse, and less tied to the particular meaning of the event for the subject). It is the precursor from which the more specific reaction of anger evolves with advances in development. Other related emotions (pleasure and joy; wariness and fear) are seen in terms of their developmental links, not merely their similarity in form.

Third, what is the function of emotion? In the view to be developed, the function of emotion will be emphasized, both in the sense stressed by evolutionists and in the way the term is used by Arnold. Arnold, Campos, and numerous contemporary writers emphasize the guiding and directing influence of emotion for individual behavior and for the integration of personality. How this guiding function evolves with development will be of special interest.

The place of emotion in the stream of behavior will also be considered. The idea of defining emotion within a complex perceptual-cognitive-physiological-behavioral reaction is an important contribution from past investigations. Developmental changes in this association are of great importance. With development there is an increasing role for subjective evaluation in this chain, and there is an increased ability to take in further information once an emotional reaction has begun.

Finally, what is the place of emotion in development? A central issue for this entire volume concerns the role of emotion and emotional regulation in general descriptions of development and for defining individual differences in development. The complement of this question, of course, concerns the influence of development on the experience and expression of emotions, both normatively and ideographically. It is these issues that we will take up first in Chapter 3.

3   Emotion and the organization of development

At the core of the latest biological, psychological and psychoanalytic models of development is an epigenetic principle which stresses the interactive nature of development, the continuing dialectic between the developing organism and its changing environment.

Schore (1994)

A general theory of development should conceive of organisms as active systems, maintaining some degree of integrity, stability, or self-regulation [and] should view change as a transition toward complexity of organization, involving multilevel functioning and organized wholes.

Santostefano (1978)

The issues pursued in this chapter concern the nature of development and the place of emotion in the study of human development more generally. A particular viewpoint on development, namely an "organizational" perspective, is advanced. The integrated and organized nature of development is illustrated, and a number of themes in early development are outlined. The implications of the general viewpoint and these particular themes for the traditional problems in emotional development are sketched here and drawn out in detail in subsequent chapters.

Two primary principles of development will be used to organize much of the discussion to follow. These two principles, synthesized from the work of major developmentalists such as James Mark Baldwin (1897), Werner (e.g., Werner & Kaplan, 1963; see also Glick, 1992), and Piaget (1952), are *unity* and *emerging complexity*. They characterize development of all dynamic systems, whether one is considering emerging life forms, an economy, the human brain, or the developing human mind (Edelman, 1992; Gould, 1989; Schore, 1994; Waldrop, 1992).

By unity one means that the organism develops as a whole (Fogel, 1993; Gottlieb, 1991; Magnusson, 1988; Thelen, 1989). One manifestation of this principle is that various domains in the developing organism (or system) do not, and indeed cannot, develop independently. In the course of human development,

38

for example, cognitive, social, and emotional development are all part of the same process.

Emerging complexity implies both that new, more complex behavior (or a new structure) emerges from what was previously present and that the new creations will show "emergent properties" (Fogel, 1993; Gottlieb, 1991; Waldrop, 1992). Development is characterized by *directionality* (toward increased complexity) and by *qualitative change*. An emerging complexity of organization is made possible by the "reciprocal interactions (co-actions) among already existing constituents," but such development is viewed as *probabilistic*, not *predetermined* (Gottlieb, 1991, p. 7). The prior behavior makes possible the new behavior but does not specify it, for the new behavior is at a level of complexity and organization not inherent in the preconditions. Precursor and outcome are related in ways that we will discuss, but one cannot say the former causes the latter. Emerging complexity is inherent in development itself (Fogel & Thelen, 1987).

The principles of unity and emerging complexity are readily apparent in the development of the human embryo from the first cell division. Indeed embryological development may serve not simply as a metaphor, but as the basic model, an instantiation of the basic nature of development itself. What begins as simple cell division, a quantitative process with little increase in complexity, moves through a series of qualitative transformations wherein an initial structurization into layers of cells (ectoderm, mesoderm, endoderm) leads to interconnected structures and systems, which then begin to function. It is no surprise that different names are given to the developing organism at different phases (e.g., zygote, blastocyst, embryo, fetus). Each phase becomes more complex than the preceding one as the organism develops in an integrated and unified fashion.

Early emotional development, too, must be approached within the framework of these principles. In particular, the study of emotional development must be integrated with the study of other aspects of development, and a primary focus must remain the description of the ever more complex organization of emotional life.

The unity of development

Understanding emotional growth and understanding human development in general are virtually the same task, since emotion is so integrated with other aspects of human functioning (Fogel, 1993; Kitchener, 1983; Magnusson, 1988; Turkewitz, 1987). It may be possible to study profitably other domains of development in relative isolation, though this seems unlikely; it is certain that studying emotional growth requires studying the whole of development.

For example, much of human emotion is social in nature, and the development of emotion cannot be separated from its social context (Fogel, 1993). Affection and rage typically have social objects. Shame requires an audience. Guilt is based on the internalization of social values. Infants smile more frequently and more broadly when they are with others than when alone. And in evolutionary perspectives (Darwin, 1872/1965; Izard, 1977; Plutchik, 1983), social communication is the primary function of all emotions. Therefore, the study of emotion is closely linked to the study of social development, and emotional life is embedded in social relationships. Numerous theorists, for example, have stressed the importance of mutual exchange between infant and caregiver in emotional development and, reciprocally, the importance of affect for all aspects of personality and social development (Fogel, 1993). Spitz (1965) put it the following way:

Affective interchange is paramount, not only for the development of emotion itself in infants, but also for the maturation and the development of the child ... this affective interchange is provided by the reciprocity between the mother (or her substitute) and the child ... depriving the child of this interchange is a serious, and in the extreme case, a dangerous handicap for its development in every sector of the personality. (p. 454)

Schore (1994) argues that even the postnatal development of the brain itself is influenced by ongoing socioaffective exchanges.

In the same way, studying emotion entails the study of cognitive development. When emotion is defined as a subjective relationship between person and event, cognition in some sense is always involved. Emotion (affect) and cognition are "nondissociable" (Piaget, 1962); they cannot be separated. Emotional development and cognitive development are two different aspects of the same process of the person–environment transaction. As Vygotsky (1962) has stated, a separation between cognition and affect "makes the thought process appear as an autonomous flow of thoughts thinking themselves, segregated from the fullness of life, from the personal needs and interests, the inclinations and impulses of the thinker" (p. 8).

It sometimes may appear to the researcher that cognition precedes or determines changes in emotional development, but this is in part illusory. It is the case that infants without certain cognitive capacities fail to show certain "achievements" in the emotional realm as well, and that retarded infants show a lag in emotional development commensurate with their lag in mental age (see Chapter 7). In this way cognitive development "influences" emotional development. Moreover, the evaluative activity that typically precedes an affective response may be viewed as a cognitive process. Some (e.g., Arnold, 1960; Lazarus, 1991), in fact, have written of emotion as the "outcome" of such a cognitive process. Infants can experience surprise, for example, only when an expectation is violated, fear only when a threat is perceived. The ontogenesis of emotion is very much the study of advancing cognition, the growth of meaning.

While this view of cognition leading emotions is in a sense valid, it is misleading in an important way, because the influence of emotion and emotional development on cognition would seem to be equally profound. Even granting that a cognitive process necessarily occurs in triggering an emotional reaction, this "cognition" is tempered by "affective memories" (Lazarus, 1991) – that is, past emotional experiences with that situation. Moreover, as Piaget and other developmentalists have suggested, affect is what cognition serves, and affective experiences alter cognitive structures (see Chapter 7). As tentative and unfirm cognitive advances make possible emotional reactions, these experiences feed back to the cognitive system. Emotion and cognition are mutually influencing in an ongoing way. And virtually all cognitive/affective development occurs within a social matrix. It is this particular organization of development, rather than just specific capacities, that is characteristically human.

The nature and organization of development

The organization of development refers to the nature of the developmental process, the way in which behaviors are hierarchically organized into more complex patterns within developmental systems, the way in which later modes and functions evolve from earlier prototypes, and the way in which the functions of parts are integrated into wholes (Breger, 1974; Emde, Gaensbauer, & Harmon, 1976; Fogel, 1993; Sameroff, 1983; Santostefano, 1978; Thelen, 1989; Vygotsky, 1962; Werner & Kaplan, 1963). It refers to relationships between systems – physiological and psychological, or cognitive, social, and affective – and subsystems within these (Brody & Axelrod, 1970; Cicchetti & Beeghly, 1990; Emde et al., 1976; Schore, 1994; Sroufe & Waters, 1976). It refers to the consequences of earlier adaptations for later adaptation (Erikson, 1959; Magnusson, 1988; Mahler, Pine, & Bergman, 1975; Sander, 1975, in press; Sroufe, Egeland, & Kreutzer, 1990). And it refers to the smooth and synchronous flow of the stream of behavior and to the tendency for this flow to be increasingly under the control of psychological (anticipation, memory, intentionality) as opposed to physiological processes (e.g., Emde et al., 1976).

A distinctive feature of this developmental viewpoint concerns the emphasis on developmental process – on qualitative change and changing organization – in contrast to a view of development as adding capacities or quantitatively expanding existing capacities. The following example can illustrate this distinction.

When the mother (caregiver) of a 6-month-old infant puts one end of a cloth in her mouth, then dangles the loose end in front of her baby by shaking her head from side to side, the infant's attention is captured by the cloth. All activity ceases, and the baby watches the cloth intently. After a period of inspection, the infant methodically reaches for the cloth and pulls it from the mother's mouth, all without a change in the sober expression. Almost inevitably, the cloth shortly finds its way into the baby's own mouth, as does anything the infant grasps at this age.

In the same situation, a 10-month-old first watches with rapt attention, though perhaps glancing back and forth between the cloth and the mother's face. Very quickly the face brightens, and the infant, smiling or laughing, grabs the cloth from the mother's mouth. Perhaps signaled by movements of her lips, the infant attempts to stuff the cloth back into the mother's mouth, laughing heartily.

How are these two infants different? What development has taken place during the 4 months of life separating them? Is there some "thing" that the 10-month-old "has more of" than the 6-month-old? Or does it make more sense to think of the 10-month-old as fundamentally transformed, qualitatively different from the 6-month-old? It seems fairly clear on an observational level that the younger infant becomes engaged with the cloth as an entity, that for him or her the mother recedes into the background. The cloth seemingly is pulled from the mother's mouth "inadvertently," as part of the operation of securing the object. No game is discerned; the relationship between cloth and mother is lost. In other words, in the first half year infants tend to reach for objects that capture their attention, whether a brightly colored ball on the floor, the feet at the end of their legs, or a cloth in mother's mouth. They also tend to stick things they do reach into their own mouths.

The 10-month-old, on the other hand, has the ability to keep in mind both the cloth and mother and, more importantly, is able to grasp the relationship between the two. This infant must have some kind of memory (image, scheme) for the mother, must know that he or she can bring about the reverse transformation (mother without cloth), and can even cause the incongruity again. The 10-month-old operates with the aid of an advanced memory – representations of objects (people) or events that can provide a backdrop for current experience. And his or her behavior is influenced by an ability to anticipate outcome. The 10-month-old has a past and a future, as well as present experience. He or she also has some sense of permanence concerning the world, in this case that mother without cloth is still there in mother with cloth. All of this is reflected in the older infant's laughter in this situation.

There are many ways to describe the developmental difference between these two infants. The 6-month-old is, of course, busily acquiring the experience that will let the capacities of the 10-month-old emerge. There is a continuity between the two age periods. The 10-month-old's behavioral organization emerged out of the 6-month-old's pattern of organization. But one thing is clear: The 10-month-old is a vastly different and more capable infant than the 6-month-old.

To point to the fact that 6-month-olds laugh in other circumstances (Chapter 5), and argue therefore that there has been no development in the pleasure-joy system, is to miss a great deal. Tremendous development has taken place during this short time span, and the result is best described in terms of qualitative changes rather than quantitative change alone. The 10-month-old grasped the incongruity; the 6-month-old, though perhaps having a vague sense that something unusual was happening, did not grasp it. Similarly, though one can speak of "memory" and "anticipation" in infants during the first half year, such capacities are qualitatively different than those of the 10-month-old. In fact, in many ways, the functioning of the 10-month-old, guided by past experience and operating in the context of expected consequences, is more like that of an adult than that of a young infant.

Most important is the changing organization of behavior. Basically, 6-month-olds have all of the individual behaviors that we described in 10-month-olds' reactions. These infants can certainly laugh and do so often in response to vigorous tactile and auditory stimulation (Sroufe & Wunsch, 1972; see also Chapter 5). They clearly have the capacity to recognize their mother, even with a partial transformation of her face. And they have the motor skill to place the cloth back into the mother's mouth. It is not the capacities themselves, but new levels of organized complexity that best capture the developmental change between 6 and 10 months. Thus, 10-month-olds are capable of vastly more active and complex participation in the social process.

Themes in the organization of infant development

The following discussion of some specific themes in the organization of infant development is designed to illustrate certain aspects of the developmental process in more detail. In the first section principles that dominate in the early months of life are discussed. In general these principles point to the importance of "state" (the continuum from deep sleep through wakefulness to vigorous crying, which has been divided into meaningful categories) and to the increasingly active role of the infant in state regulation (Papousek, Papousek, & Harris, 1986; Sander, in press). In the first half year the infant moves from global reactions in response to internally generated state changes to more precise and coordinated reactions to state changes (which themselves are largely products of the infant's transactions with the environment). In parallel with this, the infant also moves from precursor affective states toward genuine emotional reactions.

In the subsequent major section, themes of development that are prominent in the second half year will be discussed. These themes center on the interrelated meanings of events and behavior (see Chapters 4 and 9).

Each principle or theme, while described in relation to the infancy period, would apply throughout the early years. Moreover, what is the primary principle of developmental organization – the repeated emergence of new levels of organization (converging lines of development and subsequent intersystemic reorganizations) – applies to both earlier and later development.

Themes of development in the early months of life

The physiological context of behavior. While physical maturation, state, and physiological regulation exert influence throughout the early years, they are prominent themes in the early weeks and months of life. Indeed, establishing some regularity in physiological cycles is widely considered the first adaptive task of the infant (e.g., Emde et al., 1976; Sander, 1975, in press). Wide individual differences in sleep–wake cycles, crying time, and reactivity are reported (Brackbill, 1975; Clemente, Purpura, & Mayer, 1972; Korner et al., 1989; Osofsky & Danzger, 1974; Sander, 1993). And the cyclic or transient neurophysiological state and maturation of neurofunctioning are primary determinants of behavioral expressions that later become linked with emotions (Korner et al., 1989; Parmelee, 1972; Sroufe & Waters, 1976).

For example, the rapid eye movement (REM) sleep smile of the newborn apparently reflects fluctuation in CNS arousal, a process that declines with maturation of the cortex, dropping out entirely by about age 3 months (Emde et al., 1976; Spitz, Emde, & Metcalf, 1970; Sroufe & Waters, 1976). Even early elicited smiles (see Chapter 5) are heavily dependent on state, with alert smiles ontogenetically later than smiles elicited while asleep or drowsy (Wolff, 1963). Likewise, there is wide agreement that early distress derives primarily from interoceptive stimulation (e.g., pain, hunger); infants in the first 3 or 4 weeks of life are rather insensitive to noxious external stimulation (e.g., Tennes, Emde, Kisley, & Metcalf, 1972; Wolff, 1969). This insensitivity is also reflected in the difficulty of establishing conditioning, habituation, and HR deceleration (the cardiac orienting response) during early infancy (see Emde et al., 1976, and Sameroff & Cavanaugh, 1979, for reviews).

One might say in summary that in early infancy behavior is heavily influenced by the physiological context within which the stimulation occurs. Such contextual factors include possibly enduring characteristics of the individual (temperament) and transient states of arousal. While temperament, state, and neurological maturation probably remain important, continuing to interact with experience, they become subordinated to the principles of developmental organization. For example, after the first half year hunger no longer evokes excitation or even significant behavioral change in usual circumstances (Escalona, 1968). The physiological prototypes of behavioral organization give way to psychophysiological processes (Emde et al., 1976; Sander, in press; Sroufe & Waters, 1976), as will become quite clear in our discussion of positive affect (Chapter 5) and fear (Chapter 6).

The trend toward active involvement in producing stimulation. The dramatic increase in amount of time the infant is awake and alert is a major development in the first weeks of life. Parallel to this is a psychological process, reflected in an increasing involvement with the surround and a trend toward more active participation in producing affectively effective stimulation. This trend toward active participation is perhaps the central developmental theme in all of infancy (Sroufe, 1990; Sroufe & Waters, 1976). In early infancy this tendency takes the form of arousal becoming increasingly a function of the infant's relationship with external events, rather than being in a one-to-one correspondence with the quantity of external stimulation. At first this involves sustaining attention and following changes in stimulation, but by the third month it includes processing the content of the stimulation as well. The infant is not just stimulated; increasingly, the infant creates stimulation.

In the development of positive affect, for example, gentle modulated stimulation is first effective for eliciting smiles. Here, quantity and other physical parameters of the stimulation are crucial; any stimulation that sufficiently jostles the nervous system will do. Later, smiling occurs to less intense but dynamic stimuli (e.g., nodding head and voice), and then stationary visual stimuli become effective (see Chapter 5). The content of the event is crucial; that is, the arousal is produced by a cognitive or recognition process. These smiles, common by 10 weeks, are due to the active transaction between infant and event. In this context one can speak of the beginning of true emotions. The active involvement concept also captures Watson's (1972) observation of vigorous smiling and cooing in the third month to mobiles that move dependent upon the infant's actions.

The trend toward active participation in stimulation also is apparent in negative reactions. Distress at first is produced primarily by interoceptive stimulation, later by noxious or captivating external stimulation, still later by the cessation of pleasurable interaction, and finally by stimulation with a specific negative meaning (e.g., Bronson, 1972; Escalona, 1968; Sroufe, 1977; Tennes et al., 1972). At first, any stimulation that captures and locks the neonate's attention will ultimately lead to distress. Later, only certain kinds of events have this power and depend on the infant's active efforts to make sense out of experience (see Chapters 4 and 6).

As will be discussed further in considering specific affective systems, the infant's increasingly active participation in his or her experience, based on the growth of memory and anticipation abilities, continues throughout early development; so too does the tendency for the content of stimulation (and, later, specific meaning in relation to the infant's acts) to take precedence over the quantity of stimulation. Of course, just as state and temperament remain important, the quantity of stimulation is never irrelevant; even older children may laugh with joy in vigorous play or may become distressed by overstimulation.

From global/diffuse to specific/coordinated actions. When an infant is distressed in the early months, even by a specific external source, the reaction tends to be a diffuse, total body reaction; only later is there a directed, coordinated reaction specific to the event. Charlotte Buhler (1930), in a classic work, has described the ontogenesis of negative reactions to a common early event – having one's nose wiped. At first, wiping the infant's nose tends to produce total body involvement, with flailing of the limbs. Only later do arm movements become sufficiently coordinated to bat away the hand, and a directed reaction to the nose being covered occurs even later (e.g., 7 months). It is not until about 8 months that the infant will execute an anticipatory blocking movement. Such increased organization is also seen in the clear biphasic response in fear situations at about this time. The 8- to 10-month-old infant will first show behavioral and physiological orienting (evaluation), then the negative reaction (Emde et al., 1976; Sroufe, Waters, & Matas, 1974). Negative reactions need not build gradually from general excitation by this age.

Similarly, positive reactions are increasingly characterized by a specificity and coordination of behavior. In young infants smiling and cooing often build from general activity. Later, one sees attention and anticipatory quieting, then smiling. Ultimately, smiling can occur in the absence of motility (Escalona, 1968). And with advancing cognitive development, the execution of specific intended acts, with anticipated consequences (e.g., pulling off a cover in peekaboo), are associated with positive affect. In general, anticipation and specificity in reaction are two signs of the infant's increased ability to interact meaningfully with objects and events. Such criteria are highly relevant to designating the emergence of emotions proper (e.g., pleasure, proto-anger, and wariness; and later joy, anger, and fear), as distinct from their precursors. We will return to this principle in Chapter 4.

Sensory, sensorimotor, and sensoriaffective integration: the roots of control. Early in infancy repeated stimulation is responded to with little evidence of carryover from one stimulus presentation to another (e.g., Tennes et al., 1972) or from one day to another in a habituation series (e.g., Emde et al., 1976; Sameroff & Cavenaugh, 1979). Soon, however, a cumulation of effect can be observed. For example, Tennes and colleagues (1972) reported that in the third month gradually increased motor activity and then distress were noted with several presentations of a loud horn, whereas earlier there was a decrement in responsivity over trials or no consistent response. Such sensory integration is relevant to positive affect as well, since both positive and negative affect may be presumed to involve increases in arousal (Sroufe et al., 1974; see also Chapter 6).

Tennes and colleagues (1972) also provide an example of the coordination of sensory, motor, and affective behaviors. Early in infancy, engaging visual stimulation sometimes leads to a prolonged cessation of behavior occasionally resulting in distress. But in the second month such fixations are punctuated by periods of motor activity, smiling, and cooing ("positive discharge"), as well as brief glances away, which become the dominant reaction:

This waxing and waning marked the onset of pleasurable responses . . . It represents a modulation of motor activity and of gazing, each preempting the other in alternation . . . The increased responsivity to stimulation would result in irritability, but the concomitantly occurring increased coordination between sensorimotor systems increases the capacity to sustain more stimulation over longer periods of time without distress. (p. 218)

Thus, the coordination of attention and motor activity initiates what will become positive emotion and also promotes cognitive development by helping the infant stay engaged with the stimulation. The 8-week-old infant is no longer at the mercy of all captivating stimulation, even though certain stimuli still remain preemptive, as we will discuss in Chapters 4 and 6.

The affective component is so prominent in the punctuation and regulation of early behavior that Stechler and Carpenter (1967), in a paper of fundamental importance, propose the term "sensory-affective" to replace "sensory-motor" for the initial stage of development (see also Schore, 1994). The chain is made up of sensory and affective links more often than sensory and motor links alone. Affective expression can be seen to mark, pace, or complete transactional loops in social and nonsocial encounters, as well as play a role in modulating arousal in continued engagements (Sroufe & Waters, 1976; Stechler & Carpenter, 1967; Stern, 1974, 1985). Stern (1974), for example, has described how positive affective expression and gaze aversion are coordinated to structure caregiver–infant interaction. Infant and caregiver interaction sequences are organized around the "goal" of positive affect exchanges and away from negative affect. Such a goal, which is best viewed metaphorically because it is only sometimes explicit for the caregiver and more rarely explicit for the infant (Fogel, 1993), guides the rise and fall of the interaction intensity.

Later sensorisensory and sensorimotor integrations, which Piaget (1952) described with the term "coordination of schemes," also have clear relevance for emotional development. As will be presented in Part II, the squeal of laughter in mock attack, wariness of novelty, fear, and focused anger all, in one way or another, call upon coordinated sensory impressions or the failure (interruption) of an anticipated coordination. For example, the 5-month-old laughs at loud sounds made by the caregiver when face to face (i.e., a loud sound and the caregiver's face can be coordinated) but cries when the sounds are made from behind, unexpectedly. Later, the 10-month-old described earlier laughs as he stuffs the cloth back into the caregiver's mouth, coordinating his action with a remembered visual experience. Or the infant may cry when, instead of the expected appearance of mother, a stranger steps from behind a screen, or be angry when an attempted action to secure an object fails. Coordinating the action with the memory of the desired but unattainable object leads to the experience of frustration. The tendency to impose order on experience is ever present. When order can be attained from novelty, incongruity (Berlyne, 1969), or uncertainty (Kagan, 1971), through mastery or repetition (Piaget, 1962), there commonly is positive affect; when the orderly flow of cognition or behavior is inalterably interrupted (Mandler, 1975), there often is negative affect.

These themes of physiological state, active involvement, and sensoriaffective coordination, which dominate the early weeks and months of life, will receive some elaboration in presenting the specific affect systems in the following chapters. However, continuously relevant as they are, these are not the themes or principles that best characterize development at the end of infancy. In the second half year, when many basic human emotions emerge, we are concerned with the rise of meaning – that is, with the behavioral organization of an active agent that is influenced by past experience and anticipated outcomes and that is beginning to know objects and persons as existing independent of his or her actions.

The themes of development in the second half year: meaning, context, and the dynamics of behavior

Increasingly in the second half year, whether an emotional reaction occurs and what kind of emotion occurs depend on the meaning of the event for the infant. Meaning itself is less defined in terms of the ''objective stimulus'' and more in terms of the infant's subjective experience based on past experiences and surrounding circumstances. Reactions, therefore, may not only be more differentiated and more rapid, but are more idiosyncratic – that is, based more on the specific history of the particular infant. All of this may, of course, pose problems for those trying to understand infant emotion, for the same event may lead to different reactions in different infants, or even in the same infant on different occasions. Much of this complexity is due to the context sensitivity of older infants as they process the meaning of events.

The situational context. By the end of the first year the infant no longer responds to isolated stimulus events (e.g., an approaching stranger), independent of the setting. Emotion becomes organized with respect to context. Setting (laboratory vs. home), familiarization time, preceding events (e.g., a mother separation episode), presence and location of the caregiver, and other aspects of the situation influence the reaction (see Chapter 8). With rather substantial alterations, context effects can be demonstrated in early infancy, as in Stechler and Carpenter's (1967) observation of distress in response to the sight of the mother's face decontextualized (in a *gansfeldt*) or demonstrations of negative affect in response to the totally unresponsive face of the mother (Tronick, 1989; Tronick, Adamson, Wise, & Brazelton, 1978). But in the second half year the effects are subtle and wide ranging; for example, the generally positive reaction to mother approaching with a mask, or the negative reaction to an intrusive stranger, can be influenced by the order of the approaches or other preceding events (Emde et al., 1976; Skarin, 1977; Sroufe et al., 1974).

These context effects reflect the infant's abilities to remember and anticipate experiences, and to be more differentiated from the event, which increasingly lead to the infant's subjective relation to the event. For example, HR data indicate that the sequence and setting effects just mentioned are not due to changes in state; rather, they are assumed to reflect changing thresholds for threat (Sroufe et al., 1974). Resting HRs of infants are not different in home and laboratory, suggesting that general arousal is not different in the two contexts. And HR may recover to baseline following a noxious event, even in the laboratory. Still, reactions to a given event are affected by setting or previous emotional experience. Following one emotionally arousing event, even given full autonomic recovery, the infant shows a greater (and sooner) emotional response to a subsequent arousing event. By the end of the first year, infants evaluate events in context (which includes aspects of their own experience), and their reactions must likewise be interpreted in terms of organization within context. (This will be elaborated in Chapter 8.)

Whether inferring an emotional state or determining enduring characteristics of an individual child, examining behavior in context is crucial. As Escalona (1968) suggested, "What remains relatively stable in the behavioral organization of infants is not overt behavior, but the direction and extent of behavior change in response to different states and external conditions" (p. 200). For example, two infants may seek the same overall amount of proximity with a caregiver (ignoring context), but may be quite different in terms of the circumstances in which they seek contact (their behavioral organization). One may seek proximity only following separation or when injured or threatened; another may fail to seek proximity in these circumstances, seeking it only when not threatened. Alternatively, two infants may show different amounts of contact seeking, but similarities in patterning. It is not proximity seeking alone but in context that conveys information about the quality of an attachment relationship (Chapter 10). Likewise, it is behavior in context that allows observers to infer emotional reactions in the preverbal infant, without a sole reliance on the presence of adult facial expressions.

The dynamics of emotion. By the end of the first year there is a dynamic and flow to behavior, with one reaction calling forth another; that is, behavior and experience become part of the context for further experience (e.g., Field & Fogel, 1982). For example, an expression of interest may lead to an encounter with a threatening novel object, which leads the infant to seek contact with the caregiver, which supports a return to exploration.

Animal behaviorists speak of "behavioral systems," by which they mean groups of diverse behaviors that serve common functions and that may interact with other systems. Several such systems and their interaction have been described by Bischoff (1975) – attachment, affiliation, wariness, and curiosity/exploration.

Systems entail a flexible organization of various behaviors, which commonly changes with development. For example, as Bowlby (1969/1982) has discussed, looking, clinging, crying, and smiling are all part of the attachment behavioral system because they have in common the goal of promoting proximity to the caregiver. In this sense these diverse behaviors have a similar meaning. Any of them may be used in the service of the proximity goal, and later, when following and calling are added to the repertoire, the infant may show even greater flexibility in behavioral selection.

At the same time, particular behaviors can serve multiple systems; for example, looking, depending on its integration with other behaviors and the situational context, can serve any of the four systems analyzed by Bischoff. Smiling too, if appeasement (van Hooff, 1972) and tension modulation (Sroufe & Waters, 1976) meanings are accepted, can serve exploration and wariness, as well as affiliation and attachment. Smiling certainly occurs during visual exploration and solitary play, as well as during interaction with the caregiver and encounters with strangers, even when followed by clear signs of wariness (e.g., Waters et al., 1975). Moreover, a given system can serve multiple motives, and multiple systems can be activated simultaneously or sequentially in the same external situation. Infants have been observed to smile, turn away (coy behavior), and retreat to the caregiver following approach by a stranger, only to turn and visually explore the stranger once again (Bretherton & Ainsworth, 1974). Here, the attachment system is serving both exploration and comfort seeking. Such complexity does not preclude accurate interpretation of infant behavior, but it does require that meaning be inferred from patterns or constellations of behavior in context.

A dynamic, organizational perspective can often resolve confusions or controversies that arise in the study of emotional development. As one example, there once was an active debate concerning whether infants were wary of or affiliative toward strangers (Rheingold & Eckerman, 1973). However, when an organizational viewpoint is adopted, it is possible to reconcile evidence that infants are wary of novel persons with evidence that they also have strong affiliative tendencies toward them. Neither wariness nor affiliation is the more "true" infant reaction; rather, both tendencies are complexly balanced, being influenced by the infant's age, context, and interplay with other behavioral systems such as attachment (Sroufe, 1977; see also Chapters 6 and 10).

A systems or organizational perspective is at a level of complexity commensurate with the level of complexity in infant behavior and development. The need for such complexity in a species whose adaptation is based on flexibility and opportunism has been discussed by a number of investigators (e.g., Bowlby, 1973; Breger, 1974; Bronson, 1972; Sroufe & Waters, 1976; Thelen, 1989). It makes sense that the strong curiosity/exploratory tendency is in dynamic balance with wariness – for example, that immediate approach be inhibited in the face of novelty. It also makes sense, given the social basis of human adaptation, that the presence of the caregiver be crucial in this balance.

Conclusion

Emotion has a central place in the study of development, and a developmental/organizational perspective provides an important starting point for approaching traditional problem areas in the study of emotion and emotional development. The organizational viewpoint will be used to direct our efforts to define emotion, to trace the origin and developmental changes in specific affects, to conceptualize the links between emotional development and other aspects of development and to understand the place of emotion in individual adaptation. A consideration of normative development, including the vital role of the developing caregiving relationship in influencing thresholds for threat and the balance between excitation and inhibition, lays a foundation for understanding individual differences in emotional expression and the regulation of emotion.

Part II

The unfolding of the emotions

4   An organizational perspective on the emergence of emotions

Just because development is patterned, organized and universal does not mean that there is a map, plan, or scheme for the creation of those patterns . . . Systematic developmental change processes can emerge out of the mutual constraints imposed on components of the individual-environment system.

Fogel (1993)

From an organizational perspective, it is assumed that there is a logic in the appearance of the specific affects and an orderly unfolding of emotions – from neonatal precursors and early infant forms to the more complex emotions of early childhood. This is not to deny the role of genes in the emergence of discrete affective expressions, but to argue that genes are embedded in a developmental process that is characterized by co-action and interaction of all constituent parts (Fogel & Thelen, 1987; Gottlieb, 1991; Oyama, 1985; Thelen, 1989).

The development of emotions such as fear and joy should be characterized by the same principles as all development, and given the unity in development, the same processes are expected to underlie their emergence from precursors or prototypes. Later forms should be more differentiated, more psychologically based (meaning vs. general excitation), and more complexly organized with respect to context; yet later forms should be seen to evolve from earlier forms. Thus, fear, for example, would evolve from a precursor that would in some sense be embodied in the more mature response; that is, the core of the fear precursor should still be apparent in the later fear reaction, however complex and transformed the more mature reaction may be. Precursor and emotion would be distinguished in that the former would be a more global, less differentiated response. The emotion proper would have a greater precision, and it would involve a more specific meaning for the subject. In parallel with the general course of infant development, affect-related behavior in the newborn should have a reflexive base. Over the months of infancy, affect should become more psychologically based or meaning based, as emotional development unfolds in coordination with cognitive development.

55

At the same time, studying the unfolding of the emotions should offer important clues concerning the course of cognitive development (Chapter 7) and the organization of development in general. Co-emergence of different emotions can point to probable commonalties in underlying development. The emergence of new emotions, or qualitative change within emotional systems, will likely be associated with major developmental reorganizations (Emde et al., 1976; Schore, 1994; Sroufe & Waters, 1976).

The task of Part II is to uncover the order within the unfolding of the major affect systems and to relate it to the order in early development more generally. It is presumed that the order is there and that it would be apparent within any domain of development. It also is presumed that the order is of primary importance. Far less important will be determining the exact age at which a given emotion appears. Oftentimes, that age would vary depending on the criteria used. Components within a system show notable asynchronies (Fogel & Thelen, 1987). But a convergence of data, both within the domain of emotion and in other domains of development, suggests a coherent developmental process.

Emotions as constructs

When emotions are treated as developmental constructs, an emotional reaction is said to occur when a prescribed set of circumstances elicits a range of pre-established reactions with some reliability in an infant or child; that is, emotions are inferred from numerous indications, rather than being identified with some single indicator (see also Plutchik, 1983). A variety of behaviors, preferably in combination, will be viewed as relevant, including facial expression, motor behavior, vocal responses, and autonomic changes.

Given the emphasis on the subjective relationship between infant and event in our general definition of emotion (see Chapter 2), meaning plays a critical role in emotion. It is for this reason that we would not infer fear in the newborn – despite the presence of startle, crying, head turning, or even a ''fear'' face – or pleasure when the sleeping newborn smiles. Such newborn reactions are not based on processing the content of the event, but rather are reflexive reactions in response to endogenous CNS fluctuations or simple intensity parameters of external stimulation. Thus, there is no subject–object relationship.

Further we make distinctions between newborn reactions that are not at all dependent on the content of the event, later reactions that build slowly as part of a prolonged processing of an event, and between both of these and even later immediate reactions to the meaning of a particular event. Newborn infants, after a time, will thrash and scream if their heads are restrained. And, later, infants will cry if a well-established motor pattern is interrupted for a continued period. But only at around 8 months do infants cry *immediately* upon being unable to carry out an *intended* act. Only this latter reaction will be called anger within our developmental perspective, even though the earlier reactions are in an important sense similar. The slowly building responses to blockage of a well-established pattern, which are equally important developmentally, will be considered precursors of anger. There is some arbitrariness to these distinctions (and they could be referred to as Anger 1, Anger 2, and Anger 3), but without some such demarcation, important developmental processes are obscurred.

Since an emotion is not indexed by a particular response, independent of context, it must always be inferred. But one can become increasingly confident that the emotion is within the infant's repertoire as there is a continued convergence of experimental, observational, and developmental data. The immediacy of the 8-month-old's distress reaction when he or she fails to procure a ball, coupled with independent data on the growth of intentionality during this period, allow one to infer the emotion of anger, even while awaiting evidence for the reliable and regular presence of the "anger face" in such a context at this age (Camras, Holland, & Patterson, 1993). Should such evidence be forthcoming, confidence in this construct would, of course, be increased.

The fact that determining the experience of an emotion in a nonverbal infant is complex and frequently involves a certain amount of inference does not produce a futile situation. We can say that fear, for example, emerges in the second half year, though not with the certainty that would come with accepting crying or the reliable fear face as the index of fear (which would place the emergence of fear in the newborn period, on the one hand, or after the first year, on the other). Ultimately, ties between the emergence of fear and earlier emotional development, fear and cognitive and social development, and even what is being called "fear" here and the reliable presence of the fear face can be traced. This is more consistent with the objectives of the discipline of emotional development, as defined in this book, than is determining the age at which emotions emerge by any given definition.

Ontogenesis of the emotions

Several assumptions have guided the formulation on the development of emotions to be presented. It is assumed that emotions proper do not exist in the newborn period, but that major emotions such as anger, fear, and joy become available to the infant by the end of the first year. The developmental issue, then, is to explain the origins of the previously nonexisting emotions. Within our developmental perspective it is assumed that they represent transformations of earlier, "nonemotional" reactions; that is, the stuff from which emotions arise must already be available in the early months. It is neither a case of something coming from nothing, nor a case of preformism, with the mature emotions already there in smaller form. The mature emotions will be seen to emerge from precursor emotions in the first half year of life and from prototypes or root forms of these precursors in the pre-emotional reactions of the newborn, as the infant develops in interaction with the environment.

Pre-emotional reactions, precursor emotions, and major emotions are linked by processes of differentiation as well as specification and differ both in their instigation and in their form. There is a changing role for meaning and a greater precision in the later emotions. While precursors are global reactions to broad classes of stimulation, mature forms are precise and often immediate reactions to specific, meaningful events. This position is distinct from one based on the presence of all discrete emotions at the beginning of life (or their discrete emergence in full form) and from the position that emotions simply emerge from an amorphous mass in the newborn period. It is neither a specific affect theory (Izard, 1978, 1990) nor, as will be seen, a simple differentiation theory (Bridges, 1932).

Bridges (1932) was the first to set forth formally the notion of emotional differentiation in her now classic paper on the ontogenesis of emotion. Her scheme is presented in Table 4.1. Bridges's analysis set the standard for studying emotional development, clearly suggesting an integration with general development. The idea that specific emotions evolve out of earlier, undifferentiated distress or nondistress ("excitement") states – away from global to more specific reactions – remains a part of the scheme to be developed. Some support for this concept was presented in Chapter 3, and more will be found throughout this part. However, Bridges did not specify the basis on which she inferred particular emotions in her subjects, and her formulation requires considerable elaboration and revision.

Bridges was correct in thinking that, if overly excited, the young infant's reaction would be distress, and that distress is related to arousal in a continuous fashion during the newborn period. Prior to maturation of limbic structures and, especially, corticolimbic interconnections, it probably is the case that there is only undifferentiated brain stem arousal, not arousal associated with various emotions (Gellhorn, 1968; Schore, 1994). Reactions are based on purely physical parameters of stimulation. When the newborn becomes highly aroused, for any reason, distress results. Thus, there cannot be emotions in the sense of subject–object relationship (i.e., a meaning of an event for the child) in the early weeks of life.

But as early as 1934, Florence Goodenough pointed out that very young infants are more capable and complex than Bridges supposed. "General excitement" does not cover the young infant's repertoire. In general, Bridges did not really link the specific emotions with their precursors or illustrate the process of differentiation. She did not, for example, indicate the common elements be-

Table 4.1. *Bridges's scheme for the differentiation of emotions in the first 24 months*

Birth
General excitation ("excitement")

1 Month
Excitement branches to excitement and distress

3 Months
Excitement branches to delight
Emotions present: excitement, distress, delight

6 Months
Distress branches to distress, fear, disgust, and anger
Emotions present: excitement, delight, distress, fear, disgust, and anger

12 Months
Delight branches to delight, elation, and affection
Emotions present: excitement, delight, elation, affection, distress, fear, disgust, and
   anger

18 Months
Distress branches to jealousy; affection branches to affection for adults and affection
   for children
Emotions present: excitement, delight, elation, affection for adults, affection for
   children, distress, fear, disgust, anger, and jealousy

24 Months
Delight branches to delight and joy
Emotions present: excitement, delight, elation, joy, affection for adults, affection for
   children, distress, fear, disgust, anger, and jealousy

---

tween early frustration reactions and later anger. She did not suggest the precursors of fear or other specific emotions or indicate how one emotion evolved to another. Finally, she did not call upon general development to explain why particular emotions appeared when they did. Bridges's view of the ontogenesis of the emotions can be elaborated by considering the different routes to distress, within which are the roots of later negative emotional reactions.

There has been an attempt to draw on the empirical literature and current theory in developing the reformulation to be presented in this chapter. With Bridges and others, it is assumed here that true emotions do not begin until a basic differentiation between the "self" and the surround has been made – that is, until the emergence of awareness or rudimentary consciousness (e.g., Spitz, Emde, & Metcalf, 1970). When no distinction is made between inner experience and surround, no "connections" can be made; there can be no subject–object relation, and therefore no emotional reaction as defined here. This definitional feature is essential if emotions are to be viewed as playing an integrative role in organism–environment transactions. Prior to the beginnings of awareness, however, infants can, for obvious survival purposes, communicate distress. They also exhibit a prototype of later positive emotions, a "turning toward" (Spitz, 1965), which is an orientation of the entire body and sensory apparatus toward some stimulus event.

In the various and changing arousal states and reflexive reactions of the newborn period are the roots of the later emotions. The newborn sleep smile reflects a modest fluctuation in the CNS arousal, which is the prototype of later positive affect. Sustained arousal and global distress may be produced in various ways: pain, hunger, physical restraint, arresting stimulation, or sudden stimulation. The roots of negative emotions and surprise are to be found among these various causes of high arousal. Basic negative emotions, such as fear and anger, will emerge from these early diffuse reactions to high, unmodulated arousal. They are true emergents, but one can see the prototypical core of each reaction in the various conditions that produce early distress. Again, this early distress (or quiescence) is not properly called emotion, because it is simply a function of the amount of arousal. Meaning (the subjective relationship) has no major role. (Pain itself is not an emotion, even in later life, although it may certainly lead to anger or fear; Izard et al., 1987).

Reactions such as startle and disgust are sometimes offered as examples of "emotions" that clearly occur in the newborn period. However, the startle reaction is obviously a reflex and is quite distinguishable in its morphology and character from the later surprise reaction (Ekman, Friesen, & Simons, 1985). "Disgust," wherein a newborn wrinkles up the nose in response to a bitter taste, is also best considered a reflexive reaction. The fact that it is morphologically similar to later psychological reactions does not allow inference of an emotional experience. Among other things, like the newborn smile, these reactions may occur during sleep. These newborn reactions may be prototypes for later genuine emotions, but they are not best thought of as emotions themselves.

The concept being developed is distinct from that of Bridges in that there is an effort to specify the relationship between precursors and later emotions. Emotions do emerge from early, undifferentiated positive and negative affect, but they emerge in a lawful, specifiable way. Thus, major affect systems may be traced from the newborn period, even though emotions proper are not viewed as emerging until later.

The pleasure/joy system

The pleasure/joy system provides an excellent example of an evolving affect system. What we see in the newborn period is a prototype, which is almost purely physiologically based. From this evolves an intermediate precursor, a psychophysiological process in which the infant's psychological engagement of a specific event mediates a similar physiological reaction. Finally, a more purely psychological reaction emerges in which the particular meaning of the event for zthe infant predominates. Reactions may be immediate and may be in response to anticipated outcomes; that is, they may be independent of stimulation per se.

The neonatal smile is a function of endogenous CNS events, being associated primarily with REM sleep (see Chapter 5). It is due largely to the immature status of the nervous system, being more common in premature infants and disappearing over the first 3 months of life. Even the first elicited smiles are due largely to an "artificial," reflexive production of this endogenous process. When the infant is sleeping, a chime or other gentle, modulated stimulus produces a smile some 5 to 8 seconds following stimulation as arousal increases then slowly falls again. Based on a substantial literature, we will conclude in the next chapter that these early sleep smiles and even the first waking smiles, which are also a function of quantitative features of stimulation, cannot represent emotion. Any stimulation that produces the required arousal fluctuation leads to the smile. Context or meaning are irrelevant in these neonatal smiles.

At the same time, it is assumed that this early state-related reaction is related to later pleasure. What begins as a quantitative, state-based reaction becomes a qualitative reaction, based on the content of the stimulation. When the 3-month-old smiles at a face or a dangling toy clown, the emotion of pleasure is inferred. This is an emotional reaction because the particular content of the event is crucial. With the novel clown, for example, the smile occurs only after several presentations, and substituting a new object inhibits the smile. This more mature smiling response, involving open mouth and crinkling eyes, is not due to stimulation per se, since stimulation occurs on every presentation. Rather, it is due to effortful recognition, which can occur only after some exposure. A cognitive (psychophysiological) response has superceded a physiological response (Emde et al., 1976). Still, the original arousal fluctuation prototype is retained within the more mature reaction. Tension, as well as recognition, is required for the exogenous smile, as is shown by the fact that with continued presentation of the event (noneffortful assimilation) the infant will stop smiling. All of this will be discussed further in the next chapter. Here, it is presented only to illustrate the idea of the neonatal (nonemotional) smile as a prototype for later pleasure.

Early smiles of pleasure in response to external events are culturally universal and, in this sense, may be thought of as "discrete" affects. But they do not simply appear in the absence of precursors. Moreover, they require the integration of numerous component processes, an integration that lags far behind the first appearance of the facial smile (Fogel & Thelen, 1987).

Early pleasure evolves further to the more differentiated emotion that will be called "joy." The labels given to the two emotions are not nearly as important as the developmental relation between them. *Pleasure*, as just defined, is a positive affective reaction resulting from a cognitively produced arousal fluctuation. In its early form, it requires some time (and with a novel stimulus several trials) for the reaction to unfold. The infant studies a face, focuses on the eyes, then smiles (or smiles after several presentations of a toy). The effortful study produces arousal, which is modulated when the face is recognized. What is being called "joy" is more immediate and is based not only on a particular content, but a particular meaning. In fact, the "stimulus" *is* the meaning. For example, 10-month-old infants may show an immediate joyous greeting upon the caregiver's arrival or may laugh in anticipation of her return in peekaboo. They may laugh at the sight of mother pretending to suck on their bottle. Not recognition of the object, but understanding the meaning, is responsible for the reaction. Again, however, a core arousal fluctuation process is inferred (see Chapter 5). Further advances in meaning that come with an expanding sense of self in the toddler period would lead to further changes in the pleasure/joy system (Chapter 11). All of this is consistent with the organizational principle that the same behavioral response may have changing meaning with development.

The fear system

The fear system provides another example. In the early weeks, crying is sometimes produced by "obligatory attention" (Stechler & Latz, 1966). Some stimulus captures the infant's attention, and following unbroken attention, the infant cries. It is assumed that stopping the flow of behavior leads to an increase in arousal and, ultimately, distress (Meili, 1955; Sroufe, 1984). As with early smiling, this is not considered an emotion, because the content of the event is largely irrelevant. Any event that stops the flow of behavior will cause the reaction. However, this distress reaction is a precursor of and prototype for fear, because it is due to an external event (has a perceptual base).

Later in the first half year the infant has the capacity to disregard stimuli ("obligatory attention," per se, drops out). However, certain events (e.g., a stranger's face), because of a mixture of familiar and unfamiliar elements, can capture the infant's attention. Even though glancing away, the infant is drawn back to the event. Following prolonged inspection, there is again distress. Despite effort, the infant cannot fit this event into the class of known events. This reaction to the unavoidable/unassimilable will be termed *wariness* (cf., Bronson, 1972). It qualifies as an emotional reaction, because it is determined by the content of the event. Only a very restricted class of events can elicit the response. It is a precursor of fear because of the perceptual/psychological base. The term *fear* itself, however, as was done with joy, will be reserved for more immediate reactions, based on a specific negative meaning of the event for the infant. Thus, distress upon immediate sight of a stranger (perhaps on a second trial) is due not to a failure of assimilation (and a consequent prolonged buildup of tension), but to negative meaning. There is a more immediate negative reaction, an "I don't like this" response. As will be discussed in Chapter 6, different mechanisms mediate these fear reactions than mediate the reflexive reactions of the newborn.

The anger system

Similarly, anger, which is defined as an immediate, negative reaction directed at an obstacle to an intended act (and later to certain kinds of threat), is viewed as differentiating from earlier precursors. Even in the first days of life, one may elicit a global, diffuse, flailing response in the infant by restraining his or her head. Quite analogous to obligatory attention, this reaction is due to a prolonged stoppage of behavior and the subsequent buildup of arousal. After a time, the distress occurs. Here, the blockage is physical, however, and provides a prototype for frustration reactions and anger. Again, this early reaction is not viewed as a true emotion, because of the missing criterion of meaning, or subjectivity.

A few months later, however, the failure to execute *well-established* motor patterns can cause a similar reaction. Brazelton (1969) describes this reaction as follows:

The force behind this integration can be aroused in a baby of this age by leaving him with a toy that he cannot pull into him. He is left with vision and fingers. He will play happily this way for a period. Then, his frustration *builds up* as he strains to get his mouth on it. He ends up by screaming furiously when he cannot examine it all over with his mouth and hands, as well as his eyes. (p. 131, emphasis added)

This is, indeed, an emotional reaction, involving the beginnings of meaning. It is the failure of this established action pattern that frustrates the infant, not just failure to move per se. Such a reaction of failing to execute an established motor pattern is an example of a "frustration reaction." As was the case with what we called "wariness," this negative reaction requires a building-up period. It also remains rather global and diffuse as a response. Anger, which is identified as occurring in the second half year, along with joy and fear, is a more immediate reaction, and it can occur even when a previously *untried* action fails. It is not the disruption of a well-worn behavioral pattern, but the interruption of an intended act (e.g., reaching for a ball that rolled under a couch). The response may be quite specific and explicitly directed at the source. Still, as in the joy and fear systems, anger is viewed as evolving from the frustration reaction and its precursor. Embodied in anger is the original response to the blockage of behavior. With further development "rage" emerges in the toddler period. Rage can have both the intensity of the early infant frustration reaction and the directedness of the later anger response.

Summary

Each basic emotion is seen as evolving from its own precursor apparent in the first 5 months of life. This precursor is a prototype in the sense of embodying a core feature of the later emotion. These precursor emotions (pleasure, wariness, frustration reactions) also emerge from earlier reactions to modulated or sustained arousal. While emotional expression in the young infant is limited, there are different routes to the arousal of these expressions. And in these different routes lie the origins of different emotions. The *common processes* in the development of each of the affective systems may be outlined as follows:

1. For each of these three basic systems, a physiological prototype is present in the newborn period. In each case, a broad class of internal or external events can lead to the physiological state. The reaction is due to purely physical and quantitative (gentle, modulated, prolonged, etc.) aspects of stimulation or to internal processes. It occurs reflexively. In agreement with Bridges, the negative reactions that ultimately will become anger and fear are not really distinguishable in the early weeks. However, because of the distinctive routes to distress that are involved, we can see them as forerunners of the mature reactions. Because of the limited importance of content (subjectivity, meaning), these reactions are not considered emotions proper. This is a strategic, definitional decision.
2. Following the newborn period, precursor emotions emerge (pleasure, wariness, frustration reactions). These are genuine emotions because they involve an element of meaning and a role for the content of the event. However, these emotional reactions require a period of buildup or a repetition of trials, and they are rather diffuse reactions, involving the entire body (smiling, cooing, kicking of the feet, twisting, turning, flailing, etc.). They are based on a general, rather than a specific meaning (recognition or failure of recognition; disruption of an established motor sequence). Wariness and frustration reactions still are not distinguished by qualitative differences in their expressive components (both leading to distress), although frustration reactions often may be more intense.
3. The basic emotions of joy, anger, and fear, which are viewed as emerging in the second half year, involve a more precise, immediate reaction and a specific meaning. Fear, for example, is a rather immediate recognition of threat ("I don't like that"). It is not a failure to recognize that, in persisting, leads to distress (wariness). Infant fear is in response to the specific meaning of the event. Fear and anger now are expressed differently, with avoidance in fear and diffuse attack in anger. In time, reliable differences in facial expression also emerge.
4. The more mature emotions do not displace precursor emotions. The smooth execution of behavior can still produce pleasure, unfathomability and vague

threat can produce wariness, and diffuse frustration can lead to intense distress at any age. But young infants cannot experience joy, anger, or fear as defined here.

The analysis could be extended to other emotions such as surprise, which does seem to have precursors (Baillargeon & DeVos, 1991), or to the grief reaction at the loss of an attachment figure, which may emerge from separation distress and an even earlier distress at the breakdown of the infant's own behavioral organization. (However, the distress/sadness/loss system has not been subjected to careful analysis to date.)

This formulation represents a unique position. It may be distinguished from the specific affect theory of Izard (1978, 1990), because his position implies that the emotions emerge in a rather discrete manner and that they do not exist in precursor forms. In contrast, in our developmental view of emotions as emerging from early prototypes, there is not phenotypic identity between the mature form and the early manifestation; for example, few or no elements of the fear face are seen in the distress of wariness. Prototype and mature form are related developmentally, not morphologically. While the physiological prototype is embodied in the mature emotion (arousal fluctuation in pleasure/joy; heightened arousal in anger and fear), it has become part of a transformed psychological process. Emotions do not appear; rather, they develop, and developmental changes continue even after the emergence of the mature expression (see Chapters 5 and 6).

The position is also distinct from that of Bridges. While differentiation underlies both schemes, Bridges suggests a single amorphous mass (excitation) in the early period and suggests no developmental process, whereas distinctions among the routes to arousal are pivotal here, as is a role for an increasingly active infant. By the end of the first year a number of discrete emotions, as well as blends, do exist, but these have evolved in a lawful way from precursors. Most important, there is a commonality in the developmental process across affect systems that is highlighted in the present approach.

The developmental view presented here is in accord with recent descriptions of brain development (Schore, 1994) and the development of life forms (Gould, 1989). In attempting to explain the evolution of species, Gould faced a problem in some ways analogous to our effort to understand the development of the emotions. During the Precambrian period there was an abundance of life forms, simple only in comparison with modern mammals. Gould argues that if we "wound back the clock," it would not be possible to predict which of these more than 200 phyla would survive to become today's 4 existing lines, or even to know that mammals, large mammals, primates, humans, and consciousness would ever emerge. Such developments were not inherent in the preceding life forms (though obviously they were potential), and the evolution that occurred was dependent on myriad factors that could not have been known. Today's species are indeed emergents. Does this mean that life on earth did not develop lawfully out of earlier conditions? Gould shows that it is possible to describe and reconstruct how mammalian species lawfully arose from one of these early classes. Connections between present and past are necessarily lawful.

By analogy, the fact that a knowledge of newborn patterns of arousal and affect expression does not allow prediction of anger and fear does not mean that mature and earlier forms are not related. Fear and anger are potential in the newborn's responses to captivating stimuli and head restraint, though nature could have created different outcomes. Emotions are emergents, dependent on the coordination of myriad constituent parts dynamically interacting in development. But they evolve lawfully from preconditions in the newborn period.

"Stages" in the development of affect

While the developmental outline presented in this chapter is based on available empirical literature, it is to some extent theoretically derived. There has been a deliberate attempt to draw developmental parallels across affect systems. Thus, fear, anger, and joy are presented as emerging during the same developmental period. While this parallel is not completely established, it is a reasonable working assumption that the developmental reorganization during the third quarter of life would have implications for each of the affect systems, and that major changes in affect would likewise be influential in this reorganization. During this period there are major advances in object concept, intentionality, and an understanding of causality. Coincidentally, in the positive affect system (Chapter 5), for example, the term *joy* is reserved until the third quarter to capture the capacities for anticipation and active mastery apparent at this time (Piaget, 1952; Sander, 1975; Sroufe & Waters, 1976). Although the tendency toward active participation continues throughout infancy, there seems to be a qualitative turning point here. A similar case is made with the other affect systems and with other periods of developmental reorganization.

These comments on the differentiation of emotions within evolving systems raise the question of "stages" in the development of affect. In a sense, when affect is viewed as the "force" and cognition as the "structure" of mental life (Piaget, 1952), there can be no stages of emotional development. But in an integrated view of development, affect and cognition are interdependent, and the stages of development therefore apply to both domains:

The cognitive schemes which are initially centered upon the child's own action become the means by which the child constructs an objective and "decentered" universe; similarly, and at the same sensori-motor levels, affectivity proceeds from a lack of differentiation between the self and the physical and human environment toward the construction of a group of exchanges or emotional investments which attach the differentiated self to other persons (through interpersonal feelings) or things (through interests at various levels). (Piaget, 1952, p. 21)

The "stages" outlined in the following subsections, then, are not coincidentally parallel to descriptions of cognitive development (see Chapter 7), though they have been to a large extent independently derived. The three major developmental reorganizations described, which are taken from Spitz (e.g., 1965), were in fact inspired by observations of emotional development, as were the periods of emotional development summarized in Tables 4.2 and 4.3. Parallels between the cognitive and affective sequences will be discussed in Chapter 7.

Developmental reorganizations and the ontogeny of emotion

Spitz has suggested three qualitative turning points in early development ("developmental organizers"), each marked by a change in affectivity and each reflecting a basic transformation in psychological life – the emergence of new functions and a qualitatively different process for interacting with the environment (Emde et al., 1976; Spitz, 1965). Spitz postulated, with some evidence (e.g., Spitz et al., 1970), that such converging lines of development and the consequent developmental reorganization were linked to CNS maturation.

Emde (1980; Emde et al., 1976) presented further documentation for this position, drawing on comparative literature as well as the psychological and physiological data on human infants. Developmental changes in the electroencephalograph (EEG) recordings, sleep patterns, autonomic responses, and affective expression have been shown to converge, consonant with the first two periods of reorganization described by Spitz.

Finally, recent neuroanatomical evidence (including animal experimentation and autopsy studies of human infants) confirms qualitative changes in brain development and organization roughly concordant with the stages suggested by Spitz. As reviewed by Schore, the first qualitative advance occurs with dendritic elaboration of cortical neurons in the first 3 months; the second at roughly 10 months with maturation of the frontal lobes, the development of the sympathetic nervous system, and the establishment of basic corticolimbic interconnections; the third in the toddler period, with the complete maturation of limbic structures and accelerated development of the parasympathetic nervous system (see Chapter 2). Our aim in presenting this material on brain development is not to suggest that the brain is causal in these reorganizations, but to underscore the unity of the human developmental system.

The first reorganization. During the first 3 months there is a monotonic decline in endogenous (reflexive) smiling and infantile fussiness, mirrored by a recip-

Table 4.2. *The emergence of emotions in early life*

Month	Developmental issue	Anger/frustration	Wariness/fear	Pleasure/joy
0	Absolute stimulus barrier	Distress due to physical restraint, extreme discomfort	Startle/pain, obligatory attention	Endogenous smile
1				
2				Turning toward, pleasure
3	Regulation of tension (positive affect)	Frustration reaction		
4			Wariness	Delight, active laughter
5				
6	Development of reciprocity (active participation)			
7		Anger		Joy
8				
9	Formation of an effective attachment relationship		Fear (stranger aversion)	
11				
12	Practicing (exploration and mastery)	Angry mood, petulance	Anxiety, immediate fear	Elation
18	Emergence of self	Defiance, rage	Shame	Positive valuation of self, affection
24		Intentional hurting		
36	Mastery through play and fantasy		Guilt	Pride, love
54	Identification, sex-role development, and peer competence			

rocal increase in exogenous (social) smiles. At the same time REM, which in newborns occurs both during sleep and wakefulness, becomes restricted to sleep. Sleep becomes differentiated away from a simple dichotomy of deep sleep and restless sleep to the major stages of mature sleep, and by 3 months it begins

Table 4.3. *Stages of cognitive development and related changes in the affective and social domains across the first 24 months of life*

Cognitive development (Piaget)	Affective development (Sroufe)	Social development (Sander)
0–1: Use of reflexes Minimal accommodation of inborn behaviors	**0–1: Absolute stimulus barrier** Built-in protection	**0–3: Initial regulation** Sleeping, feeding, quieting Beginning preferential responsiveness to caregiver
1–4: Primary circular reactions First acquired adaptation (centered on body) Anticipation based on visual cues Beginning coordination of schemes	**1–3: Turning toward** Orientation to external world Relative vulnerability to stimulation Exogenous (social) smile	
4–8: Secondary circular reactions Behavior directed toward external world (sensorimotor ''classes'' and recognition)	**3–6: Positive affect** Content-mediated affect (pleasurable assimilation, failure to assimilate, disappointment, frustration)	**4–6: Reciprocal exchange** Mother and child coordinate feeding, caretaking activities Affective, vocal, and motor play
Beginning goal orientation (procedures for making interesting sights last; deferred circular reactions)	Pleasure as an excitatory process (laughter, social responsivity) Active stimulus barrier (investment and divestment of affect)	
	7–9: Active participation Joy at being a cause (mastery, initiation of social games) Failure of intended acts (experience of interruption) Differentiation of emotional reactions (initial hesitancy, positive and negative social responses, and categories)	**7–9: Initiative** Early directed activity (infant initiates social exchange, preferred activities) Experience of success or interference in achieving goals
8–12: Coordination of secondary schemes and application to new situations	**9–12: Attachment** Affectively toned schemes (specific affective bond, categorical reactions)	**10–13: Focalization** Mother's availability and responsivity tested (demands focused on mother)

Table 4.3. (*cont.*)

Objectification of the world (interest in object qualities and relations; search for hidden objects) True intentionality (means–ends differentiation, tool using) Imitation of novel responses Beginning appreciation of causal relations (others seen as agents, anticipation of consequences)	Integration and coordination of emotional reactions (context-mediated responses, including evaluation and beginning coping functions)	Exploration from secure base Reciprocity dependent on contextual information
12–18: Tertiary circular reactions Pursuit of novelty (active experimentation to provoke new effects) Trial-and-error problem solving (invention of new means) Physical causality spatialized and detached from child's actions	**12–18: Practicing** Mother as secure base for exploration Elation in mastery Affect as part of context (moods, stored or delayed feelings) Control of emotional expression	**14–20: Self-assertion** Broadened initiative Success and gratification achieved apart from mother
18–24: Invention of new means through mental combination Symbolic representation (language, deferred imitation, symbolic play) Problem solving without overt action (novel combination of schemes)	**18–24: Emergence of self-concept** Sense of self as active (active coping, positive self-evaluation, shame) Sense of separateness (affection, ambivalence, conflict of wills, defiance)	

with a non-REM period. Moreover, there are coincidental changes in the EEG. A host of other changes occurs, including the disappearance of some reflexes. This first "organizer" (major reorganization), which includes a beginning recognition of objects, is most obviously marked by the presence of the reliable social smile (see Chapter 5) and represents the infant's basic distinction between the "in here" and the "out there." There is a beginning recognition of repeatability in the surround and "awareness moving toward anticipation" (Spitz, 1965; Spitz et al., 1970). There can be pleasure as the infant finds familiarity in the "out there" and disappointment when the contact is broken. To Spitz, the first true emotions occur at this time because reactions now reflect a relation between the infant and the surround. The very fact of the exogenous (externally elicited) smile reveals such an awareness, because such elicited smiling occurs in response to only highly familiar events (e.g., the face) or following a number of presentations of a novel event. The infant "recognizes" the particular event. This is a qualitative turn in development. Before this time, and in keeping with its limited cortical development (e.g., Chugani, 1994), the infant's behavior seems to fit a discharge, hydraulic, or homeostatic model. Now, seeking and maintaining contact with stimulation become more prominent (Emde et al., 1976).

The second reorganization. The new sensitivity to reliability in the surround moves development forward at an ever increasing rate, until the press of development forces a second reorganization. In part this process can be viewed as the capacity for recognition leading to recall memory, object permanence, and other cognitive/motivational advances, as the infant can begin coordinating experiences. Recognition is essential for the experience of repeatability of events and for the categorization of experience. Experience becomes more organized as current and previous events can be related and as events are engaged with expectation.

Ultimately, infants in the first year can act with regard to objects not visually present, can affectively respond to their loss or recovery, and can experience this affective reaction in connection with the event. This is a new level of awareness (see Emde, 1980). In Spitz's view (1965), this second reorganization is signaled by stranger anxiety – the failure of the stranger's face to match the stored image of the mother. A broader view of recall memory and expectation, as associated with the differentiation of persons, object relations, and fear in general, seems more defensible (see Chapter 6 and also Emde et al., 1976). Whether a fear of strangers reflects anxiety over the loss of mother is contestable (e.g., Emde et al., 1976).

Still, the view of a major developmental reorganization in the third or fourth quarter of the first year seems descriptively accurate, with implications for positive affect, as well as for fear, anger, surprise, and separation distress. At the physiological level, the size of limbic structures such as the hippocampus rapidly become adult-like at this time, and one finds rich interconnections between frontal cortical and limbic systems (Nelson, in press; Schore, 1994). The perception of certain "events" would immediately tap into reservoirs of affective experience.

The third reorganization. As an intentional being in a world with permanent objects that can be acted on in planned ways, the infant moves toward a third reorganization. Many theorists have described the emergence of the autonomous self in the second year with *awareness* of the self as a separate being (e.g., Mahler et al., 1975; Sander, 1975; Schore, 1994). For Mahler, for example, the infant's moving out into the world (''practicing'') necessarily leads to the awareness of separateness (Chapter 11). Spitz emphasizes more the infant's discovery of will. In any case, the increased capacity for internal representation, object mastery skills, and increased mobility converge to support the infant's use of the caregiver as a secure base for exploration. Being able to represent the caregiver mentally (to know he or she is accessible even when not immediately within reach) frees the infant to explore at a distance. This experience in mastering the surround on one's own in turn leads to the emergence of a sense of autonomy and to a qualitative change in the child's cognitive transactions with the environment, including inner affective control, again supported by CNS maturation (e.g., Emde et al., 1976).

Such developmental reorganization is supported by evidence that during this developmental period infants typically recognize themselves in a mirror, whereas earlier they do not (Amsterdam, 1972; Lewis & Brooks-Gunn, 1979; Mans, Cicchetti, & Sroufe, 1978). It is also supported by apparent changes in the cognitive domain (e.g., Piaget's stage 6, the transition from sensorimotor behavior to representational thought, and Lenneberg's [1967] biological readiness for language) and in the affective domain (see Chapter 11). Spitz argued that this third major developmental reorganization was marked by negativism. More generally, it can be argued that defiance, shame, affection, and positive valuation of the self evolve only with the emergence of the autonomous self. For example, while infants certainly become attached in the first year and express joy and pleasure upon greeting, exploring, and interacting with the caregiver, true affection is perhaps best conceived as an emotion experienced by a well-differentiated self with regard to a clearly represented other. Nonelicited ''love pats'' are quite common in 18-month-olds, rare in 12-month-olds.

A fourth reorganization. Extrapolating from Spitz's system, a fourth organizer would also be marked by major affective changes, advances in cognitive development, and further differentiation of the self concept. Such a nodal point is suggested by the 3-year-old's capacity for fantasy play, role taking, and beginning identification (Sroufe, Cooper, & DeHart, in press). It is only after the infancy period, when with continued differentiation of the self there is identification and internalization of standards, that we may properly speak of guilt, love, and pride, which evolve from the emotions of the preceding period. The more separated infant is capable of a greater connectedness and a wider range of emotions (Chapter 12).

Schore points to a fourth stage in brain maturation at the end of the toddler period, dependent, as is all earlier development, on the young child's socio-emotional experience. He points to a shift from sympathetic to parasympathetic dominance, underlying emotions such as shame, and a shift from right-hemispheric to left-hemispheric advances, supporting the emergence of language. By the end of the period a balance is achieved between excitatory and inhibitory systems. This will be discussed further in Chapter 11.

Eight periods of infant affective development

Drawing on the work of a number of investigators (e.g., Campos et al., 1989; Escalona, 1968; Mahler et al., 1975; Sander, 1975; Sroufe & Waters, 1976), a further differentiation of eight phases of affective development can be delineated and related to parallel phases of cognitive and social development. As shown in Table 4.3, there is initially a period of rather absolute nonresponsivity, which Tennes and colleagues (1972), following Benjamin, refer to as a passive stimulus barrier (Period 1). During this period, infants are relatively invulnerable to external stimulation. Next, there is a period of turning toward the environment (Period 2). This is a period of relative vulnerability, since the infant is open to stimulation and has available only preadapted arousal modulation devices (Tennes et al., 1972). These devices include the beginning coordination of attention, motor activity, and smiling and cooing, which help bring an end to the distress of obligatory attention (see Chapter 3). The act of "turning toward" contains the roots of interest and curiosity, as well as positive affect.

The crowning achievement of Period 2, the reliable social smile, ushers in the period of positive engagement (Period 3), roughly 3 to 6 months (e.g., Escalona, 1968). It is interesting that in Sander's (1975) stages, which are based on observations of social development, this same period is referred to as "reciprocal exchange," characterized by "sequences of affectively spontaneous back and forth exchanges" with much smiling. Since during this phase there is awareness and "anticipation" (Spitz, 1965), motor expectations, and secondary circular reactions (Piaget, 1952), there can be disappointment and failures of assimilation. Consequently, such negative emotions as frustration reactions and wariness can be experienced. But the social smile and the generally increased responsivity elicit positive engagement from the caregiver (e.g., Emde et al., 1976; Sroufe & Waters, 1976; Stern, 1974), and many general schemes can be exercised without disruption. Probably based on maturation, infantile fussiness has disappeared (Emde et al., 1976), and the infant has the capacity to actively avoid noxious stimulation (Tennes et al., 1972). The infant smiles and coos at his or her own feet and toy giraffe, and especially at the caregiver. For the first time the infant laughs in response to vigorous stimulation (Chapter 5). "Pleasure has become an excitatory phenomenon" associated with states of high excitation (Escalona, 1968, p. 159).

The social awakening continues in Period 4 (7–9 months), when the infant participates in social games (Sroufe & Wunsch, 1972) and makes "persistent efforts to elicit social responses" (Escalona, 1968, p. 188), even from other infants (Goodenough, 1934, p. 258). In the first half year infants will look at another infant and perhaps smile. But now they will vocalize, touch, cajole, and otherwise try to elicit a response from their partner. Infants also intentionally initiate interactions with the caregiver (as witnessed by their persistence until they get a desired response), explore the caregiver's person (Mahler et al., 1975), and, with budding intentionality, produce consequences in the inanimate environment (Escalona, 1968; Piaget, 1952). As there is increasing meaning in the infant's transactions with the surround, emotional reactions become more differentiated late in this phase, with an initial hesitancy in the face of novel objects (Schaffer, Greenwood, & Parry, 1972) and sober faces for strangers (e.g., Emde et al., 1976). This is the period of active participation, engagement, and mastery. It is also the period in which infants begin to become aware of their emotions. Joy, fear, anger, and surprise emerge as its products.

Although infants continue to manifest strong affiliative tendencies toward people, including strangers (e.g., Bretherton & Ainsworth, 1974; Rheingold & Eckerman, 1973), an exclusive preoccupation with the caregiver may follow in Period 5 (e.g., Sander, 1975). This is accompanied by a temporarily subdued affective tone (Sroufe & Wunsch, 1972) and an intensification of stranger fear (Sroufe, 1977; see also Chapter 6). This is the period of attachment, when integrated positive greetings to the caregiver emerge, when the caregiver's presence becomes a source of security, and when emotional expression becomes highly differentiated and refined. By the end of this stage one can see gradations of feeling, ambivalence, and moods, as well as the rather clear, deliberate communication of emotion.

In what can be called a practicing phase (Mahler et al., 1975), an attachment–exploration balance phase (Ainsworth, 1973), or a phase of self-assertion (Sander, 1975), infants are often again ebullient in Period 6 (roughly 12–18 months). For example, increases in expressions of positive affect have been observed to occur between 10 and 13.5 months (Rothbart, 1989). And young toddlers actively explore and master the inanimate environment.

But as Mahler and colleagues (1975) have described, this rather complete confidence and sense of well-being cannot endure unchallenged. Inevitably, moving out into the world leads the infant to an awareness of separateness from the caregiver – a necessary but temporarily deflating step in the formation of self-concept (Period 7; see Chapter 11). To maintain the newfound sense of autonomy in the face of anxiety over separation and the increasing awareness of his or her limited power is the emotional task of the 2-year-old (Chapter 11). This task is ultimately resolved with the development of play, fantasy skills, and, finally, identification with caregivers (Period 8; Breger, 1974; see Chapter 11).

Conclusion

A considerable amount of information and a very complex developmental scheme have been introduced in this chapter in a very condensed fashion. In subsequent chapters many of these topics will be treated in a more expanded way. At this point, the major objective was to illustrate the need for some complexity in any adequate model of emotional development. The Darwinian emphasis on specific, universal emotions is not incompatible with organismic developmental theory. There are specific emotions, and these may emerge in the individual's repertoire in their mature form in a rather constricted period. But such an emergence is not inconsistent with a developmental history – that is, with the process of differentiation. The brain, too, undergoes qualitative change during postnatal life. Long before mature corticolimbic interfaces are in place, the infant has arousal mechanisms and primitive limbic structures to support early affect expression.

To accurately describe the ontogenesis of the various emotions, and the course of emotional development more generally, it is necessary to consider both continuity and discontinuity. As has been suggested, no emotion suddenly appears full-blown in humans; yet the periods of rapid reorganization of behavior bring forth transitions such that a reaction, fleeting and irregular before, or occurring only in certain delimited circumstances, now becomes highly reliable, even in response to events previously impotent with respect to the affect in question. In the view presented here, there is a lawful ontogenetic trail for all of the classic emotions, originating in early infancy. At the same time there are qualitative changes in emotion and affective expression that capture and reflect reorganizations in psychological development (see also Emde et al., 1976). Whether one wishes to call the greeting reactions of the 10-month-old "joy," or the aversive reactions of the 10-month-old "fear," they are qualitatively different from earlier expressions of positive and negative affect. Yet they have their roots in these earlier expressions. They also are logically related to later affective reactions, as emotional life continues to evolve. As a consequence, the discussion in the following chapters will be built around evolving systems, and will point to relations between these systems and emotional development beyond the infancy period.

Ultimately, an understanding of the developmental processes underlying the evolving affect systems will be brought to bear on the problem of individual differences in emotional development – that is, individual patterns of behavioral/affective organization. The assessment of individual differences will also focus on the qualitative turning points in early development, each having an affective core. As there are prototypes for the various emotions, there are prototypes for the individual organization of emotional development. These are individual patterns of early behavioral/emotional organization, which are elaborated into individual personality structure – individual ways of expressing and containing impulses, desires, and emotion.

5 The development of joy: a prototype for the study of emotion

> Certain smiles are not triggered by social events, are not conditionable, and are related to REM states of drowsiness. Other smiles are clearly responses to caretakers, appear to be anticipatory reactions, and appear at times of high alertness. The latter smiles are inferred to be emotional, the former are not.
>
> Plutchik (1983)

The developmental course of pleasure and joy is revealed by decades of solid research on infant smiling, which focused on its occurrence, its progressive changes in form, and its evolving meaning. Perhaps more than is the case for any other problem area, research focused on the nature and significance of infant smiling and laughter has revealed fundamental developmental processes. These processes are central to understanding normative affective development, individual emotional life, and the ties between the two. One cannot, for example, understand that at the core of smiling is arousal regulation and miss the importance of this process for studying individual differences.

There are no doubt several reasons for the important contribution made by research on smiling. First, much of the research carried out in the 1960s and 1970s was faithfully descriptive, a necessary cornerstone for any body of meaningful developmental research. Second, studies were addressed to ages across the span of infancy, often employing a longitudinal format. Third, smiling was approached from a variety of perspectives – ethology, social learning theory, cognitive theory, psychoanalytic theory, and genetic field theory (Spitz et al., 1970; Sroufe & Waters, 1976). From such a confluence it was readily determined that the smile had intimate ties with cognitive development, that it had multiple meanings that changed with age and even circumstances, and that it had biological significance.

There is a final and more important reason for the preeminence of smiling research, which centers on its integrative significance. The mature infant smile is both physiological and psychological, cognitive and affective, social and personal. It reflects the transaction of an active, meaning-seeking infant with his or her changing and unfolding environment. And it not only reflects and punctuates such encounters, but actually influences environmental reactions. Above all, it reflects the degree and quality of connectivity with the environment and the infant's emerging evaluation of that connection.

The goal of this chapter is to draw on smiling research to describe how the genuine emotion of pleasure evolves from pre-emotional states in the newborn period and, with further developmental progression, leads to the emotion of joy in the second half year. In so doing, the critical concept of a developmental prototype will be clarified.

Specific tasks for the chapter include tracing changes in the meanings of the smile during the course of development, revealing the relationship between early (endogenous) smiles and later smiles, relating developmental changes in smiling to general principles of development, and elaborating the function of the smile *for the infant*. In emphasizing the function for the infant we nonetheless keep in mind the communicative function of the smile, which no doubt played a central role in its evolution. The two levels of explanation are complementary. An attempt will be made to integrate the various perspectives regarding functions proposed for the smile, and the physiological, social, and cognitive components of smiling. As Kagan (1971) stated, the smile "serves many masters," and even after the mature smile emerges at 5 to 12 weeks of life the meaning of this ever present behavior changes with development. A common thread in this development can be seen, however, in the relation of the smile to its psychophysiological correlates.

An examination of developmental changes in morphological and dynamic features of smiling, from its earliest beginnings to the emergence of laughter by age 4 months, reveals a striking relationship between smiling and mechanisms of arousal, attention, and the modulation of tension. In addition, even after the emergence of mature smiling and laughter, the importance of such tension modulation mechanisms is apparent in progressive changes in the nature of situations potent for eliciting positive affect. (Insofar as the term *arousal* denotes a physiological rather than a psychological construct, the term *tension* is preferred. The distinction between my use of this term and the classic psychoanalytic use will become clear in discussion.)

The ontogenesis of smiling and laughter

Early smiles

The very earliest smiles have been called "endogenous" (e.g., Spitz et al., 1970) or "spontaneous" (Wolff, 1963) because they occur in the absence of known stimulation, most commonly during sleep. Emde and his colleagues have shown that these low-intensity smiles, which involve simply turning up the corners of

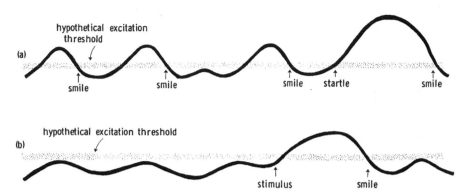

Figure 5.1. Schematic illustration of the excitation–relaxation cycle showing hypothetical threshold and relationship to overt behaviors.

the mouth, are not related to gastric activity or to vegetative drive state (e.g., time since feeding; Emde & Koenig, 1969). Rather, they are correlated with spontaneous (CNS) discharge of subcortical origin.

A wide variety of evidence is pertinent to Emde's position. The first smiles occur in bursts almost exclusively during REM sleep, especially when the eyes are first closed and in the middle portion of REM episodes, periods that are characterized by low levels of background cortical activity (Emde & Koenig, 1969; Wolff, 1963). One may also produce multiple small smiles by gently rousing a deeply sleeping infant toward wakefulness, thus reproducing the conditions of REM sleep. These first smiles are inversely related to other spontaneous behaviors (e.g., they do not occur when the infant is stirring or for about 5 minutes following startle; Takahashi, 1973; Wolff, 1963). Finally, they are more frequent in premature infants and have been found to occur in a microcephalic infant without a functioning cortex (Emde, McCartney, & Harmon, 1971; Harmon & Emde, 1972), and they decrease in frequency with age over the first 3 months of life (Spitz et al., 1970).

The conclusion that emerges from these data is that endogenous smiles are rather completely dominated by the state of the organism. They are associated with low, oscillating states of excitation of subcortical origin, with the smile occurring as the excitation rises above, then falls below, some threshold. (See the schematic of the excitation–relaxation cycle in Figure 5.1a.) As the cortex becomes functional these endogenous smiles decline, which is why, for example, they are more common in premature newborns. One might even say that the declining of these smiles permits an external view of the developing cortex.

It is important to note that the first elicited (exogenous) smiles are also obtained when the infant is asleep; that is, stimuli that do not effectively elicit smiling during the waking state in the first week of life are effective when the infant sleeps (Wolff, 1963). This is perhaps because of the relatively low levels of motor and cortical activity present before and after stimulation in this state. Stimulation increases the level of excitation above some threshold, with the smile occurring as relaxation follows, between 6 and 8 seconds after stimulation (Wolff, 1963). This would seem to be analogous to gently jiggling the sleeping infant, though here the rousing is due to an auditory stimulus (see Figure 5.1b).

The very earliest *waking* smiles are elicited by low-level tactile and kinesthetic stimulation (light touches on sensitive areas, blowing on the skin, gentle jiggling of the infant; Emde & Koenig, 1969; Watson, 1924/1970). These first elicited smiles, like the spontaneous (endogenous) smiles, are low-intensity responses to mild stimulation, typically involving only the corners of the mouth (see Table 5.1). Oster and Ekman (1978) have reported that these early smiles result from the action of a single muscle, while progressively later smiles involve the action of multiple muscle units.

According to Wolff (1963), the first smiles readily elicited when the infant is awake (perhaps in the second week) occur when the infant is satiated following feeding. The infant is drowsy and glassy-eyed ("intoxicated"). The response is of slightly larger magnitude (as drowsy REM smiles are of larger magnitude than those occurring during REM sleep; Emde & Koenig, 1969). Primarily, the mouth corners are drawn back further; it is neither the grimace of the first week nor the alert smile of 4 weeks. Auditory stimulation, especially high-pitched voices, are very effective elicitors at this time. Thus, by the second week of life the expression of positive affect is less dependent on low levels of modulated stimulation; still, the effectiveness of external stimulation depends on a generally low level of background excitation or activity.

By the third week of life, the first alert smiles occur. While awake and with focused attention, the infant smiles more actively, especially at voices, according to Wolff's data. This alert smile involves a brightening and crinkling of the eyes with the mouth pulled into a "grin," and its latency is now only 4 to 5 seconds poststimulation. This all suggests a steeper gradient of excitation and faster recovery. At this time a nodding head accompanying vocal stimulation is more effective than the voice alone, implying a greater capacity to accommodate stimulation. For the first time the infant's directed attentional processes play at least some role in engendering the excitation. There are wide individual differences in the ages at which these and other smiles appear, probably due in part to gestational age. Still, the sequence and the relationships between state, latency, and the magnitude of the response are as described.

The progression continues in the fourth week, during which the caregiver's voice is especially effective, even causing an interruption of feeding for the smile. In this and in other ways the smile has become more independent of the

Table 5.1. *The development of smiling and laughter*

Age	Response	Stimulation	Latency	Remarks
Smiling				
Neonate	Corners of the mouth	No external stimulation		Due to CNS fluctuations
Week 1	Corners of the mouth	Low level, modulated	6–8 seconds	During sleep, boosting of tension
Week 2	Mouth pulled back	Low level, modulated, voices		When drowsy, satiated
Week 3	Grin, including eyes	Moderate level, voices	4–5 seconds	When alert, attentive (nodding head with voice)
Week 4	Grin, active smile	Moderate or moderately intense	"Reduced"	Vigorous tactile stimulation effective
Weeks 5–8	Grin, active smile, cooing	Dynamic stimulation, first visual stimulation	3 seconds or less	Nodding head, flicking lights, stimulation that must be followed
Weeks 9–12	Grin, active smile, cooing	Static, visual stimulation, moderately intense	Short	Trial-by-trial effects, effortful assimilation, recognition; static at times more effective than dynamic
Laughter				
Month 4	Laughter	Multimodal, vigorous stimulation	1–2 seconds	Tactile, auditory, most effective
Months 5–6	Laughter	Intense auditory stimulation, as well as tactile	Immediate	Items that may have previously caused crying
Months 7–9	Laughter	Social, visual stimulation, primarily dynamic	Immediate	Tactile, auditory decline
Months 10–12	Laughter	Visual, social	Immediate or in anticipation	Visual incongruities, active participation

organismic state. The first smiles to a silent moving face occur, and during visual tracking of a slowly moving object (producing a "hypnotic-like" state), a sudden movement of the hand across the field of vision elicits a startle smile. These developments represent the roots of the infant's own involvement in tension production, though the smiles are primarily still in response to stimulation per se, as opposed to stimulus content. Also during the fourth week, patty-cake (three vigorous claps of the infant's hands), which had not elicited any smiling at 3 weeks, became the most effective stimulus employed for seven of Wolff's eight subjects, and remained so across the first 3 months, even producing smiling in fussy infants. The smile elicited by such vigorous stimulation is a maximal smiling response, close to a chortle. Wolff does not report the smile latency here but does say, "Smiling intensity increases with repetition, the response latency becomes shorter, and the baby's excitement increases" (p. 126).

There is something special about the ability to cope with this degree of stimulation. The active smiling that it engenders suggests that even at this early age some cortical modulation of the stimulation-produced (global) arousal is possible, by virtue of the infant's increased ability to assimilate at least portions of the impinging stimulus situation and to follow changes in the stimulation (see the section entitled "Summary and Model"). As the degree of excitation increasingly becomes due to the infant's "engagement" of the stimulus, we speak of the infant's efforts to "stay with" the stimulus as engendering tension (Sroufe & Waters, 1976). It is not yet a matter of processing stimulus content, however, and the patterning of the stimulation remains an important determinant of the response.

Wolff concluded his detailed observations in the fifth week. At that time the voice waned in its effectiveness, and the nodding head became the first visual stimulus to consistently elicit smiling. Smiles could be elicited up to 23 trials in a row, and could be reinstated and maintained for many more trials if the experimenter put on a mask, then sunglasses over the mask, then removed the mask, and the like. The masked face with wagging tongue was more effective than mask alone. All of these observations point to the need for a *dynamic* visual event to provide sufficient stimulation for smiling to occur. This remains the case until 3 to 4 weeks later when the infant alone can produce the same effect by actively engaging and elaborating the content of "meaningful" stimuli.

Scheme formation and recognition

The presentation of a stationary face does not consistently elicit smiling until about 8 to 10 weeks (Ambrose, 1961; Gewirtz, 1965; Spitz et al., 1970), although by 5 weeks it is potent when in motion (Wolff, 1963). This is indeed an important developmental landmark, probably reflecting the first formation of a true visual scheme. Spitz and colleagues (1970) showed that the emergence of smiling to a stationary face is paralleled by the decline of endogenous smiling and infantile fussiness and by important developmental changes in both the EEG and sleep patterns associated with maturation of the cortex. As discussed in Chapter 4, all of this points to a qualitative turn in development, at which point the infant becomes dramatically more responsive to the surround. The elicited smile no longer depends entirely on the parameters of the external stimulation. Instead the conditions necessary to occasion smiling can now clearly arise as a function of the infant's *cognitive engagement.* The involvement of cognitive activity is suggested by several lines of evidence, including the observation that institutionalized infants are delayed by several weeks in reaching peak responsiveness to the immobile face (Gewirtz, 1965), as are infants with Down syndrome (Cicchetti & Beeghly, 1990).

During the period from about 5 to 8 weeks, the infant seems to be most responsive to dynamic visual stimulation (the nodding head and Wolff's masked face with wagging tongue); thus, Salzen (1963) found with an 8-week-old subject that rotation increased the effectiveness of cardboard stimuli and that blinking lights were more effective than a static display. The infant's increased capacity to attend to and follow contrast and change mediate the smile, but still the excitation seems to derive primarily from stimulation, rather than the processing of a stimulus configuration (content). At this time there is little specificity of the stimulus content.

Increasingly, however, stationary but "meaningful" visual stimuli become more effective (Shultz & Zigler, 1970; Zelazo & Komer, 1971). Thus, Shultz and Zigler (1970) found with 3-month-olds that a stationary toy clown was more effective in eliciting smiles than a moving clown, in clear contrast to earlier ages. Employing Piaget's (1952) concept of recognitory assimilation, Shultz and Zigler argued that the infant can more readily "master" the stationary clown. The tension–relaxation cycle produced by "effortful assimilation" (Kagan, 1971; Piaget, 1952) reflects a fundamentally different process than excitation produced by stimulation; it is more cognitive than sensory and represents a more active role for the infant. The infant, through his or her own cognitive activity is producing the tension–relaxation process that previously resulted only from random CNS fluctuations or from quantitative aspects of environmental stimulation.

The following observations attest to the fact that effortful assimilation (tension production and release) is central in these smiles of the 8- to 12-week-old. First, stimuli once effective in eliciting smiles lose their potency over time. In normal home-reared infants, for example, immobile faces decline in effectiveness after age 3 to 5 months (Ambrose, 1961; Gewirtz, 1965; Kagan, 1967; Spitz et al., 1970; Takahashi, 1973). Similarly, within a single experiment, repeatedly presented stimuli decline in potency, after having been effective for a number of trials. The infant scrutinizes the stimulus with neutral affect during the initial trials, then smiles for several trials before returning again to affectively neutral looking. Piaget (1962) argued that there is initially a process involving accommodation followed by smiling with accommodation and assimilation. Thus, first there is effort without assimilation (neutral affect). Then there is both strong effort and assimilation (smiling). Finally, with repeated exposure there is ease of assimilation, little cognitive effort, and again neutral affect. If a novel aspect is introduced during the series of presentations, there is renewed orienting to the transformed stimulus, with a decline in positive affect if the infant still had been smiling to the original stimulus. This is followed by smiling to the altered stimulus on subsequent trials and again a decline (Kagan, 1971; Shultz & Zigler, 1970; Sroufe & Wunsch, 1972; Zelazo, 1972; Zelazo & Komer, 1971). Moreover, older infants smile sooner than younger infants to the same novel stimulus situations, suggesting a shorter accommodation phase (Zelazo, 1972).

Kagan (1971) summarized the situation with respect to the declining smile to faces with age in the following way:

The smile declines because his schema for a face becomes so well articulated that all faces or representations of faces are immediately recognized as such. There is *no tension; no effort is required for assimilation*, and hence, no smile. (p. 153, emphasis added)

Similarly, Zelazo (1972; Zelazo & Komer, 1971) attributed the curvilinear trends within experiments using auditory and visual stimuli to changes in the ease of assimilation. Thus, these investigators see a role for tension (effort) in the ''recognitory'' smiles.

The development of laughter

Infant laughter, which is strikingly similar to adult laughter and readily distinguished from earlier chortling smiles, may first be elicited reliably at about age 4 months. In comparison with smiling, laughter requires a greater and typically more rapid buildup of tension (see also Thompson, 1990). Most often the laugh occurs immediately or within 2 seconds after the cutoff point of the stimulation. Clear developmental trends have been found in the nature of items potent for producing laughter. Closely paralleling the case for smiling in the first quarter year of life, the elicitors of laughter proceed during the first year from intrusive tactile and auditory stimulation to interesting sociovisual events (Sroufe & Wunsch, 1972). (The following conclusions are based on the longitudinal study of 10 infants and the cross-sectional study of 96 infants.)

The trend from age 4 to 6 months is from laughter at vigorous stimulation to laughter at less vigorous but more ''provocative'' tactile and auditory stimulation (see Table 5.1). At first, physically vigorous stimulation is most potent. Of 28 items in our battery (see Table 5.2), laughter was produced in one-third of the 4-month-olds only by a vigorous kissing of the stomach and the "I'm gonna get you" game (looming approach with talking, building somewhat slowly but abruptly terminating with tickling the ribs). Both involve intense tactile stimulation. Five-month-olds laughed in addition at the mother vocalizing a resounding "BOOM BOOM BOOM." One-third of the 6-month-olds laughed at a swelling, loud "Aah" with abrupt cutoff, at being rather gently jiggled, and being tickled under the chin, and at the three items successful at 4 and 5 months. Thus, by 6 months a range of stimulating auditory items and less intense tactile items had become effective. Also, this was the first age at which one-third laughed at a visual item (mother approaching with cloth-covered face; a dynamic visual stimulus).

In the second half year a new trend emerged, with laughter occurring in response to social and more subtle visual stimulus situations, and with the intrusive, vigorous items declining in potency. For example, one-third of the 8-month-olds laughed at peekaboo (performed without sound) and at their own faces being covered, as well as to mother's approach with covered face, mother shaking her hair, mother crawling on the floor, and at pulling a dangling cloth from mother's mouth (see Chapter 3 for a detailed example of the latter item). These items all involve a transformation of the infant's internal scheme of the mother and a coordination of the altered image with the memory of the familiar image. The only clearly potent auditory or tactile item was "kissing the stomach."

This trend continued month by month, with 12-month-olds laughing at the greatest proportion of the visual and social items. They laughed most to the items that provide an obvious element of cognitive incongruity: mother "walking like a penguin," approaching with a mask, sucking on the baby's bottle, and the game of sticking out her tongue (and pulling it in as the infant reaches), as well as to each of the social and visual items successful at 8 months. (In all, one-third or more laughed in response to 9 of the 14 social and visual items.) They also laughed at 4 tactile and auditory items, but when infants in the last quarter laughed at such items it was clear that the item had been transformed; for example, they laughed *in anticipation* of the mother actually kissing the stomach (so it is not in reaction to the physical stimulation). Similarly, the oldest babies often laughed hardest when stuffing the cloth back into the mother's mouth. Clearly, then, with laughter as with smiling, the response progressively becomes a product of the cognitively sophisticated infant's active engagement and elaboration of novel experiences (see Sroufe & Wunsch, 1972, for further detail).

A steep, sharp tension fluctuation is required to produce laughter; the re-

Table 5.2. *Instructions for individual items*

Auditory

1. Lip popping: Four pops in a row, then pause. Starts with lips pursed, cheeks full.
2. Swelling "Aah": Starts low, builds to loud voice, abrupt cutoff. Six-second pause.
3. Using a loud, deep voice pronounce, "Boom, boom, boom," at 1-second intervals.
4. Mechanical type of sound, varying voice pitch from low to high and back down again.
5. With mouth 1 foot from baby's ear, whisper, "Hi, baby, how are you?" Avoid blowing in ear.
6. With falsetto voice (like Mickey Mouse) say, "Hi, baby, how are you?"
7. With lips relaxed, blow through them as a horse does when tired.

Tactile

8. Blow gently at hair for 3 seconds. Blow from the side, across the top of the head.
9. Four quick pecks, on bare stomach.
10. Gently stroke cheek three times with soft object.
11. Place baby on knees facing away. Five vigorous bounces.
12. Hold baby waist high, horizontal, face toward floor and jiggle vigorously for 3 seconds.
13. Using finger, gently tickle under baby's chin for 3 seconds.
14. Open mouth wide, press lips on back of neck, and create suction for 2 seconds.

Social

15. Focus baby's attention on your fingers. Walk fingers toward baby, then give baby a poke in the ribs. If laughter is achieved, do another trial not followed by poking.
16. Playing tug: Allow baby to grasp yarn, then tug three times, trying not to pull it away. Pause and repeat.
17. Put cloth in mouth and lean close enough for baby to grasp it. Allow baby to pull cloth out and replace it if this is his or her tendency. Place the end of the cloth in baby's hand if this is necessary.
18. Say lyrically, "I'm gonna get you" (make the "I'm" quite protracted), while leaning toward baby with hands poised to grab. Then grab baby around stomach. If laughter is achieved, do another trial not followed by grabbing.
19. Stand at baby's side. Put cloth over baby's face. If baby does not uncover his or her face immediately, uncover for him or her. Do not drag cloth across baby's face. Emphasis is on baby getting out from underneath.
20. Stick out tongue until baby touches it (make baby's hand touch it if necessary). Quickly pull tongue back in as soon as he or she touches it.
21. Using black cardboard, get baby's attention with face uncovered, cover face for 2 seconds, uncover quickly and pause 3 seconds. Do not say, "Peekaboo."

Visual

22. Using a white cloth, proceed as in number 28.
23. Use one of baby's favorite toys. Focus his or her attention on it (out of reach). Cover it for 2 seconds, uncover quickly.
24. Sucking baby bottle: First make sure that the baby is not hungry, then take bottle, bring toward your lips, take three pretend sucks, lower bottle.
25. Crawling on floor: Place baby in highchair or infant seat. Crawl across, not toward, his or her field of vision. Stand, return to starting point.

Table 5.2. (*cont.*)

26. Penguin walk: Stand with arms extended to sides, walk in an exaggerated waddle across baby's field of vision. Return to starting point walking normally.
27. Shake head vigorously at a distance of 1 foot from baby's face three times. Do not allow hair to touch baby.
28. Obtain baby's attention. Hold mask up so he or she can see it. Place mask in front of your face, lean slowly to within 1 foot of baby's face, pause 2 seconds. Lean back slowly, remove mask slowly.

Extra items
29. Crawl behind baby, ostentatiously chasing, slapping hands on floor.
30. Lift baby slowly to position overhead, looking down back. Minimize tactile and kinesthetic aspects.
31. Mirror image: To reduce peekaboo effects move baby slowly in front of full-length mirror. Hold for 3 seconds, remove slowly, then pause for 4 seconds.
32. As in number 18.
33. As in number 15.

Note: Pauses between trials are 4 seconds unless otherwise stated.

sponse, of course, is maximal. (See Rothbart, 1973, and Thompson, 1990, for similar tension release interpretations of laughter.) Observations with the "swelling Aah" item illustrate this. First, this item (and the loud vocalization, "BOOM BOOM BOOM") sometimes produced crying in infants before the age of onset of laughter. When this occurred, *the same* item was especially likely to produce laughter the following month (the infant now having an alternative response to such a marked tension fluctuation, and a greater capacity to tolerate high levels of excitation; see also Fogel, 1982). Second, if, instead of swelling the sound in a positively accelerated function with an abrupt cutoff, it was swelled, tapered, and reduced in loudness, the item did not produce laughter, presumably because the tension fluctuation was blunted. Similarly, other items that build to a climax are maximally potent for laughter (e.g., the best item, "I'm gonna get you," with looming presence and a poke in the ribs). If the "I'm gonna get you" item is done in deadpan voice it is not effective. If it is drawn out and swelled ("IIIIIII . . . m gonnnnnnna"), then abruptly concluded ("GETCHU!"), it is maximally effective.

Granting the importance of a steep gradient of tension and rapid recovery, the laughter of older infants to the mother sucking on their bottles or walking "like a penguin" reflects a rapid coordination of schemes and processing of incongruity, a cognitively generated analog of a rapid and pronounced arousal fluctuation. The physical stimulation per se is of low intensity. The intensity of the experience comes from the meaning imposed by the infant. This is a remarkable development, with profound implications, fully comparable to the qualitative developmental change reflected by the smile of recognition at 3 months (see the later section on "function"). These developments reflect the increasingly active involvement of infants in creating their own experience.

As was the case with smiling studies, trial-by-trial effects for laughter also are quite revealing. Laughter reliably builds from smiling on earlier trials (often with an initial trial or two of neutral expression) and fades again to smiling on later trials (Sroufe & Wunsch, 1972). As effortful assimilation is implicated in recognitory smiles, faster effortful assimilation or effortful assimilation of more features of the situation, and therefore a steeper tension fluctuation, is implicated in laughter. Whether smiling or laughter occurs is also influenced by context, salience, and background stimulation (see Chapter 8). In general, one of the most remarkable developments over the first year of life is the rapid increase in the capacity to tolerate arousal or tension (Fogel, 1982; Schore, 1994). This is reflected in the developmental changes in smiling and then laughter.

The growth of mastery: from passive recipient to active agent

In the development of both smiling and laughter the infant's progress is from response to intrusive stimulation, and to stimulation mediated by active attention, toward smiling and laughing in response to stimulus content, and finally toward an ever more active involvement in producing the stimulus itself. Kagan (1971), for example, found that 2-year-olds smile following the solution of a problem (e.g., finding an embedded figure), with smiling more likely the more difficult the problem solved. In this circumstance the stimulus for smiling is clearly a product of the child's mental processes, not the picture on the page. At the same time, we find that with development it becomes increasingly difficult to elicit smiling to simple repetitive stimuli or static stimuli. "Effortful assimilation" increasingly involves more than recognition.

With our laughter items, it was noted that in the second half year those in which the infant participated became more potent (pulling the cloth from mother's mouth, reaching for the protruding tongue), and that infants laugh at social participation items only when participation is accomplished (e.g., when they are sufficiently developed to tug reciprocally when playing tug with mother; Cicchetti & Sroufe, 1976). Later, infants laugh more at their own productions (attempting to stuff the cloth back into mother's mouth). Likewise, Mayes and Zigler (1992) found that 9- to 11-month-olds routinely smile and laugh while practicing motor tasks such as pulling to a standing position. Informal observations suggest that the tendency to laugh in situations in which the infant is agent, rather than recipient, increases into the second year of life, with, for example, infants laughing more vigorously at covering the observer's face with a cloth than at having their own face covered.

Piaget (1952, 1962) introduced the concepts of both recognition and mastery with regard to smiling and laughter, and investigators of early scheme-related smiling have generally used one term or the other (Shultz & Zigler, 1970; Zelazo & Komer, 1971). In light of the preceding discussion, "mastery" would seem to be the broader concept (with recognition considered a form of mastery), since it can encompass early smiling with recognition, the smiles following problem solving and laughter in response to incongruity and games. It also implies an active role for the infant in engaging the surround. One of the most remarkable facts regarding human nature lies in the clear and obvious joy of infants in mastering skills and engaging the environment.

Summary and model

Early elicited smiles, though manifesting progressive changes, are in an essential way more closely related to endogenous REM sleep smiles than to smiles reflecting effortful scheme formation. First, gentle, modulated tactile and auditory stimulation, which makes no requirements for directional attention or analysis of content, is most effective (see Table 5.1). In the absence of background "noise," such stimulation, by its rhythm, intensity, and modulated quality, externally reproduces the fluctuating CNS states that occur in association with REM smiles, especially, for example, when the infant is drowsy or entranced. Later, as the infant matures, he or she can orient to or be "captured" by more complex or changing stimuli, even when the level of background excitation is moderately high. Smiling occurs in the alert state, to more vigorous stimulation, and to dynamic visual or visuoauditory stimulation that requires directed and sustained attention. These smiles are of shorter latency and larger magnitude (and involve more muscle units), reflecting both the greater background stimulation and the cognitively engendered tension. With the increasing importance of scheme formation in occasioning smiles, it is no longer stimulation per se that produces the tension → relaxation → smile, but the infant's effort in processing stimulus content.

Relatively little environmental stimulation is involved when an infant is visually presented a novel object (e.g., a dangling clown). But in the case of a 10-week-old, considerable stimulation (tension) results from the infant's *own efforts* of engagement and accommodation. When, in time, these efforts lead to relatively rapid assimilation, the cognitively mediated smile results. This progression toward an increasing role for cognition and meaning in producing positive affect continues throughout the first year of life, with even laughter occurring in the absence of vigorous stimulation by the end of this time.

It is proposed that cortically mediated (content-based) tension increases and recovers rapidly, producing the "arousal jag" (Berlyne, 1969) required for smiling (and later laughter), and that this occurs against the backdrop of slowly recovering global arousal produced by stimulation per se. Chance (1962) has presented neuroanatomical and neurophysiological evidence for distinguishing between two components of arousal produced by external stimulation: a non-specific component that affects the "state" of the animal and a specific component that conveys the signal value of the stimulus. Relevant, then, are both the developing ability to maintain orientation in the face of higher levels of stimulation and the ability to assimilate "meaningful" aspects of the stimulation. As the infant becomes more actively involved in his or her transactions with the environment, there is no longer a one-to-one correspondence between stimulation and arousal. *The content of the event, and therefore the relationship between the infant and the event, becomes primary.* It is for this reason that 10-week-olds' smiles can clearly be labeled emotional reactions by our definition. It is because of the level of engagement by the infant, concluded to be present in such circumstances, that the psychological experience of pleasure is inferred from smiling at this time.

Early pleasure is posited to derive from the modulation of tension around some moderate level. Although the distinction may seem arbitrary, neonatal smiles, while reflecting a comfortable arousal level or a pleasant state, are not considered to indicate a genuine emotion because they do not involve even the beginnings of meaning. Of course, the beginnings of meaning do come out of such arousal fluctuations. However, it is only when the smile is mediated by a cognitive process – a connection between the infant and the surround (an awareness) – that the emotion of pleasure is inferred. Interestingly, there are qualitative changes in the smile itself at this time (open mouth, crinkled eyes), perhaps reflecting the steeper gradient of tension in cognitively mediated smiles.

Joy is distinguished from the pleasure of the 2- to 3-month-old, requiring a more active mastery and a higher level of meaning (which probably includes awareness of the affect itself). Laughter, the most intense expression of positive affect, requires a steeper gradient and a more rapid fluctuation than does smiling and in the present analysis is related to delight (Period 3) or joy. Joy is placed on the developmental chart (Table 4.1) in the third quarter of life (Period 3). Given the laughter of the 5-month-old, this again may seem arbitrary. But the intensity of elation by 9 months is qualitatively different than that seen earlier (e.g., Schore, 1994; Termine & Izard, 1988). Also, it is in the third quarter of life that infants laugh in anticipation of mother's return in peekaboo, laugh at a variety of social games, laugh at visual spectacles across a distance, and begin to lose interest in mere stimulation. In short, the meaning of the event in relation to the infant becomes dominant, in comparison to mere stimulation. Affectivity has progressed from being due to mere parameters of stimulation, to a combination of stimulus features and infant attentional and processing efforts, to rec-

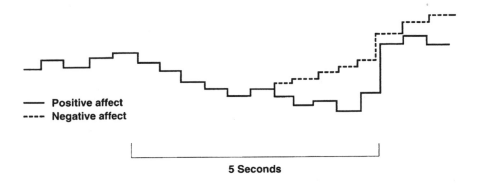

Figure 5.2. Schematic illustration of heart rate change associated with positive and negative responses to approach by a masked adult.

ognition of the stimulus content, to the meaningfulness of the particular event. Of course, meaning becomes even more dominant in the fourth quarter, with visual incongruities paralleling social games in potency for eliciting laughter. Ultimately, in the second year, an understanding of meaning from previous experiences may be carried forward in the form of a positive mood.

The tension modulation hypothesis

Our work on the development of laughter was conceived with a tension modulation hypothesis in mind (Sroufe et al., 1974; Sroufe & Wunsch, 1992). Thus, a range of items was selected that varied in sensory modality, physical intensity, and apparent incongruity of content. Also, items were included that were similar to those previously reported to produce fear (loud sounds, loss of balance, looming approach, and masked approach), since these would be expected to produce the requisite tension and therefore laughter in a secure context (see Chapter 8 and the section on "function" later in this chapter). Other research findings confirmed the importance of this construct (Field & Fogel, 1982).

Psychophysiological antecedents of smiling and laughter

Figure 5.2 is a schematic of observed HR changes during both aversive and positive reactions to masked approach. In this situation either mother or a stranger calls the infant's name, presents the mask, covers his or her face, then slowly leans to within reach of the infant. In each case there is an initial HR deceleration of large magnitude, and at this point we cannot predict the infant's reaction from either physiological records or videotaped overt behavior. In an aversive situation, as when a stranger approaches in the mother's absence, a tachycardia (acceleration) follows the deceleration, becoming more pronounced with crying. In the typical case the HR acceleration precedes the crying (Vaughn & Sroufe, 1979). With the mother presenting the item, unless the infant has been previously frightened, the deceleration to her approach continues right to the point of smiling, laughing, and reaching; it is followed, of course, by tachycardia associated with the vigorous muscular discharge (see also Emde, Campos, Reich, & Gaensbauer, 1978). These HR patterns are very reliable, and they suggest that dramatic orienting and appraisal are an intricate part of both fear and strong positive affect (Fogel, 1982). We refer to "engaging" and "evaluating" the stimulus situation and "engendering tension" (see Chapter 8).

Laughter and smiling in infants with Down syndrome

The longitudinal observation of infants with Down syndrome (Cicchetti & Beeghly, 1990; Cicchetti & Sroufe, 1976) support the tension modulation concept. These infants lag considerably behind normal infants in the onset of laughter (by 4 months or more), and laughter remains rare. In time, however, they do laugh at items in the same order reported by Sroufe and Wunsch (1972) for normal infants. Also, they will frequently smile at situations eliciting laughter in nonretarded infants and, again, in the same order. Especially with the nonreflexive, more cognitively sophisticated items, infants with Down syndrome seem unable to process the incongruity with sufficient speed to produce the "tension jag" required for laughter (although the differential smiling suggests developmental changes in comprehension). This notion is supported by the long latencies to smile and laugh in these infants. It is also interesting to note that extreme abnormalities in muscular tension seen in some of these infants can be related to laughter. The four most markedly hypotonic (flaccid) infants in the sample did not laugh at all before age 13 months and then very rarely. Parallel differences in development have been found in studies of fear in these infants (Cicchetti & Beeghly, 1990; see also Chapter 7).

The concept of tension modulation

The tension modulation concept being proposed must be distinguished from concepts rooted in drive reduction or the closed hydraulic energetics of classic psychoanalysis. Tension, as described here, is not always present and seeking discharge, and it is not necessarily aversive. Tension is a natural consequence of the infant's engagement of novel stimulation.

In a secure context, infants actively seek to reproduce incongruous, tension-producing situations. Therefore, notions of tension "relief" or "reduction" are deliberately avoided. The position is distinct from Ambrose's (1963) ambivalence position (laughter is not viewed as expressing a mixture of pleasure and fear) and even from other cognitive positions, such as Kagan's (1971), which imply that processing incongruity necessarily involves a negative component:

The smile that accompanies recognition of a face required, first a buildup of tension during the brief period of uncertainty that the infant must experience . . . The smile can reflect the assimilation and the accompanying drop in the tension . . . the infant who smiles may have a capacity to build up a tension . . . and to be relieved of it. (p. 155)

The formulation presented here, which is similar to Kagan's, is unique in assuming that the initial orienting, appraisal, and tension production is not affectively charged and that affect is determined by context as well as by stimulus discrepancy. We emphasize the fact that the same stimulus situation can lead to either strong negative or positive affect depending on the infant's context-based "evaluation" of the incongruity. Within broad limits, no set amount of tension automatically leads to negative affect, and infants are not best viewed as seeking to be relieved from tension.

While the tension modulation process being discussed is primarily psychological, it is elaborated from an earlier physiological process. Spitz's notion of the physiological prototype (e.g., Spitz et al., 1970) is germane here. While the excitation–relaxation cycle underlying the early endogenous smile represents a spontaneous CNS discharge of subcortical origin, and later smiles are primarily under the influence of cortical processes, there are still autonomic and muscular components. The process has been transformed and elaborated with development but still embodies the earlier physiological component (see Chapter 4). Arousal modulation has become tension modulation, but the core excitation fluctuation remains a part of the more mature response.

The function of the tension regulation mechanism

The tension regulation process, which is so apparent in every phase of the development of smiling and laughter and which has such striking overt behavioral and physiological manifestations, must be of functional consequence. In particular, the functional significance of this mechanism *for infants*, as they transact with the environment, remains to be specified. (The communicative function will be discussed in a subsequent section.)

For survival and adaptation it is of fundamental importance that the human organism have special capacities for dealing with situations of uncertain consequence. Ethologists (Bowlby, 1973; Freedman, 1965) have stressed the survival value of wariness concerning the unknown. Wariness, or hesitation and guardedness in the face of something unfamiliar, serves the function of protecting the human from being harmed by a malevolent creature or situation. On the other side, however, the developmental value of transactions with novel and unknown aspects of the environment must also be emphasized. A major adaptive advantage of humans is opportunism – capitalizing on new discoveries and taking advantage of novel occurrences. Also, engaging novel situations enhances cognitive development. Through failures of assimilation, schemes become both broadened and differentiated by accommodation (Piaget, 1952), and the infant's view of the world becomes more perfectly adapted to its present environment.

Careful study reveals that the infant's motivation concerning the unfamiliar, perhaps especially toward strange persons, is quite complex (Bronson, 1972; Sroufe et al., 1974). For example, infants, even in the second half year of life, clearly have strong affiliative tendencies toward unfamiliar persons (attending to them, smiling at them at a distance, exchanging objects; Bretherton & Ainsworth, 1974; Rheingold & Eckerman, 1973; Sroufe et al., 1974). And yet they also show avoidance or subtle signs of wariness (e.g., gaze aversion, "worried facial expression") and do not smile when a stranger actually attempts to make physical contact, especially if familiarization time is kept to a minimum. The tendency to express wariness is as well documented as the affiliative tendency (see Chapter 6).

Not surprisingly, the human infant is equipped with capacities appropriate to this complex motivation and to the saliency of unfamiliar stimulus situations. The most widely discussed capacity has been the *orienting response* (OR). When confronted with a novel stimulus situation of moderate intensity (or change or termination of stimulation), a complex of motoric, sensory, and autonomic reactions occurs (e.g., orientation of the sensory receptors, muscular quieting, HR deceleration, increased blood flow to the brain), which heightens the capacity to process and respond to environmental information (Graham & Clifton, 1966; Sokolov, 1963). While this highly adaptive process is now well known, it is nonetheless remarkable. For an opportunistic organism whose adaptation is based on a flexible use of the environment, it is critical that distracting motor activity cease when orienting to a salient, novel stimulus situation.

But when orienting is so dramatic and total, it is likewise important that there are mechanisms to terminate it and to allow rapid response to the situation. Behavioral avoidance, gaze aversion, and the expression of positive affect are behavioral components of processes available to the infant for this purpose. A positively toned tension release process is particularly advantageous for the infant. Positive affective expressions "foster continued appraisal of nonthreatening events and enable the child to respond rapidly and appropriately to changes in stimulus conditions" (Thompson, 1990, p. 382). Positive emotion allows the baby to remain oriented toward the situation, and at the same time to express well-being and encourage others to continue or repeat engaging events.

The hypothesis that smiling and laughter are closely associated with a tension release mechanism was originally derived from an analysis of the close relationship between fear and laughter. For example, we observed that in different contexts the same stimulus situations (e.g., mother approaching wearing a mask) could prove equally potent for producing either crying or laughter (see Chapter 8). But consider the different consequences of negative and positive affective expressions.

Following orienting and tension buildup in an *insecure* context, crying and active avoidance serve both the set goals of an attachment behavior system (attracting the parent) and the function of modulating arousal (see Chapter 10). However, this occurs at the expense of further engagement of the event. Indeed, infants who have cried on one trial of social approach by a stranger wearing a mask cry or avoid the situation even sooner on subsequent trials (Waters et al., 1975).

In a *secure* context, the tension produced by the same social approach may lead to positive responses. When the function of modulating arousal is served by tension release with positive affect (or by subtle aversive behaviors such as gaze aversion or coyness), the infant is not taken out of contact with the situation. Infants who smile during one encounter with a provocative stimulus situation typically engage the event more readily on subsequent encounters. The maintenance of contact and interaction ultimately promotes assimilation. For the infant, then, the function of the tension release mechanism with which positive affect is associated goes beyond modulating prevailing levels of arousal. It serves, in addition, to help the infant maintain commerce with novel or provocative stimulus situations and thereby promotes both cognitive and emotional growth. As will be discussed in Chapter 8, there is an important clue here for the study of individual differences.

An important corollary function concerns the release of overt behavior. During the orienting and appraisal period the infant is "captured" or "frozen" by the incongruous stimulation. When the mother or the stranger engages in masked approach toward an infant, the infant ceases ongoing activity, quiets, and stares intently at the masked face. When mother is the agent (or sometimes the stranger following mother) the face then brightens, the infant smiles or laughs, then reaches. The reach and smile may occur simultaneously, but the reach never precedes the smile. This suggests both that the smile is the final point of the appraisal process (Bowlby, 1973; Sroufe et al., 1974) and that the tension release → smile terminates inhibition of overt motor behavior. (In my current formulation of this process, smiling and laughter are viewed as components of the tension release process, rather than as instrumental in tension release.)

Other explanations of infant smiling

The emphasis on the close association between smiling and tension modulation is not to deny the important social or communicative roles of the smile – for example, sharing emotion and eliciting approach from others (Vine, 1973). In fact, this is the most likely function underlying the evolution of the smile in humans. As will be discussed later, it is complementary to the tension modulation function. The social interpretations make sense of the overt expressive components of tension release (as opposed to a nonfacial response); that is, they explain why we smile rather than flex our toes when we experience pleasure.

Moreover, the tension modulation interpretation does not deny the insightfulness of previous investigators regarding the relationship of smiling to recognition, mastery, and other cognitive constructs (Kagan, 1971; McCall, 1972; Shultz & Zigler, 1970; Zelazo, 1972; Zelazo & Komer, 1971). The present view is consistent with these cognitive positions but, in answering the question of *why* the smile occurs with mastery or recognition, stresses a different level of analysis, one that underscores the developmental links between early endogenous and later exogenous smiling.

There is heuristic value in the tension modulation notion for encompassing all of the data on smiling and laughter in the first year of life, as well as in pointing to the emergence of behavioral coping mechanisms early in infancy. Neither a communication position, an innate releasing mechanism position (Ahrens, 1954), nor learning positions can encompass the findings on smiling to repeatedly presented nonsocial stimuli (see also Zelazo, 1972). And the recognition mastery hypothesis stops short of specifying the facilitative role of smiling/tension release in the process of mastery.

Social interpretations. Increasingly during the first year, the smile becomes primarily a social behavior. It is a major component of the infant's greeting behavior, is performed differentially to caregivers, and is more frequent when the infant is in the presence of people than when alone (Ainsworth, 1973; Fogel, 1993; Jones, Collins, & Hong, 1991; Vine, 1973; Wahler, 1967). Indeed, because of the ease with which smiles are elicited by social stimulation, 10-week-olds' smiles have been referred to as "social" smiles (as distinguished from spontaneous smiles). The smile clearly plays important roles in eliciting approach from others, in communicating well-being, and in promoting interaction essential to the development of mother–infant attachment (Ainsworth, 1967; Bowlby, 1969/1982; Schore, 1994; Stern, 1974). The first smiles to the face suggest to the caregiver that "my baby recognizes me," which supports the caregiver's ongoing engagement and effectiveness in providing appropriate stimulation. Thus, the early "social" smiles help ensure input or *aliment* for the cognitive processes that will eventually lead the infant to true social recognition.

Moreover, the smile has an important place in the development of reciprocity. First, the smile rewards caregiver behaviors, encouraging the repetition of actions and promoting interactive chains. Thus, the social function of the smile complements the function of positively toned tension release by providing opportunities for infants to exercise their tendency to perpetuate novel stimulus situations. The positively toned tension release both helps the infant stay engaged *and* encourages caregivers to continue the event. In addition, as a behavior each partner can exhibit, as well as elicit from the other, the smile has an important place in the learning of mutual effectance and emotional sharing (Schore, 1994). Finally, smiling/tension release, as well as gaze aversion, may have a special role in modulating arousal within face-to-face interactions, which are crucial for the development of reciprocity (Brazelton, Koslowski, & Main, 1974; Field & Fogel, 1982; Robson, 1967; Tronick, 1989; Waters et al., 1975; Zaslow & Breger, 1969). Affective development clearly contributes to social and cognitive development, while at the same time changes in the meaning of the smile reflect cognitive growth. In sum, the smile has numerous roles in social functioning, but these roles are complementary to the tension release interpretation.

The smile as learned

Much of the discussion of social functions suggests important roles for learning, broadly conceived, in the metamorphosis and differentiation of the smile during infancy. Differential greeting, reciprocity, elicitation of maternal approach, and efforts to reproduce events that occasioned smiling all point to the importance of learning experiences for both the infant and the caregiver. Likewise, the waxing and waning of smiling with the repetition of a stimulus, which Piaget would conceptualize in terms of accommodation and assimilation, clearly involves learning and memory.

It is also clear, however, that traditional models of learning, classical and instrumental conditioning, are not at all adequate in accounting for the acquisition, development, and functioning of the smile in early life. Difficulties with the classical conditioning position were outlined by Gewirtz (1965): (1) Atypically, the smile response is elicited by a wide range of unconditioned stimuli (visual, auditory, and tactile-kinesthetic). (2) Gross stimuli (e.g., the face) presented unchanging for long periods elicit repeated smiles (vs. a reflex). (3) The supposed conditioned stimulus (e.g., aspects of the caregiver) elicits smiles initially and does not permit discrete presentation. In addition, Watson (1972) has pointed out that infants smile more to a full face than to a profile, a view closer to that which would be associated with nursing. These results seem to discredit the notion that infants smile at visual stimuli because of their association with unconditioned stimuli or drive reduction.

At one time it was thought that patterns of smiling in infancy might be accounted for primarily by operant conditioning; that is, infants smile because they are reinforced for doing so. Since Brackbill (1958) demonstrated scheduling effects, it was apparent that smiling rate was at least responsive to contingencies. Now it is clear, however, that despite the influence of contingent reinforcement (Brackbill, 1958; Zelazo, 1971), it is of secondary importance to recognition-assimilation and subsequent habituation (Zelazo, 1972). Thus, in Zelazo's (1971) important study, smiling rate was initially high for the contingent social reinforcement group (where the experimenter engaged in talking, smiling, and touching after each smile), the noncontingent social reinforcement group (a control which Brackbill did not have), *and* the unresponsive experimenter group. Moreover, smiling decreased in *all* groups over trials, including those subjects being reinforced, though with the latter there was more marked "scalloping" across days.

Moreover, reinforcement cannot be used very readily to explain smiling patterns associated with inanimate objects. Reinforcement is secondary to cognitive factors in producing the typical sequence over trials of neutral affect, positive affect, then neutral affect again to novel stimuli. If the change from neutral expression to smiling is due to something inherently reinforcing in the stimulus situations, then smiling should continue rather than cease with repeated presentation. The more compelling explanation remains effort with nonrecognition, changing to recognition, changing to recognition without effort. Positive affect is inherently part of the mastery experience.

Also germane are Bloom's findings with vocal behavior (Bloom, 1975; Bloom & Esposito, 1975). When proper controls were instituted it became clear that social facilitation, and not reinforcement, accounted for vocalization changes. Usual baseline procedures in operant studies of smiling and vocalization (an unresponsive adult) actually suppress social behavior (Tronick et al., 1978). Therefore, a return to normal interaction ends a suppression of affect, and subsequent noncontingent responsiveness is as effective as contingent responsiveness in overcoming this suppression. Experimenters who failed to use controls had the illusion of operant effects, but the results were due to stimulation per se. According to Bloom, reciprocity in caregiver–infant relationships is best characterized in terms of synchrony, not reinforcement. "For early social development the operant conditioning paradigm has ecological validity only in structure and not in function" (1975, p. 6). Caregivers do not teach infants to smile, but they may provide the conditions in which smiling readily occurs (see Chapter 9).

Conclusion: principles of development revealed by smiling research

In tracing the ontogenesis of smiling and laughter, not only are continuing roles for meaning and tension apparent, but certain basic principles of development are illuminated.

First, development is typically marked by repetitions of similar trends during different developmental periods. For example, the evolution in the first 3 months from stimulation-produced excitation to cognitively produced tension (wherein the infant imposes meaning on the stimulation) is elaborated and transformed, but in a basic way repeated, in the final quarters of the first year in the development of laughter. Again, there is a progression from a response based on stimulation (laughter to being tickled and to loud sounds) to a reaction based on the infant's cognitive elaboration (e.g., laughter to mother sucking on the infant's bottle). There is an *increasing flexibility* (e.g., concerning the range of situations that may produce laughter) and *increasing organization*, in the sense that the reaction is not merely a spillover of accumulating excitation, but a focused, sudden, and precisely timed response, which sharply punctuates the stream of behavior. This is the principle of directionality in development (see Chapter 3).

This observation is certainly consonant with Piaget's (1952, 1962) concept of functional invariants in the development of cognitive structures. Throughout the sensorimotor period and beyond, the sequence of accommodation, assimilation, *differentiation*, consolidation, accommodation . . . is repeated as the child's cognitive structures become organized and adapted to the environment. In a dialectic manner, the end point of a developmental sequence is the starting point for a repetition of that sequence. Earlier development paves the way for later development. Given the close ties that both the organization of behavior and the expression of affect have to cognitive growth, similar invariants should be expected to operate throughout their development as well. The observation that smiling in response to stimulation per se gives way to more active involvement, leading to a similar progression in the development of laughter, is only one example.

Parallel to this first principle is a second, the tendency of the infant to move toward incongruity and to find pleasure in cognitive challenges. As Piaget (1952) illustrated, the infant begins life already as an active participant in his or her own development, seeking stimulation and engaging novel experiences. With development the infant becomes an increasingly active agent, *producing* as well as mastering the situations that promote both cognitive and social growth. The observation of this mastery principle in action, complete with the emotions of pleasure, delight, and joy, promotes a very different view of the developing child than one emphasizing external reward (Overton & Reese, 1972; White, 1959). Development is its own impetus.

A third principle concerns the *unity* of development. The tension modulation function places the smile within a constellation of important mechanisms for dealing with novel aspects of the surround. In doing so, a close relationship is seen between the constructs of joy and fear and between smiling and wary behaviors, both of which serve important functions by mediating infants' inter-action with their environment (Waters et al., 1975). Such a relationship under-scores the significance of emotion in human adaptation.

Rather than being competitive hypotheses, the proposed concept of tension release, with its close ties to cognitive processes, and the social theory of the smile are complementary. Infants' active participation in their own development is nurtured by the social world. As positively toned expression of affect supports infants' strong tendency to maintain contact with novel stimulation at the edge of their cognitive capacities, so also does the range and continuity of engaging affect and behavior with which caregivers respond to infants' signals of well-being and pleasure (Schore, 1994). By the very nature of the nourishment they require and the role each plays in providing for the other, cognitive and socioe-motional aspects of development are inseparable. Again, development is seen as an integrated whole. The cognitive underpinnings of developmental changes in the processes signified by the smile are clear; strongly implied also is the role of the attachment relationship and interaction with a sensitive, responsive caregiver in expanding the infant's tolerance of tension and in promoting ex-pansion of schemata (see Chapter 8 and beyond). In a reciprocal manner, cog-nitive changes promote exploration, social development, and the differentiation of affect; and affective-social growth leads cognitive development, as in the caregiver's renewed closeness with the infant upon the beginnings of "recog-nition" smiles. Neither the cognitive nor the affective system can be considered dominant or more basic than the other.

Cognitive and social factors promote evolution from the pleasant physiolog-ical state reflected in the neonatal smile and the pleasure of early recognitory smiles, to the joy of mastery and engagement. Although dramatically trans-formed, the prototypical excitation–relaxation process remains embodied in the more mature forms. As we understand this developmental process, we move closer to an integrated conceptualization of the socioemotional and cognitive growth of the infant.

6   The development of fear: further illustration of the organizational viewpoint

What do we mean when we say that the infant is fearful? We mean that there exists a set of behaviors in a particular context that we use to infer that the infant is fearful.

Lewis and Rosenblum (1974)

Two stimulus situations that, when present singly, might arouse fear at only a low intensity may, when present together, arouse it at high intensity . . . the presence . . . of an attachment figure . . . makes an immense difference to the intensity of the fear aroused.

Bowlby (1973)

The emerging of fear from its predecessors further reveals fundamental processes of development. It illustrates especially well the phenomenon of changing mechanisms underlying related affective reactions as they develop and, in particular, the increasing role of meaning. As was the case with the pleasure/joy system, what I will call fear does not exist in the newborn period and yet develops from precursors in early infancy. Moreover, fear, like other emotions, continues to evolve through the toddler period and beyond, with advances in cognitive development. Rather than thinking of fear as something that suddenly appears at a given age, an organizational viewpoint underscores a developmental sequence of qualitative changes, with fear emerging over the course of infancy along with fundamental changes in the basis for emotional arousal.

The developmental process is remarkably parallel in the pleasure/joy system and what we will call the wariness/fear system. The first reactions in each system are due to simple accumulating excitation, independent of the specific content of the event. For this reason such early reactions are not considered emotions. A few months after birth, however, the content of the event has become an important determinant of negative reactions, as was also the case with smiling. At this point negative reactions sometimes are due to a mixture of familiar and unfamiliar elements. Some subjectivity is involved, in that the infant's past experiences play a role in determining what is familiar and unfamiliar. The particular event is important for the infant's engagement and consequent feelings of distress. This is, therefore, a true emotion as defined in Chapter 4, a precursor of fear. As was done with the pleasure/joy system, however, the term *fear* will be reserved for reactions in the second half year when the event has a particular and rather immediate negative meaning for the infant (see Table 4.2). It is not a failure to assimilate, but a rather immediate recognition of threat (e.g., Lazarus, 1991, p. 236).

In the discussion to follow, the term *wariness* will be used to label the emotional reaction that is the precursor of fear. Analogous to pleasure in early infancy, which is the result of "recognition," wariness is a response to the failure to "recognize" when assimilative efforts are activated strongly (a reaction to the unknown; Sroufe, 1979a). Obviously, negative reactions to the unknown continue throughout life. Thus, the wary reaction is a precursor in that it is a developmentally early form of the more mature reaction, not in the sense that it is replaced and disappears. This is the same sense in which diffuse distress is the precursor of anger and the smile of pleasure in recognition at 3 months is a precursor to the joy of mastery in the second half year.

Fear reactions proper, in response to strange or aversive events, emerge in the second half year (roughly 9 months). These reactions are more immediate. Unlike early wary reactions, they do not unfold slowly following sustained inability to make sense out of the event. Fear is a *categorical negative reaction*, based on the meaning of the event for the infant and drawing on affectively toned memories (Emde, 1980).

"Stages" in the development of early fear reactions

Obligatory attention

Infants as young as 10 to 15 days have been observed to become distressed following unbroken inspection of a visual stimulus. Stechler and Latz (1966) termed this "obligatory attention" (Table 4.2). In the early weeks, infants usually visually fixate on an object for a brief time, with greatly reduced activity. Then, typically, they lose the target, requiring an adjustment by the experimenter. Occasionally, however, a young infant does get locked onto some stimulus. In these situations of unbroken attention, an initial long period of inactivity is followed by increasingly vigorous activity and hard crying (Tennes et al., 1972). As described earlier (Chapter 3), this negative response is replaced in a few weeks by smiling and cooing, as sensory and motor activity become more coordinated.

Should these early negative reactions be termed *fear?* One might argue for this, since they involve an interaction between the infant and an external stimulus, and they end with crying. The rise in arousal is due to the disruptive influence of an external perception. This will also be true of reactions that will be termed *fear,* but in a dramatically transformed way. The excess of arousal here seems to be due merely to the infant's being "captured by" the stimulus and unable to continue the flow of behavior. The content of the stimulus is largely irrelevant. Any stimulus with suitable contrast or other salient features will do, regardless of past experience with similar objects. The reaction is more "reflexive" than based on meaning. There is no awareness of the content of the event. No judgment or categorization of the event is required, and the reaction must build over time. The relative lack of importance of "meaning" in this reaction contraindicates labeling it with a psychological construct such as *fear.* Still, this reaction may be viewed as the *prototype* of wariness and fear. The later reactions will involve psychological arrest and unmodulated tension.

Wariness

What Bronson (1972) and others (e.g., Schaffer, 1974) have called "wariness" is similar to this precursor reaction, yet in an important way different. After prolonged inspection (up to 30 seconds) of a stranger's immobile, sober face, 4-month-old infants frequently show great distress. Bronson has discussed this as a reaction to the unassimilable unfamiliar. It could also be seen as a further case of obligatory attention, but here the attention arrest derives from a mixture of familiar, attractive elements and unfamiliar elements. The content of the event is important. Four-month-old infants frequently can divert their attention from noxious stimulation (Tennes et al., 1972), and they appear to try that in this situation (Bronson, 1972). But an unfamiliar human face is a very attractive stimulus, presumably because of an established general face scheme and the possible "pre-potency" of the face in early life (e.g., Robson, 1967). They look away from the face and then quickly look back again, their eyes often snapping directly back to eye-to-eye contact as though drawn by a magnet. The engagement cannot be broken. There is no modulation of the tension, and so again, distress results (Sroufe, 1984). A better case could be made that this is a fear reaction because the content of the event, the mixture of known and unfamiliar elements, is critical. Certainly, this reaction (wariness) is an emotional reaction as defined in this book; it is based on a subjective relationship between infant and event, a beginning awareness, with attendant feelings of unpleasure. Psychologically, it is closer than obligatory attention to what we will call fear. Still, the absence of a specific meaning for the infant leads us to prefer the term *wariness* to *fear* in labeling these reactions. Again, we are dealing basically with a gradual buildup of tension.

A number of distress reactions reported in early infancy may be viewed in terms of the concepts of wariness or obligatory attention. For example, there have been numerous reports of gradually building distress reactions in response to the still and unresponsive face of the mother (Tronick et al., 1978). These have been interpreted as being due to "unfulfilled social expectations," even when observed in the first weeks of life. However, such a reaction in the newborn is probably better viewed as a special case of obligatory attention. One does not need expectations or other cognitive mechanisms to explain distress to blinking lights in the neonate (whose cortex is essentially nonfunctional), so it seems prudent not to involve them in explaining distress to the mother's unresponsive face. It has not been shown, for example, that mother's face is any more potent than another face in the newborn period.

When distress reactions to the still face occur at 4 months, an age when they are found quite reliably, they might parsimoniously be viewed as due to a mixture of familiar and unfamiliar elements, as in other instances of wariness. The infant would be pressed to assimilate this event due to its high salience and familiarity; yet, the unresponsiveness is so unusual that, ultimately, the assimilation/accommodation effort fails. Unmodulated and increasing arousal leads to distress. While this is clearly an emotional reaction, it does not seem to be different in kind from other cases of continued arousal when assimilative efforts are strongly elicited but are not successful.

Thus, obligatory attention may be involved for the newborn and wariness for the 4-month-old. The notion that the same response (distress to the mother's immobile face) can be mediated by different processes – that is, have different meaning – is completely consistent with the well-established developmental principles outlined in Chapter 3. One cannot take the presence of early distress to imply the cognitive processes underlying the later response. Distress to this event should be much more common in 4-month-olds than in the first weeks, and it appears to be so.

Neither distress due to obligatory attention nor that due to the mixture of known and unknown (wariness) is considered fear proper, partly because each requires time for the buildup of tension and the negative reaction. Bronson (1972) has described how up to 30 seconds is required for the distress reaction to the stranger's face in 4-month-olds (very brief procedures being impotent). Similarly, Tronick and colleagues (1978) describe a slowly unfolding process in which the infant maintains punctuated engagement for some time before becoming distressed in the "still face" experiments. This is in stark contrast to the rather immediate negative reactions shown by infants in the third or fourth quarter of life. It is these immediate reactions that will be called "fear."

Fear

Along with Bronson (1972), Lazarus (1991), and others, I will use *fear* here to refer to a categorical, negative response. Rather than the inability to assimilate an event, fear is due to the event being assimilated to a negative scheme. In the second half year, for example, infants commonly show negative reactions to intruding strangers without the infant having a lengthy period of study. Despite a number of critiques of this literature (e.g., Rheingold & Eckerman, 1973), it is rather well established that many infants will show such reactions by 9 months, and almost all will do so sometime in the first year (e.g., Emde et al., 1976). The data are clear that when strangers intrude on infants, especially picking them up, without mediating their approach with a toy or game and without a prolonged familiarization period, the majority of 10- to 12-month-old infants show some degree of negative reaction (see the later section on reactions to strangers).

Is the negative reaction to strangers fear? Unlike the wary reaction described previously, this reaction is not strictly due to a failure to assimilate. One could argue that there is failure of a particular kind of assimilation – that is, a failure to work the stranger into the category of meaningful objects (Meili, 1955). However, there is a compelling alternative, drawing on cognitive developments in the second half year, including changes in object concept and categorical thinking (Chapter 7). Rather than positing any failure of assimilation, it may be argued that the stranger is in a sense assimilated as an object, but assimilated to a negative scheme. If infants are distressed at an initial approach by a stranger, the negative reaction occurs more quickly on a second trial (Bronson & Pankey, 1977; Waters et al., 1975). From a failure of assimilation position this presents a paradox. How can failure of assimilation occur more rapidly (virtually immediately)? It seems more reasonable to suggest that rather than (faster) failure of assimilation/accommodation, a categorical negative reaction is involved. The intrusive stranger is perceived as a member of a class of aversive events, and such a judgment is made quite quickly following one exposure. As a categorical reaction, based on the relationship of the event to the infant, this negative reaction can qualify as fear (see also Emde et al., 1976).

Fear has been located on the developmental chart (Table 4.2) at about 9 months. This is consistent with developmental data on fear in a variety of situations (e.g., Lazarus, 1991; Lewis & Michalson, 1983; Scarr & Salapatek, 1970) and, specifically, the data showing HR acceleration and obvious aversive behavioral reactions to a looming stimulus (Cicchetti & Beeghly, 1990; Cicchetti & Sroufe, 1978; Yonas, 1981; Yonas, Cleaves, & Petterson, 1978) at this time, as well as to the "visual cliff" (Bertenthal, Campos, & Barrett, 1984; Schwartz, Campos, & Baisel, 1973; see the next section). It is in accord with the general finding that negative emotional reactions become more intense, more rapid, and more persistent during this period (Thompson, 1990). It also is consistent with a developmental shift in infants' reactions to novel objects at this age: Nine-month-olds hesitate noticeably before reaching if an object is novel (Schaffer et al., 1972). Finally, it is congruent with cross-species work showing that fear reactions emerge at the conclusion of "socialization" imprinting, the time when social preferences are established (e.g., Columbo, 1982). For humans this is a protracted period. However, it is well advanced by the second half of the first year, with clear preferences for primary caregivers emergent at that time.

The role of meaning in infant aversive reactions

The research on "looming" stimuli is quite instructive with regard to the role of meaning in the development of fear. The most carefully controlled experiments (e.g., Yonas et al., 1978) use a shadow-casting apparatus, so that extraneous stimuli such as noise or wind are excluded. What the infant experiences is solely the visual information for impending collision – that is, an exponentially expanding dot that in the end covers the visual field. Based on his research, Yonas concludes that fearful reactions to this event occur in the second half year.

At times, others have reported reactions to looming stimuli much earlier than that reported by Yonas. Bower, Broughton, and Moore (1970) and Ball and Tronick (1971), for example, reported "defensive reactions" in the first weeks of life. The Bower study, however, failed to control for the extraneous features noted earlier or for reactions of the mother, who was holding the infant and could see the stimulus. Ball and Tronick had better procedures but failed to control for head movement. The head tilting back, in following the upper edge of the stimulus configuration, could cause the immature infant's arms to go up, giving the appearance of a defensive reaction (Yonas et al., 1978). Still, these studies suggested that some reaction might be occurring in newborns.

Later, Cicchetti examined newborns with proper controls in place (see Cicchetti & Beeghly, 1990). There was still very occasional crying, and in agreement with Bower there was consistent blinking (the latter occurring even in newborns with Down syndrome). But there were no motoric defensive reactions. Moreover, the reactions in retarded or nonretarded newborns occurred only on "impact" (i.e., after the dot had fully expanded) and only with sustained attention, suggesting a built-in reflexive reaction or perhaps representing another instance of obligatory attention. Since the blinking reactions are as common in infants with Down syndrome as with normal controls, it is suggested that this is a subcortical, reflexive reaction, as opposed to being due to an abstraction of meaning. Thus, newborns can be observed to show negative reactions to the loom with precise procedures, but such reactions are best viewed within the domain of precursors or prototypes for fear, rather than as fear itself.

Cicchetti's developmental data (Cicchetti & Beeghly, 1990) suggest that these early reflexive reactions drop out, to appear later in a different, more reliable form. This is quite analogous to the waning of the endogenous smile and the emergence of the social smile. By the second half year, by about 8 or 9 months, normal infants show anticipatory reactions to the loom (see also Yonas, 1981). These reactions occur as the loom approaches and often even involve blocking movements of the arms or ducking to the side. Moreover, the reactions become faster on subsequent trials. This is the same age at which HR accelerations in response to the loom appear. It is these reactions, based on the meaning of the event, that are properly called fear. It is these reactions that appear quite late in the repertoire of the Down syndrome infant (i.e., in the second year), the delay being completely congruent with the degree of cognitive retardation (Cicchetti & Beeghly, 1990; Cicchetti & Sroufe, 1978; see Chapter 7).

As we saw with the pleasure/joy system, the changing meaning of the event for the infant is again crucial in the differentiation of later emotion from its precursors. Very young infants obviously discriminate the looming stimulus from its opposite, and in certain cases even cry. But infants do not respond immediately, do not respond in anticipation, and do not respond faster on subsequent trials in the looming situation until the second half year. Only then may it be claimed that they are responding to the meaning of the event. Once again we have a case of what appears to be the same response (crying to a visual looming stimulus) being based on different mechanisms at different ages.

The central role for meaning in determining fear is also well illustrated by work with the "visual cliff" (e.g., Bertenthal et al., 1984; Campos, Emde, & Gaensbauer, 1975). In this situation the infant is coaxed to cross a glass table top with another surface either directly beneath it or some distance below. Thus, on the "deep" side the infant has the illusion of a visual drop-off, whereas on the "shallow" side no drop-off is perceived. With this situation, Campos and colleagues, using both behavioral criteria and the criterion of HR deceleration (a well-established correlate of attention; see Chapter 5), have demonstrated that 5-month-olds differentially attend to the deep side of the cliff. That is, they look more and orient more to the deep side. They do not show negative affect, however. By 9 months, in contrast, normal infants characteristically show great HR *acceleration* to the deep side, and they often refuse to cross and may cry. Thus, young infants discriminated the deep and shallow sides, but only by about 9 months is there a threatening meaning and therefore a fear reaction.

Emde and colleagues (1976) provided substantial documentation, including comparative and physiological data, for a developmental shift in the fear system at this very time. Fear reactions emerge rather precipitously across species at comparable developmental points (Columbo, 1982). Their emergence is paralleled by notable brain maturational changes, especially the integration of corticolimbic systems (Schore, 1994; see also Chapters 2 and 4) and perhaps interhemispheric connectivity (Thompson, 1990). At this time there is a shift to HR acceleration in response to stimulus events with negative meaning (including approaching strangers; Campos et al., 1975; Waters et al., 1975). Emde et al. (1976) refer to this as an "anticipatory" acceleration, because it happens without any physically noxious stimulation; that is, it is based on meaning. All this supports the view of fear as emerging in the second half year. Schore (1994) points to further brain developments in the second year (e.g, the maturation of the parasympathetic system), which he says lead to a new potential capacity, the tendency toward a fearful mood.

It should be stressed again, as discussed in Chapter 4, that a general agreement on 9 months as the "age of fear" is not critical. What is far more important is an appreciation of the developmental process. The sequence just described captures the increasing tendency of the infant to find meaning in the event. The categorical response at 9 months is qualitatively different from the emotional reaction at 4 months, which is due to a gradual buildup of tension. The 9-month-old's response is not an impersonal failure of assimilation; it is a subjective recognition of negative meaning.

The importance of meaning, of course, continues to expand after 9 months. Increasingly, context is taken into account by the infant, including past experience in the situation, availability of the caregiver, and even more subtle cues. Further work with the visual cliff may serve as one example of this elaborated role for meaning. In a typical study (Sorce, Emde, Campos, & Klinnert, 1985), 12-month-olds were prompted to cross the deep side of the visual cliff, which was arranged to be only a foot deep. On the other side was the mother and a very attractive ferris wheel toy. Moreover, in one condition the mother was smiling and animated; in other conditions she showed fear, anger, or sadness. When the mother's face showed joy, three-fourths of the infants crossed, even though they had looked at the drop-off. When the mother showed fear, no infant (of 20) crossed. (Only 2 of 20 crossed in the "anger face" condition and 48% crossed in the "sad face" condition.)

The infant's looks to caregivers for affective information are referred to as "social referencing" (e.g., Boccia & Campos, 1989). Studies show that such referencing occurs specifically in situations that are ambiguous (Gunnar & Stone, 1984). These studies illustrate the sensitivity of 12-month-olds to affect expressed by others, no doubt based in part on their own experiences with such emotions by this age. The point is that they also illustrate the vital role for meaning in determining the infant's reaction. The same situation may have vastly different meaning and therefore produce completely different reactions depending on surrounding circumstances. It is quite doubtful that 9-month-olds would be so influenced by this subtle contextual information. As stated throughout, the emergence of a reaction does not mark a developmental end point, but simply a qualitative turn in the developing affect system.

In an important program of research, Gunnar (e.g., Gunnar, Leighton, & Peleaux, 1984) has shown that the meaning of aversive events, and therefore the likelihood of fear, is strongly influenced by additional factors with older infants – namely, predictability and controllability. When the infant was given control over the operation of a mechanical monkey, as opposed to experimenter operation, a dramatic reduction in fear reactions was noted. Such factors might also be important in determining experiences of anger.

By 12 months one also sees the appearance of negative moods, parallel in time to the emergence of positive moods (Chapter 4). The infant can be apprehensive even upon entering a situation, prior to any noxious events. Separation distress that emerges reliably in the second half year (Kagan, Kearsley, & Zelazo, 1978; Schaffer & Emerson, 1964) becomes separation anxiety. And infants may be petulant and angry at the caregiver who has returned after a separation. That is, it is not the event (caregiver's return) that directly produces the negative affect; rather, anger at the separation is available when there is later opportunity for expression. Likewise, infants by 1 year may remain generally timid after a noxious experience, even when positive experiences are interpolated (see Chapter 8).

Reactions to strangers

Reactions to strangers in the second half year of life represent a special case of negative emotional reaction, being in some ways similar to anxiety and in others similar to fear. Anxiety aspects of the reaction (see Chapter 8) include the fact that it is greatly reduced when there are response options open to the infant (e.g., when he or she is free to move about) and that it generally occurs only when the stranger intrudes on the infant's space, especially attempting a pickup. On the other hand, the response can be immediate, especially with several presentations of the stranger, and there is a specific object of the distress, namely, the stranger. In most ways, stranger distress fits the definition of a categorical response: "I do not like this" or "I do not like what is happening here." Therefore, infants certainly can show fear in response to strangers, and when they do show such immediate negative reactions it is at the same age that fear is seen in other situations. This is why such reactions were given as an example of fear in the earlier discussion of stages.

However, given the complexity of infants' reactions, it may be even more reasonable to drop both the terms *stranger fear* and *stranger anxiety*, substituting instead *stranger reactions*. Strangers may be a source of anxiety or fear, but to the infant they are much more than that.

A controversy developed during the 1970s concerning whether the phenomenon of stranger fear was real or epiphenomenal. Some pointed to the clear and obvious affiliative reactions to strangers (smiling, showing toys) to suggest that infants were not wary or fearful of strangers at all (Rheingold & Eckerman, 1973). They argued that negative reactions were inferred by investigators too eager to see such responses or were due to maternal absence (not stranger reactions per se). With mother present, they pointed out, few infants were frankly distressed in the usual study. Thus, it was argued, the notion of stranger fear at least should be discarded as a developmental milestone.

Elsewhere I have discussed the literature on stranger reactions in great detail (Sroufe, 1977). Here, I can only summarize the argument to initiate a discussion of a developmental perspective on stranger reactions. To begin with, positive reactions do not contraindicate negative reactions. Infants may be both positive and negative toward strangers. From an organizational perspective, the affiliative, wariness/fear, exploratory, and attachment systems are expected to interact dynamically. Infants can be affiliative under some circumstances and apprehensive in others. Affiliation and wariness may even oscillate. Infants rarely make full, spontaneous approaches to strangers, and Bretherton and Ainsworth (1974) described a pattern in which infants who do make such full approaches immediately retreated to the caregiver. The affiliative gesture activated the wariness/fear and attachment systems. In our own research (Waters et al., 1975), we demonstrated that infants tended to smile at strangers across the room, but virtually no infants smiled when the stranger reached to pick them up. Moreover, infants who smiled when the stranger was across the room were *more likely* to show negative reactions at pickup; that is, rather than contraindicating negative reactions, the initial positive greeting (becoming engaged) may have promoted the subsequent negative reaction. Alternatively, perhaps the greeting and the aversion reflect a common developmental process, with those showing both the immediate initial smile and the later aversion simply being more advanced than those showing neither. With age (from 6 to 10 months) there is an increase in both positive and negative reactions. Novel persons are highly salient for infants and therefore elicit affective reactions. But the particular reaction depends on circumstances. The answer to the question, Are infants affiliative to or wary of strangers? is, obviously, both.

One can arrange procedures to obtain almost any result; context has a dramatic effect on reactions to strangers (Sroufe et al., 1974; see Chapter 8). If one allows the infant to become familiar with the surroundings, introduces the stranger gradually, has the stranger utilize a familiar format in approaching the infant (e.g., block play or peekaboo), and allows the infant control over the pacing, one will observe very few negative reactions (Gunnar et al., 1984; Mangelsdorf, Watkins, & Lehn, 1991; Skarin, 1977; Sroufe, 1977). If, on the other hand, the approach occurs in a novel setting, occurs very rapidly, and the stranger attempts to pick up the infant, the majority of 10-month-old infants will show negative reactions during the intrusion (Emde et al., 1976; Waters et al., 1975).

In the usual laboratory study, where procedures are deliberately rather innocuous, few infants will cry. More (perhaps 50%, depending on intrusiveness and other factors) will show a milder negative reaction (averting the gaze, exhibiting a cry face, pulling back). These mild forms have been reliably coded and have been validated by showing associated HR acceleration and by differentiating responses to mother's approach from those to a stranger's approach (Waters et al., 1975). When mother approached, video coders (without knowledge of who was approaching) did not score any negative reactions; nor was there HR acceleration; yet half of the subjects showed negative reactions to strangers. Since mothers did the same standardized approach, the negative reactions to strangers cannot be due to a "stilted" approach procedure, as was suggested by Rheingold and Eckerman (1973). Indeed, the behavior would be more "strange" for mothers than for strangers.

Determining whether the concept of negative reactions to strangers in infancy is valid would be of limited interest were it not for developmental implications. If one were to dismiss the entire concept, an important developmental process would be obscured. Regardless of whether one concludes that infants are more affiliative or more fearful of strangers (a rather simplistic conclusion in either case), of primary importance are the developmental changes. Few infants in the first half year show the signs of apprehension just discussed, while many infants do by 8 or 9 months. Especially when such observations are coordinated with other data on both negative reactions and developmental changes in positive affect, important information is gained about emotional development. There is a rather precipitous increase in negative reactions to strangers at about 8 months, based on cross-sectional data (Sroufe, 1977; Waters et al., 1975), quite parallel to changes in the pleasure/joy system.

Finally, do most babies show a negative reaction to strangers at some age? The most pertinent data come from a longitudinal study by Gaensbauer (see Emde et al., 1976). He found that each of 14 infants showed a frankly negative reaction to intrusion at some point during the study, though the age of onset ranged from 6 to 11 months. Moreover, following the onset of the negative reaction, 11 of 14 infants showed aversion for two consecutive months, 8 of 14 infants for three consecutive months. It is clear that negative stranger reactions are common in infancy. It is also clear, however, that the term *8-month anxiety* (Spitz, 1965) is inappropriately specific and that cross-sectional studies are inappropriate to demonstrate the universality or stability of the response. A study based on 9-month-olds alone, for example, would include some infants not yet showing the reaction and others who had passed their peak reaction.

Does this literature in general, and the Gaensbauer study in particular, suggest that we should consider stranger fear as a developmental milestone? For a number of reasons I think this is inadvisable. Rheingold and other critics made a valuable point in stressing that an emphasis on negative reactions is misleading. The subjects in Gaensbauer's study also could have been described in terms of the onset of greeting and showing toys to strangers, revealing the same developmental trends. All of these advances in development co-occur. The most remarkable development of the second half year is the rapidly differentiating response to people and the increasing complexity in the organization of social behavior. The concept of stranger fear sells short this more noteworthy development.

More important, the milestone idea itself is misleading. It has led some critics to believe that stranger fear is "good" – for example, that it indicates a good attachment relationship (the more stranger fear or the earlier the stranger fear, the more attached). This does not follow either logic or observation. Nor is the converse true; absence of stranger fear does not necessarily indicate a strong attachment. The problem with the milestone concept is that it is too easily incorporated into quantitative or static trait views of the child (where earlier, or more, are viewed as better).

From an organizational perspective stranger reactions are best viewed in terms of developmental issues, ones that all infants will face. A central issue in the second half year is differentiation of the child's social world. From this perspective, neither age of onset nor even degree of fear is most salient. Rather, qualitative aspects are most important, especially the organization of wariness/ fear with the attachment, affiliative, and exploratory behavioral systems.

Stranger fear and attachment

Drawing from ethological theory, Ainsworth and her colleagues (Ainsworth, 1973; Ainsworth & Wittig, 1969; Bretherton & Ainsworth, 1974) provided an important conceptualization of the relationship between attachment and aversion to strangers, which illustrates the principle of interactive systems outlined in Chapter 3. Central to the definition of attachment in this conceptualization are the attachment–exploration balance (with the caregiver as a secure base for exploration) and the specificity of need for contact with the caregiver when distressed. Thus, in the caregiver's presence, and with adequate familiarization time, most 12-month-old babies would be expected to engage in toy play with a stranger (even including eye contact, after a time). Such play would not indicate a failure of attachment, since it may be supported by the infant's use of the attachment figure as a secure base. Nor would it necessarily indicate a good quality attachment relationship, because the issue of preferential treatment under stress remains open. However, some babies are completely preoccupied with the caregiver at virtually all times, hovering near him or her and avoiding (without warming up to) the stranger. This suggests a maladaptive attachment relationship, not because of the preferential treatment of the caregiver, but because, with only mild stress, the caregiver's presence should be sufficient for the dominance of the infant's exploratory and affiliative tendencies; that is, the infant's negative evaluation and wariness in these circumstances suggest insecurity concerning the attachment figure.

On the other hand, following the distress of being briefly left alone, 12-month-old infants would be expected to specifically require contact with an attachment figure. Contact with the stranger may even be persistently resisted, with the baby becoming fully settled only when contact with the caregiver is reestablished. In this instance, it is the very infants who appear to be readily settled by the stranger (who give the appearance of being able to substitute the stranger for the mother when distressed) who show the maladaptive pattern. These babies tend to avoid the mother on reunion, as well as fail to return to active play and exploration, confirming that they are not simply placid and contented (see Chapter 10).

This discussion illustrates both that the relationship between attachment and wariness/fear is complex and that understanding one of these systems is relevant for understanding the other. Securely attached infants may in certain contexts be less apprehensive of a stranger than some babies; in other circumstances they may be more resistant to contact with strangers than another group of babies. The quality of the attachment is defined by this patterning of behavior, not by the age of appearance or amount of stranger aversion without consideration of context. These statements are more than speculative; Ainsworth's characterization of individual differences in quality of attachment has been substantially validated. The patterns of secure and insecure attachment she describes, including responses to strangers, are typically stable across a 6-month period (Main & Weston, 1981; Waters, 1978) and have notable predictive validity (see Chapters 10 to 12).

Arousal modulation in aversive situations

In Chapter 5 we discussed positively toned arousal modulation and its role in promoting development. Obviously, capacities and procedures for modulating arousal in aversive situations are equally important. Such capacities evolve markedly in the first year of life and continue to unfold during the toddler period.

The neonate has a built-in capacity to withdraw from stimulation, which has been referred to as an "absolute stimulus barrier" (see Chapter 4). In the face of noxious stimulation (e.g., the sounding of a loud horn), newborns amazingly will fall asleep after a few presentations (Tennes et al., 1972). Also, following surgical procedures (e.g., circumcision) they enter a period of deep sleep. It has been argued that such mechanisms protect vulnerable infants from overstimulation at a time when they have no voluntary coping mechanisms. It also has been considered a prototype for later psychological defenses (Spitz et al., 1970).

Over the first few months the infant evolves a functional waking capacity. This is simply to turn away from the source of the stimulation. In some ways this is a waking analog to the stimulus barrier mechanism of the newborn period, because like the early built-in mechanism, turning away rather completely terminates contact with the stimulation. However, turning away does allow the possibility of reengaging at a later point, and this procedure of divesting and reinvesting attention has been frequently observed, especially in infant–caregiver interaction. In the course of stimulation by the caregiver, the infant becomes highly aroused, it then turns away, and, if the caregiver cooperates by waiting, in time returns attention to the caregiver and is stimulated anew (e.g., Brazelton et al., 1974; Stern, 1974). This can be a remarkably serviceable technique for the young infant, even though its success depends on the cooperation of others (see Chapter 9).

In the second half year the infant evolves much more flexible and subtle capacities for modulating arousal, techniques that allow the infant to remain engaged with moderately threatening events in a more ongoing way. Waters and colleagues (1975) provided an example of such modulation in a study of stranger reactions. They employed a standard situation in which a strange adult approached an infant from across a room in a step-by-step manner. As discussed earlier, 10-month-old infants show a variety of reactions to such a procedure, with half of them showing some negative reaction. One common reaction is quite remarkable. Infants watch the approaching stranger, with brief glances away (usually down and to the side) followed again by looking. Concurrent HR recordings provide insight into the possible function of this gazing behavior with respect to the control of arousal and emotion. These gaze-averting infants at first watched the stranger soberly, with a brief HR deceleration (orienting, attention) followed by a slower, larger acceleration. When the HR acceleration was near peak, the infants averted their gaze. With the gaze aversion, HR again declined, and the infants returned their gaze to the stranger once again (Figure 6.1). This process seems to reflect an early coping mechanism. The precisely synchronized relationship between gaze aversion and the peak HR acceleration (arousal) prevents a disorganizing distress reaction and allows the infant to maintain contact with the event. Infants showing this pattern exhibited less fear of the stranger on a second trial. Such mechanisms perhaps represent the roots of delay and other coping strategies described in the preschool years (Bridges & Grolnick, 1995; Murphy, 1962; Murphy & Moriarty, 1976). In any case, it is a flexible technique under the control of the infant.

As competent as these 10-month-olds are, equally dramatic changes occur in

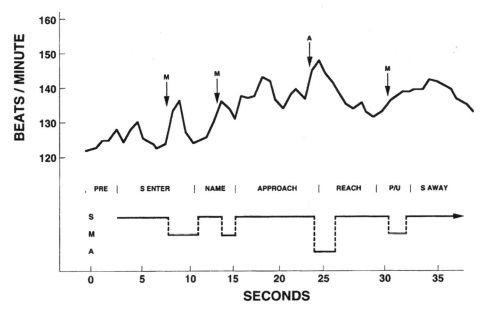

Figure 6.1. Visual regard behavior and continuous heart rate (two-beat averages) for a 10-month-old male infant rated "wary" at reach and pickup during a standard stranger approach sequence. The letter S denotes looks at stranger; A denotes looks away; M denotes looks to mother; P/U indicates point at which the stranger attempts to pick up the infant.

the next few months. For 10-month-olds (and certainly for younger infants), crying in a stressful situation appears to be an all-or-none response. When they begin crying, it is very difficult for them to stop. But even by 12 months infants have much more capacity to stop crying to take in new information. In our attachment studies (e.g., Sroufe & Waters, 1977a, 1977b), we commonly saw 12-month-olds controlling their emotion, fighting back their tears when the caregiver was briefly out of the room. This is suggested not only by pouts and cry faces, which appear and evaporate, but by elevated HRs and subdued play during separation (Mahler's "low-keyedness"). Most revealing, such infants may burst into tears upon the mother's return, something we do not observe in younger babies. In general, infants are much more fluid in their emotional expression by the end of the first year (Thompson, 1990).

Many emotional regulation capacities in infancy involve the caregiver, and these too evolve over the first year (Bridges & Grolnick, 1995). Newborn crying in the face of arousal is a primitive technique that at first further arouses the infant. Nonetheless, by securing caregiver ministrations, it commonly has the end result of bringing arousal once again within tolerable limits. Later, as discussed, the caregiver may read the infant's glances and turns away as signals, then act to reduce arousal. Then, in the second half year, the infant begins to direct signals explicitly to caregivers, ultimately including reaching for, calling, and approaching them. These are forerunners of the more sophisticated social-referencing skills mentioned earlier, which assist arousal modulation in the 12-month-old. These topics will be pursued further in Chapter 10.

Conclusion

As was the case in discussing the pleasure/joy system (Chapter 5), in examining the ontogenesis of fear the developmental process has been emphasized. The focus is not on establishing the age at which true fear appears, but rather on the sequence of changes in the fear system. There is an unfolding of more mature reactions from earlier precursors in pace with an expanding role for meaning. Different investigators may argue that the early forms or even the later form should or should not be called fear. Regardless of terminology, if the developmental aspects of the phenomenon are appreciated the coordination of changes in the fear system with other aspects of development can be seen. When the present developmental definition of fear is accepted, parallels in the emergence of fear, joy, and anger are apparent, and changes in all three systems are coordinated with developmental changes in intentionality, object concept, and other aspects of cognitive development. This is the topic for the next chapter.

7   The interdependence of affect and cognition

Knowing is inherent in feeling.
                    Kellerman (1983)

Throughout this book intimate ties between affect and cognition are apparent, both as we consider the unfolding of the emotions and as we examine the child's developing ability to control and modulate emotion. This could not be otherwise. Affect and cognition are mutually influencing, two aspects of the same process. While appraisal of an event may be necessary for the activation of emotion, events achieve significance when amplified by affect (Lichtenberg, 1989). As Piaget and Inhelder (1969) put it:

There is no behavior pattern, however intellectual, which does not involve affective factors as motives; but, reciprocally, there can be no affective states without the intervention of perceptions or comprehensions which constitute their cognitive structure. Behavior is therefore of a piece, even if the structures do not explain its energetics and if, vice versa, its energetics do not account for its structures. The two aspects, affective and cognitive, are at the same time inseparable and irreducible. (p. 158)

In a paper devoted to the relation between "affectivity and intelligence," Piaget (1962) made the point that there "is no such thing as a purely cognitive state . . . There are no acts of intelligence, even of practical intelligence, without interest at the point of departure and affective regulation during the entire course of an action, without joy at success or sorrow at failure" (p. 130). Similarly, there can be no purely affective state. Even the simplest forms of affect presuppose some discrimination and hence "a cognitive element" (p. 131). One cannot say that affect causes or precedes cognition, nor can one say that knowledge precedes affectivity. They are "non-dissociable." While others had argued that intellect supplied the means and affect established the goals, Piaget went further by arguing that "there is also a comprehension of the goal; and in the means there is also the value of the means, which is not only cognitive, but affective" (p. 131).

This emphasis on the inseparability of affect and cognition follows rather directly from Piaget's constructivist/structuralist point of view. In Piaget's theory early mental structures arise from the infant's actions, not from static properties of objects. Since all actions have affective components, these early structures or schemes are affective as well as cognitive. Reciprocally, perception of the external event (i.e., a cognitive process) is required to activate these "affective schemes" once formed. As Kellerman (1983) has stated, "Affect and cognition are fused" (p. 336).

Current views of brain development and functioning also underscore the nondissociability of emotion and cognition (Schore, 1994). In "expectancy-based memory systems" affective and cognitive "information" are interwoven in storage and retrieval. "The connections existing between the limbic system and prefrontal cortex offer a material basis for relationships between emotional and cognitive spheres" (Changeux & Dehaene, 1989, p. 98).

The Bowlby–Ainsworth theory of attachment, which will be discussed in Chapter 10, provides an excellent illustration of the interplay between affect and cognition in development. In this position, attachment is an emotional construct; yet it is rooted in cognitive processes. While attachment itself is defined as an affective bond, there are "necessary conditions" for the emergence of this bond between infant and caregiver. Ainsworth (1973) cites among these conditions a discrimination of the caregiver from others and a recognition of the person "as having a permanent and independent existence even when not present to perception" (p. 28), that is, the concept of object in Piaget's sense. Moreover, the evolution of the early attachment relationship to what Bowlby (1969/1982) calls a "goal-corrected partnership," in which the infant understands the caregiver's goals and can attempt to alter those goals, as well as his or her own behavior in terms of those goals, is obviously dependent on cognitive development. At the same time the deeply emotional attachment relationship is the focal point of infant behavioral organization; therefore, it must have implications for cognitive growth, if for no other reason than its service in exploration (Bretherton & Bates, 1985; Jacobson & Edelstein, in press; see also Chapter 10).

The interdependence of affect and cognition is emphasized at the outset in this chapter, because for the sake of exposition much of the discussion will center on cognitive "influences" on emotional development and (to a lesser extent because of the limited data base) the "influence" of affect on cognition. In reality, the influence is mutual and ongoing. In fact, given the unity of development, any such segregation is always to some extent a distortion.

Coordination in the sequencing of cognitive and affective development

One way to point out the close ties between affective and cognitive development is to compare the developmental stages proposed by Piaget with the phases of affective development presented in Chapter 4 (see Tables 4.2 and 4.3). For additional comparison, Sander's (1975) "issues" in social development are also presented. Theoretical ties between cognition and affect are clear from this comparison. For example, in Piaget's stage 2 (1 to 4 months) the first acquired adaptations are seen; behavioral searchings produce new results, and functional assimilation assures the repetition of new responses. During this stage, there are anticipatory nursing postures and later anticipatory sucking on the basis of visual cues. The apex of the stage is visually guided reaching. In the present scheme, this is the period of the first emotions, which entail primitive recognition, coordination of schemes, awareness, and primitive anticipation. The exogenous smile (Chapter 5) is testimony to functional assimilation and to rudimentary coordination of attention and motor behavior (Tennes et al., 1972) or, in other cases, to the coordination of the visible stimulus with a representation of that same event being constructed. Another example is the distress reaction of the 4-month-old following prolonged inspection of a stranger's face (wariness – the failure to coordinate familiar and unfamiliar elements).

Piaget's stage 3 (4 to 8 months) marks the first step toward intentionality. There is now a forward-looking adaptation rather than simply repetition of the old, but goals are established only after means are put into effect. For the first time, interruption in Mandler's sense (1975; see also Chapter 2) is possible, and consequently early in this stage there is distress when a well-practiced behavior cannot be exercised, and by the end of the stage there can be anger. Also, in this stage there is the joy of being an active agent.

Fear and surprise emerge at the beginning of Piaget's stage 4 (8 to 12 months). Here, the infant can coordinate schemes, which includes the coordination of present experience with categorically represented past experience and with anticipated consequences. Such a capacity underlies both the infant's searches for hidden objects and what were referred to as fear reactions in Chapter 6. Moreover, at this stage, the infant has true intentionality and an understanding of the relationship between means and ends; that is, the infant knows that to do one thing he or she must first do another. Expecting to find a hidden toy, the infant can be surprised (or angry) at a misexpected result. In addition, by this stage novelty presents a problem for understanding rather than the simple opportunity to exercise schemes; therefore, surprising outcomes motivate continued engagement of the event. A complementary example is Schaffer and colleagues' (1972) study on the development of hesitance. Stage 3 infants (5 or 6 months) will reach immediately for any objects, but after 8 months there is a striking, qualitative change in response to novelty. Nine-month-olds, for example, stop, scrutinize, and deliberate before reaching.

By the end of stage 4, the world is more objectified, less tied to the infant's actions. For example, there are anticipatory reactions (e.g., crying when mother puts on her coat). In the affective domain we see the onset and formation of attachment, deferred emotional reactions (e.g., anger and crying on mother's return), the onset of moods, the strong influence of context, and affect as part of that context. In general, affect becomes less tied to specific events and itself becomes a determinant of behavior. By this time the infant has the capacity to appraise or evaluate an event (see Chapter 8).

What is called the mastery or "practicing" phase (cf. Mahler et al., 1975) in the socioemotional domain, wherein infants begin exploring the world on their own with periodic returns to the caregiver, corresponds closely to Piaget's stage 5 (12 to 18 months), characterized by the discovery of new means through experimentation, pursuit of the novel, and provoking new results. Causality becomes detached from the child's own actions, and people and objects become independent centers of causation. Clearly, these developments are closely tied to the emergence of self-awareness (Chapter 11), which leads, ultimately, to affection, shame, defiance, and positive self-evaluation after 18 months. These developments are based on the emergence of symbolic representation and the functioning of schemes internally, independent of actions (Piaget's stage 6). There is a representation of the self.

Cognitive underpinnings of emotion and emotional development

Throughout the preceding chapters there has been the implicit assumption that expanding cognitive capacities and the unfolding of emotions proceed together, which often is viewed as cognitive development underlying emotional development. Only with recognition ("awareness") is there pleasure and disappointment or wariness. Only with some development of causality, intentionality, object permanence and meaning are there joy, fear, and anger. Surprise (misexpectation) is so closely rooted in cognitive development that it has been referred to as the "epistemological" emotion. It cannot appear before memory development is sufficient to allow a firm expectation concerning an event. Moreover, the distinctions between what were referred to as the mature emotions in Chapters 4 to 6 and their precursors were tied to cognitive factors. Fear, for example, in contrast to wariness, was referred to as a categorical negative reaction, dependent on assimilation to a negative scheme. And the effects of event sequence, setting, and other aspects of context to be discussed further in Chapter 8 obviously reflect cognitive processes.

Perhaps the most compelling empirical evidence for the specific link between cognitive factors and affect expression is found in studies of positive affect. So compelling is the case that Zelazo (e.g., Zelazo & Komer, 1971) has referred to the smile as a "window" to the infant's cognitive development. The onset and course of smiling to the face – from (1) irregular to (2) reliable but general to any face to (3) differential in recognition of the caregiver – is an obvious case in point. After smiling to any human face at 10 weeks, the infant selectively smiles to highly familiar faces by 4 to 5 months, as the face scheme becomes differentiated. A further development, the greeting reaction to caregivers that appears late in the first year, is dependent on categorical recognition (Vaughn, 1977). The enthusiastic response to the caregiver's entry is immediate, suggesting assimilation to a uniquely positive scheme, based on a recorded history of positive interaction.

Also, there are developmental trends in the nature of events that elicit positive affect; previously adequate stimuli lose their effectiveness, while more sophisticated and subtly incongruous events become more potent (Kagan, 1971; Sroufe & Wunsch, 1972). Age differences in the speed of response and number of trials to produce affective reactions (e.g., Sroufe & Waters, 1976; Zelazo, 1972) also reflect differing abilities to assimilate information. Trial-by-trial effects within experiments (see Chapter 5) suggest scheme formation, effortful assimilation leading to positive affect, and, finally, effortless assimilation and disinterest. It is the tension generated through mental effort that is expressed in positive affect.

There are also data suggesting that surprise reactions emerge after 8 months, as a cognitively based theory would predict. Charlesworth and Kreutzer (1973) have summarized findings with regard to surprise, including Charlesworth's own data. In the Vaughn and Sroufe study described earlier (Chapter 4), these findings were corroborated. Video recordings of the babies' postures and facial expressions indicated that the masked appearances of caregivers and strangers from behind a screen clearly disrupted the babies' ongoing stream of behavior; that is, the babies "misexpected" the events. When classic facial expressions of surprise were seen, they always followed the onset of the misexpected events. More often, elements of facial expressions showing surprise (e.g., raised brows, lowered jaw) were seen. These elements of the surprise expression were seen in babies as young as 8 months, though only one baby in the 8-month-old group ($N = 12$) displayed the stereotyped surprise facial expression. Interestingly, no 8-month-old failing to show "person permanence" (i.e., those infants who seemed to forget the game and their mothers when they disappeared behind the screen) showed even the elements of the surprise facial expression; only those who maintained active anticipation did.

Not surprisingly, a number of investigators have sought the affective correlates of object concept development. For example, Cicchetti and Sroufe (1978), in their sample of Down syndrome infants, found a relationship between stage 4 object permanence (wherein an infant will search for an object that has been completely hidden) and laughter to certain items. Establishing a connection between advances in object concept and aversive reactions has proved to be more difficult. Several investigators have failed to find a relationship between stranger fear and object permanence (see Sroufe, 1977, for a review). One study did report a relationship between person permanence (where a person is hidden) and stranger reactions; that is, infants exhibiting wariness of a stranger more actively searched for mother when she was hidden (Paradise & Curcio, 1974). However, this finding remains tentative. The more frightened infants may have been more motivated to find mother, since the person permanence assessments always followed stranger approach.

One explanation for the difficulty of finding the cognitive basis for aversive responses to strangers may be the very integrity of development researchers are seeking to establish. The situation is most likely one of mutual influence between affect and cognition, not linear causality (from cognition to affect). An infant does not "achieve" the stage 4 object concept, then suddenly manifest separation protest or stranger aversion. Rather, as discussed in Chapter 3, affective experiences support emerging and tentative cognitive advances. The affective reactions associated with separations (and other encounters with unavailable objects) serve to crystalize the beginning object–child relationship. The child's sense that the object is separate, is outside his or her sphere of influence, is as much a product of emotional reactions as the emotional reactions are a product of cognitive development. It is a matter of mutual determination.

The role of stimulus novelty ("cognitive incongruity")

Following Piaget (1952), a number of writers have emphasized scheme formation, as well as assimilation and accommodation, in the face of novel stimulation (e.g., Kagan, 1971; McCall & McGhee, 1977; Zelazo, 1972). With repeated exposure, infants form mental representations (models) of their experience. Such models exist in primitive form in the first half year. By the second half year they not only are more refined but are readily accessible for comparison with immediate experience (in contrast to earlier recognition memory). An incongruous or "discrepant" event, then, is one that activates existing structures but cannot be assimilated to them. Such a discrepant event is highly salient and creates a state of arousal. If resolved, such a state leads to positive affect; if unresolveable, it may lead to negative affect.

The "discrepancy hypothesis," as it has been called, emphasizes the degree of discrepancy and has been used in explanations of many developmental phenomena (Kagan, 1971; McCall & McGhee, 1977). Developmental changes in infants' reactions to people have been a primary case. With development infants clearly react differently to what is externally the same event – the appearance of an unfamiliar person. Those who championed the discrepancy hypothesis argued that these changes parallel advances in cognition. Such cognitive advances are reflected when the 3-month-old smiles at all faces, caregivers and visitors alike. Any face can be assimilated to the general face scheme that is being constructed by the young infant. Later, smiling to the immobile face declines; the general face scheme is well developed and there is no discrepancy (Hoffman, 1985). Differential smiling to caregivers appears as the scheme becomes differentiated. Now, any appearance of the caregiver's face is moderately discrepant from (and can be assimilated to) the emerging specific scheme of the caregiver. Then, in the second half year, further cognitive advances are reflected in the emergence of reliable aversive reactions to strangers. The argument is that the stranger's face is too discrepant from the well-formed schemes of familiar faces, and assimilation and accommodation cannot resolve the discrepancy. The ready access to the differentiated scheme underlies aversion to strangers in brief encounters (see also Spitz, 1965).

As we will discuss in Chapter 8, the discrepancy explanation has power, but it is not adequate to explain stranger reactions and is fraught with conceptual problems. In emphasizing the amount of discrepancy in the stimulus event, it raises an unsolveable methodological problem (the circularity of defining moderate discrepancy as a difference just large enough to lead to a reaction), and it leaves out critical subjective factors. Still, it is presented here because it does illustrate a close interplay between cognition and affect.

Emotional development of infants with Down syndrome

The study of mentally retarded children provides one entrée into the relationship between cognitive and affective development. Infants with Down syndrome provide a unique research opportunity. These children are identifiable at birth, are etiologically homogeneous, and yet have a range of outcome from near normal cognitive functioning to severe retardation. They represent a natural experiment, as it were, for tracking the interweaving of cognitive and affective development from the beginning of life.

Cicchetti conducted a landmark research project on the development of positive affect and fear in children with Down syndrome (Cicchetti & Beeghly, 1990; Cicchetti & Sroufe, 1976, 1978; Mans et al., 1978). More than 150 infants and children were studied, many longitudinally. One group of 25 was seen monthly for the first 2 years of life. Cognitive development was assessed through multiple testings with the Bayley Mental and Motor Scales and the Uzgiris–Hunt scales of cognitive development. Systematic observations of smiling and laughter were made each month using the procedures developed by Sroufe and Wunsch (1972) with normal infants. These infants, and others, were also observed responding to the visual cliff (p. 162), "looming" stimuli (p. 160), and Ainsworth's attachment procedure (chap. 10). Subsequently, their play and language were assessed (e.g., Motti, Cicchetti, & Sroufe, 1983).

The original findings with regard to the development of smiling and laughter were quite clear. As reported in Chapter 5, the first finding was that, as expected, these infants as a group lagged behind in the development of exogenous smiling and laughter. When the social smile did appear in these children, it was less intense and less engaging (see also Emde, Katz, & Thorp, 1978, p. 352). Laughter itself was quite rare, presumably because it requires rapid cognitive processing of the event and production of a sufficient "arousal jag" (Berlyne, 1969). The modal onset of observed laughter was 9 months in Cicchetti's studies, compared with 4 months for normal infants. The most extremely hypotonic (and retarded) infants did not laugh at all in the first year. Despite this late onset and relative low frequency of laughter, these infants nonetheless laughed at items in the same order as the normal subjects of Sroufe and Wunsch; that is, they laughed first at the intrusive auditory and tactile items and only later at the more subtle social and visual items (refer to Table 5.2). This ordering was even more clear when smiling was used as the index of positive affect. Most important, Cicchetti's most comprehensive and robust indicator of affective development (age of smiling to three social or visual items) was strongly related to the Bayley scales of mental and motor development and to the Uzgiris–Hunt scales. The overall correlation between the Bayley mental development index and the affective index was .89, which is clearly at the limits of reliability of these instruments. This relationship between cognitive and affective development was also found at the level of detailed observation; for example, only when the infants reciprocally tugged in the "playing tug" item (no. 16, Table 5.2) was laughter observed. As discussed in Chapters 3 and 5, without discerning the game, there can be no laughter. All of this is strong evidence of the close link between affect and cognitive development.

Relationships obtained between advances in level of object concept and causality and positive affect expressed to the social and visual items in this study were crucial for establishing that such relationships are not fortuitous. With rapidly developing normal infants some parallel changes in different domains of development would be certain to occur. The fact that they are temporally related even within the slower development of these retarded infants, as well as the strong concordances for individual infants, confirm an interrelated developmental process.

The development of fear in children with Down syndrome was also shown to be closely tied to cognitive development. Again, in comparison with available norms, these children were, as a group, quite delayed in the onset of separation reactions, fearful reactions to the visual cliff, and anticipatory aversive reactions to looming stimuli (see Chapter 6). Anticipatory defensive reactions have obvious cognitive (meaning) underpinnings, which was confirmed by the fact that they occur earlier on a second presentation of the rapidly approaching stimulus.

It is such reactions that were notably delayed in infants with Down syndrome, not the blinking that occurs in the newborn period. As with smiling and laughter, the delay was completely consistent with the assessed level of cognitive development on the Bayley scales and with the level of object concept on the Uzgiris–Hunt scales. It also was related to the index of positive affect, suggesting that a common developmental (cognitive) process is involved in positive and negative affect. A failure to cross the visual cliff, and other negative reactions in that situation, were likewise related to cognitive developmental level. Only the most cognitively advanced infants showed such reactions when tested the month after the onset of crawling (the time when normal infants show fear on the cliff).

Throughout the sensorimotor period, the affective development of these children moved through the same phases as that of normal children, though at a slower rate. In a follow-up study of some of Cicchetti's children, Spiker (1990) was able to show that these children also enter a phase comparable to the "terrible twos," with defiance and oppositional behavior. While this is counter to the myth of the affable Down syndrome child, it is not counter to the experience of the children's parents. This period of negativism coincided with the child's approximation of a mental age of 2; that is, typically by age 3 or 4 years.

Similarly, when a subset of these children was seen at age 4 to 5 years, a remarkable concordance between affective and cognitive assessments was again observed (Motti et al., 1983). For example, the level of symbolic play correlated both with enthusiasm in play and with affective sharing of play with the caregiver ($r = .73$ and .45, respectively). Performance on the Bayley scales at age 2 years strongly predicted both affective (.58 with enthusiasm) and cognitive (.72) assessments at ages 4 to 5, as did the affect assessment obtained at 10 months. This total data set makes obvious the interdependence of affect and cognition.

The main conclusion from the Cicchetti research is that Down syndrome children exhibit an essentially normal pattern of behavioral organization and development. Cicchetti has argued that the slower pace of development of these children affords a clear view of the basic nature of all development. The integration of cognitive, social, and emotional aspects of development is apparent when the process is drawn out. Five-year-old Down syndrome children may show a developmental lag of 1, 2, or 3 years, but their behavioral organization is similar to that of younger nonretarded children. One observes the same dedication to exploration, the same sharing of delight in discovery, and the same joy in mastery (or pride in creation) as in normal young children, although the expressions may be muted. The role of affect in both guiding play and the interactive or discovery chain is similar; for example, the child struggles to open a box, tries different methods, persists, then exclaims, "I did it!" with a smile to the caregiver. Except for the child's physical features, the hypotonia, and the commonly delayed language development, the play of these children cannot be distinguished from that of normal, younger children. They are attached to their caregivers and use them as a base for exploration; they affectively engage the surround; and within the limits of their cognitive development, they are imaginative, creative, and certainly exuberant. Like normally developing children they exhibit a period of negativism, and they are capable of anger, fear, and guilt. These reactions occur in comparable contexts to the circumstances that arouse such emotions in normal children.

Cognitive development and the continued unfolding of the emotions

The preceding discussion has emphasized the cognitive concomitants of joy and fear, emotions normally appearing in the first year. The continued unfolding of the emotions is also intrinsically linked with cognitive development. Certain emotions require some capacity for the representation of relationships with others (e.g., grief, affection). Some require an evolving sense of self (e.g., shame). Other emotions require a comparison of behavior with an internalized standard (pride, guilt). Each of these makes demands on cognition (though again they reciprocally influence cognitive development). One cannot, for example, experience anxiety until a threat to the self (however primitive that self might be) is perceived, or feel the shame of the self exposed until there is some sense of self-awareness.

Anxiety, though not a discrete emotion, is an interesting case, because new bases for anxiety emerge with development. As detailed by Breger (1974), the prototype for anxiety is a feeling of helplessness within a separation experience. To the infant such a separation experience represents a loss of a vital part of his or her primitive ''self-system,'' which in the first year includes the caregiver. Such an anxiety experience rests on the beginning recognition of the caregiver as an independent ''object.'' Then, in the second year, cognitive advances allow the basis of anxiety to move beyond literal separation to fear of loss of love (psychological separations such as may occur in scolding in some circumstances). Later still, the young child may experience anxiety because he or she violates known prohibitions, even without an adult present (which we refer to as guilt). This is a more abstract sense of disconnection, but the prototypic sense of self-loss remains. Ultimately, one may think of adult existential anxiety as a threat to the integrity of the individual. Throughout, this progression is interwoven completely with cognitive development.

Hoffman (1985) has pointed out specifically how the bases for emotion change with an advancing understanding of causality. A toddler who falls may express anger at a caregiver who is present, as though he or she caused the accident; not so a preschooler. Likewise, toddlers say they are sorry to their mothers who look sad, as though the sadness were their responsibility (Zahn-Waxler, Radke-Yarrow, & King, 1979). Again, such behavior would not occur in the preschool years, though by then there would be more evolved guilt reactions.

Both empathy and aggression/hostility are clearly tied to cognitive development. While infants are capable of neither, both unfold from precursors in infancy to fairly evolved capabilities by the end of the preschool period (Eisenberg, 1989; Hoffman, 1979). Research has suggested that both empathy and aggression are object centered and impersonal during the toddler period (Bronson, 1981). For example, the child sees another toddler trying to reach for an object. Since the object is near the first child, he or she pushes it within reach of the partner who can then grasp it. Such instances of behavior were interpreted by Bronson in terms of the child's need for cognitive closure. The child in the second year is able to recognize the intended act and to know what its outcome is supposed to be – the child cooperates in the completion for the sake of completion, as though the intention were his or her own. Such behavior is probably not true empathy, being a response to the action sequence and not the feelings or goals of the other. At this age there is little visual checking with the other or sharing in the resulting feelings. Still, in this object-/action-centered behavior lie the roots of later empathy-based prosocial behavior. It represents the beginnings of role taking.

Bronson noted similar, object-centered precursors of aggression. In toddlers, aggressive encounters nearly always involved objects – issues of joint possession. One child has, the other takes, or both children reach an object at the same time and a struggle arises. Again, at this age there is little concern about the other. When the object is obtained, the "hostilities" are over, although one child may be distressed. While "unintentional," it is likely that children learn from such early encounters that forceful actions often will be successful. Children later disposed to be hostile and aggressive will have the requisite tools. Other research shows that by the end of the toddler period, children are responsive to the "possession rule" (Brownell & Brown, 1985). Twenty-four-month-olds less often try to take objects already possessed by a peer and more often negotiate than do 18-month-olds. Also, they more often relinquish an object to a partner who was previously playing with it.

In many ways true empathy/altruism and hostile aggression draw on the same cognitive advances – namely, the child's understanding of the feelings of the other person. To be empathic and altruistic involves knowing what the other child feels and desires, then responding in terms of those feelings. Likewise, to be exquisitely hostile requires an understanding of the other's circumstances and the likely effects of one's behavior. For example, one unpopular 5-year-old boy was playing with an African mask, growling at nearby children. One girl was frightened by this, shrinking back. The masked boy selected this child for intensified approach, driving her away in tears. The same understanding, of course, could have led him to take off the mask and reassure the child, which other 4- to 5-year-olds have been observed to do (Kestenbaum, Farber, & Sroufe, 1989).

The reciprocal influence of affect on cognition

Virtually all of the research presented in the preceding sections, being correlational in nature, could just as well have been presented in terms of the "influence" of affect on cognition, or more simply as evidence that emotional and cognitive development proceed as one. As one example, the finding that the most hypotonic Down syndrome children lag substantially in both affective expression and mental test performance could well be viewed in terms of a compromised cognitive development due to an impoverishment of emotional experience. Many of the cited authors, of course, realize the arbitrariness of the presentation followed, but proceeded as they did for purposes of exposition. It is, nonetheless noteworthy how seldom findings are viewed or questions are posed from the alternative perspective.

There are a number of ways that the "influences" of affect on cognition could be conceptualized. Hoffman (1985) has outlined three of these and marshals support from work with adults and older children. First, affect may initiate or disrupt information processing or result in selective processing. Second, affect may organize recall. Across the lifespan one's affective state promotes the recall of information that is congruent with that affect. Hoffman believes that this organizational feature may underlie the young child's learning of scripts (e.g., what you do at McDonald's; see Nelson & Grundel, 1981), because such situations commonly have a strong affective base. Third, affect contributes to the formation of emotionally charged categories and schemes. When new stimuli are assimilated to such categories, past affect is transferred to them. In Fiske's (1982) conception, "Affect may generalize from experiences with prior instances to the category as a whole and hence back to new instances" (p. 61).

Possible roles for affect in infancy have centered on affect as the infant's primary medium of communication and meaning and as the basis for early concept formation (e.g., Kellerman, 1983; Stechler & Carpenter, 1967). Kellerman takes the position that "concept formation exists at first as affective tonal representation. This idea is an oblique reference to the proposition that cognition is derived from uncrystallized affect; that is, thought is the consolidation in language of a feeling, mood, or cluster of emotions" (p. 319). He goes on to discuss the intonational or inflectional nuances in infant babbling. Such tonal and inflectional variations give meaning to the infant's phonemic productions to both the infant and the other. And this (shared) meaning is affective (see also Brazelton & Cramer, 1990; Stern, 1985).

Affect may be viewed at times as promoting, inspiring, or calling forth cognitive effort. We have discussed the role of positive affect in sustaining contact with novel events (and therefore promoting assimilation) in Chapter 5. Several investigators reported that the spontaneous use of the infant's most complex behaviors are observed in pleasurable interactions with the caregiver (Escalona, 1968; Stern, 1974). Charlesworth (1969) showed a similar influence for surprise. Surprising events were engaged over and over, without the usual habituation so common with repetitive events. In these ways emotional reactions mediate contact with the environment.

Another example of emotional factors inspiring cognition is provided by the work on "caregiver permanence" in comparison with object permanence. Sylvia Bell (1970), in a landmark study, demonstrated a décalage (unevenness of progress) between caregiver permanence and object permanence that was influenced by the security of attachment. As will be discussed in Chapter 10, securely attached infants are active in exploration and in seeking contact following separation, as well as readily settled by the caregiver when distressed. Anxiously attached infants show poor exploration, are difficult to settle, or are avoidant of the caregiver upon reunion following a brief separation. In Bell's study securely attached infants showed a more advanced level of caregiver permanence compared with object permanence (cf. Piaget's stages of object concept, especially search behavior), while anxiously attached infants showed a more advanced level of object permanence, or no décalage. Different procedures were used for testing person permanence and mother permanence in Bell's study, so the study is subject to criticism as a test of whether mother permanence *generally* precedes object permanence (Jackson, Campos, & Fischer, 1978). But the procedures were the same for both groups of infants, so group differences really cannot be explained away by this procedural critique. Moreover, the results were replicated by Chazan (1981). One may also argue that securely attached infants were more motivated to find their mothers. This is simply saying, however, that the affective tie promoted expression of the infant's most advanced capacities. This is close to Bell's interpretation, which emphasizes the cognition-enhancing influences of the positive infant–caregiver relation. The caregiver is a very special object for these securely attached children and is associated with a history of positively toned exchanges. Such a history promotes the growth of understanding of the caregiver as a separate, independent object. The relationship between the quality of attachment and later development will be a major topic in Part III.

It also has been reported that affectivity may be used to reveal advances in cognitive development, further illustrating the unity of development. Haviland

(1975), in a remarkable paper, illustrates how those assessing cognitive growth in infants, including Piaget and infant testers, repeatedly rely on interest, surprise, and other expressions of affect to determine level of cognitive performance. For example, in one of Piaget's famous examples, Laurent's knowledge of object permanence is inferred not simply from his actions with the matchbox. Rather, it was because he showed interest in the box, was surprised and then disappointed by the disappearance, and showed eager expectation concerning the return. Likewise, Laurent's anger when Piaget repeatedly made his bottle disappear suggested knowledge beyond that of a younger infant. Even the absence of affect was used by Piaget to infer a lack of appreciation of the permanence of the object. Cicchetti and Hesse (1983) have elaborated on this idea. In a similar vein, Yarrow and his colleagues (e.g., Yarrow, Rubenstein, & Peterson, 1975) studied what they call "cognitive-motivational" variables, acknowledging with Piaget that secondary circular reactions, creating a spectacle, and so forth are not possible without the sustained affective investment of the infant.

Others have demonstrated that affective measures are useful predictors of later cognitive performance. Birns and Golden (1972), for example, found pleasure in the task to be a better predictor of later cognitive performance than were early cognitive measures. Likewise, Cicchetti and Sroufe found that laughter to a preselected set of items at age 9 months (using a median split) predicted the Bayley scores of a group of Down syndrome infants at 16 months with no overlap between groups. Early laughter to complex events is an excellent predictor because it taps the motivational, attentional, affective, and cognitive capacities (e.g., the competence) of the infant. *Emotion is necessarily integrative.*

Conclusion

The interdependence of affect and cognition is abundantly supported by diverse pieces of evidence. This is despite the fact that there is rather little support for simple linear causality, either from cognition to affect or affect to cognition. The two are better viewed as complementary aspects of a unified developmental process, with cognition serving affect and affect inspiring cognition. The mutual impact of emotional experiences and cognitive development will be an important area for further research. One route to answering the most pressing questions will probably be detailed longitudinal studies of individual cases. A key hypothesis is that qualitative advances in cognitive functioning may be stimulated by critical (affectively laden) transactions with the environment. Only when such transactions can be recorded in some numbers, in the context of densely scheduled cognitive assessments, can the expected relations be demonstrated. The richest studies would be equally concerned with the ongoing reciprocal influence of cognitive advances on emotion.

8 Meaning, evaluation, and emotion

[Emotions] arise in response to the meaning structures of given situations, to events that are important to the individual, and which importance he or she appraises in some way.

Frijda (1988)

Arousal is a valuable behavioral catalyst and organizer but ... heightened and prolonged arousal can be disorganizing emotional regulation is essential to enlisting emotive processes into the organized and psychologically adaptive higher-order control of behavior.

Thompson (1990)

Subjectivity and meaning are critical for understanding all aspects of emotional development (Emde, 1980; Lazarus, 1991). They are central to the very definition of emotional reactions, which have as their core a relationship between the infant and the particular event. They underlie the unfolding of mature emotions from their precursors, because this process is based on the growing meaning of events for the infant. Likewise, they are pivotal for explaining why one emotion rather than another is aroused, especially in what seem to be similar situations. Finally, as will be developed, subjectivity and meaning are essential to conceptualizing individual differences in emotional life.

In this chapter we review the role of subjective factors and meaning in emotion as a transition to examining individual differences in emotional expression and regulation. By the end of the first year it is not events themselves, but what infants make out of them that determines emotional reactions and individual reactivity. Moreover, dramatic individual differences in the meaning of events and of emotional arousal itself have become established. This is especially true with regard to situations that are novel or incongruous, which are critical in human adaptation.

Over the course of infancy (and beyond) there is both an increasing specificity and an increasing subjectivity of meaning. For example, the difference between fear and wariness is a difference in specificity, fear being a categorical reaction to a particular event. At the same time, fear reactions, in contrast to earlier

131

wariness, reflect an increasing subjectivity, the relation of this event to the particular infant. It is not that the frightened infant literally sees something different when looking at a stranger than does a nonfrightened infant (who is younger, less advanced, more or less experienced with strangers, or more secure). The stimulus array is the same, but the meaning is different.

There are no pure perceptions by 10 months. Events are related to previous events in terms of past as well as present meanings. When the infant sees a stranger in a white lab coat, historically associated affect is automatically part of the perception. Moreover, the infant does not see the stranger, then remember past experiences; the past experiences are part of the "seeing" (see also Schore, 1994, p. 315). We are still dealing with cognitive activity, but cognitive activity in which affect is inherently involved.

Critical, then, both in the development of the emotions and in what may be called individual emotional development is the meaning found by infants in their transactions with the environment. This imbuing of events with meaning is what is meant by the term *evaluation*, a subjective mental process. Consistent with the developmental overview provided in Chapter 4 and the cognitive considerations in Chapters 5 to 7, evaluative capacity is clearly apparent in the second half year, though it has earlier roots and evolves considerably with the development of symbolic capacity. Evaluative capacity strongly influences the unfolding of the affect systems. In addition, as will be developed, it is vitally important in determining the nature of the affective response in any given situation.

The evaluative capacity is a key process underlying commonalties in the developmental course of various affect systems, and it is a central concept in explaining the intimate relations between affect systems. A close tie between laughter and fear, for example, has been understood by philosophers for centuries. And in most early accounts an interpretive process was given a key role in determining the emotional reaction. Kant (1790, cited in Berlyne, 1969), for example, described laughter as "a sudden transformation of a strained expectation into nothing." Only a change in the interpretation of the event lies on the fine line between laughter and fear. We, too, were aware of this close relationship as we began our studies of affect development.

One of the initial discoveries in our own studies on the development of laughter (Sroufe & Wunsch, 1972) was that the same kinds of events previously reported to produce fear were the best elicitors of positive affect. John B. Watson (1924/1970) and others had listed loss of balance and loud noises as two major unconditioned fear stimuli; yet these were among the best laughter stimuli, especially in the first half year. Masks have also been used widely in studies of fear (Hebb, 1949; Scarr & Salapatek, 1970). In our studies, however, in which the masked approach was done by the infant's mother in a playful home context (vs. an experimenter in the laboratory), the mask produced uniformly positive affect with 10- to 12-month-olds. Loud noises, loss of balance, and masks may all produce fear *or* joy. This was a very provocative observation.

Others (e.g., Ambrose, 1963) had interpreted laughter as a mixture of fear and joy ("ambivalence"). Our interpretation, in contrast, emphasized that laughter was the maximal positive response. That laughter reflects a purely positive affect was suggested by the fact that it built from smiling on early trials with a given salient event, then faded again to smiling with continued presentation. It seemed unlikely that negative elements would be noticed only after several trials, and then would be disregarded later. That the same items could elicit both laughter and fear strongly suggested a link, but it could not be the case that laughter generally was a partial or mixed fear response.

Developmentally, the relationship between strong positive and strong negative affect also was striking. The age at which laughter emerged in response to the masked approach by mother is roughly the same age at which fear appeared in response to the masked approach by the stranger. Also, as discussed in Chapter 5, items that produced distress early in infancy (usually very intrusive events) were likely to produce laughter the following month. Finally, a parallel developmental course between fear and joy was highlighted in describing the studies of retarded infants (Cicchetti & Sroufe, 1978). Not only are more severely retarded infants comparably retarded in assessments of both positive and negative affect, but the developmental trends in these two domains are completely parallel; that is, infants who show, for example, a 5-month delay in anticipatory negative reactions to a looming visual stimulus also show a comparable lag in onset of smiling or laughter to our visual and social items (refer to Table 5.2). And, in general, infants with Down syndrome, who as a group show little laughter, also show little fear in infancy. The most extremely hypotonic infants show neither in the first year (see Chapter 7). Clearly, the same developmental processes and some common mechanism(s) underlie both strong positive and immediate negative affect.

Determinants of joy or fear in the face of novelty

Tension, a part of Piaget's (1952) equilibration process, was given a central role in the explanation of laughter presented in Chapter 5. The infant cognitively engages the novel event, accommodative efforts ensue, and tension is generated as a natural by-product. When such effort leads to (rapid) assimilation, smiling (or laughter) results. But must tension always be associated with pleasure? Obviously not. Disequilibrium and uncertainty at times produce distress, and Hebb (1949), Berlyne (1969), and other prominent theorists made such a construct the basis for explanations of fear. We presented a similar position in describing wariness (Chapter 6). A major question, then, concerns how disequilibrium can sometimes lead to distress and sometimes to joy. Cognition plays a role, but so do other aspects of development, as well as the history of emotional experiences.

The discrepancy hypothesis (Chapter 7), proposed by Kagan (1971) and other developmentalists, stresses the amount of discrepancy or assimilability. In this view, positive affect occurs in cases of "moderate discrepancy" when, because the stimulus is not too unlike familiar stimuli, the infant is able to alter its mental structures so that the discrepant event fits. A more discrepant event would lead to accommodative failures and fear.

This purely cognitive position has been criticized for its inherent circularity. (If the infant shows positive affect, the event must have been moderately discrepant.) It is difficult in advance to define what would be moderately discrepant, given the complexity of most socioemotional situations and a host of experiential differences among individuals. Moreover, the position has been shown to be wanting on an empirical basis, by demonstrations of quite different reactions by the same infants to the same stimuli in different contexts.

My own view emphasizes context-based evaluation (Sroufe, 1984; Sroufe, Waters, & Matas, 1974). Engaging a discrepant or novel event produces arousal or tension. But no particular amount of arousal is automatically distressing. Discrepancy alone can play only a partial role in determining affective expression. Stimulus factors such as intensity, discrepancy, novelty, complexity, and salience (see Berlyne, 1969) influence primarily the degree of attention and arousal production and thus the *magnitude*, but not the direction, of the affective response. Loud sounds, because of their intensity, and a masked approach, because of the degree of incongruity and saliency for the older infant, produce sufficient arousal for *either* strong positive or strong negative affect.

Whether the *direction* (hedonic tone) of the affect is positive or negative depends on the infant's capacity for modulating tension (e.g., developmental level) *and* security of context. Stechler and Carpenter (1967) have stated this same viewpoint as follows:

Discrepancy and its various synonyms are *quantitative* terms and provide no implication of directionality. Further information, beyond the fact of discrepancy, is required to predict whether the arousal will have a positive or negative hedonic *quality*. It is predominantly the qualitative aspects of affect which are most difficult to explain via the informational model. (p. 173, emphases added)

They go on to say that information must be described not only in terms of its processing load but also in terms of its *meaning*. Thus, the expression of positive or negative affect depends both on arousal (which includes assimilability) *and* the infant's context-based evaluation.

This two-factor model of affect is supported by substantial evidence. In an early study we found significantly more negative reactions (both in overt behavior and HR acceleration) to strangers in the laboratory, where such an event would be evaluated more negatively, than at home (Sroufe et al., 1974). Based on a discrepancy model (strangers being more discrepant in the home), Kagan (1971) had predicted the opposite. Moreover, when infants were given time to become familiar with the laboratory (10 minutes), the same stranger, approaching in the same sequential manner, produced significantly fewer negative reactions (50% vs. 93% with only 30 seconds of familiarization time). The stimulus discrepancy of the stranger wasn't changed, only the context in which the stimulus was presented.

Moreover, a basic finding in the stranger fear literature is that if an infant is distressed by an initial stranger approach, he or she will become more distressed and sooner distressed on a second approach, even if fully settled between episodes. It does not make sense to think that the stranger becomes more discrepant on the second occasion (a faster failure of assimilation); rather, the infant's threshold for threat is lowered. Distress on the first trial becomes a context for evaluating the second approach. There is in fact no failure of assimilation at all. The event is rather immediately recognized as one that the infant does not want. The infant's evaluation is negative.

A series of studies with masked faces provided additional evidence (Sroufe et al., 1974). As stated earlier, in a playful home context, with mother putting on the mask in the infant's view and then approaching, smiling was universal in 10-month-olds and 50% laughed. The same procedure, however, produced much less laughter (18% to 33% in a number of studies) in the laboratory, though most infants still smiled. Moreover, if the observations were made in the laboratory following a brief separation from the mother, which would dramatically alter the infant's evaluation of the situation, smiling was greatly reduced to mother with mask, and there was *no* laughter. Also, if a stranger approached with the mask first, infants were subsequently less likely to smile at mother. Some even cried. On the other hand, when the mother went first, this increased positive reactions to the stranger (see Sroufe et al., 1974). Finally, three infants were tested when separated from their mothers (though playing contentedly in a high chair). Under these conditions masked approach by a stranger produced crying in all three infants. Virtually any result, from uniformly positive to uniformly negative affect, can be produced with the masked approach procedure by varying context.

The role of evaluation

Cognitive considerations alone cannot handle this array of results. It seems unlikely that mother with mask is more discrepant in the laboratory or following either a separation or masked approach by a stranger than at home, or preceding either separation or stranger approach. In fact, for example, having seen the mask previously (on the stranger), one would think it would be less discrepant (more familiar) when mother then wore the mask. And it seems unlikely that a stranger with mask is more discrepant in mother's absence than in her presence. In addition, in studies of stranger reactions it has been found that infants are less likely to be negative when sitting on mother's lap than when she is sitting a few feet away (which would make comparing of faces and noting discrepancy more possible). In the home, we have had mothers put nylons over their faces, bark like dogs, walk like penguins, and do other outlandish things. The infants squeal with delight. Clearly, discrepancy alone cannot account for this entire body of findings.

To handle these data, concepts like *context-based evaluation* or *changing threshold for threat* are required. As another example, consider a situation in which the caregiver picks up a 14-month-old by the heels. This is extremely arousing: But since the agent is the caregiver and 14-month-olds have a great tolerance for arousal, the threshold for threat is high. The event in context is positively evaluated. Laughter results. Following a stranger approach or a separation experience in the laboratory, however, this *same* procedure produces distress, even in the same infant on the same visit. This is not because the infant now fails to recognize the event. A more reasonable interpretation is that the degree of arousal associated with this familiar but stimulating event is no longer tolerable. Factors such as the presence of the caregiver, the opportunity to become familiar with surroundings, and a favorable sequence of events may not make events less discrepant (or less arousing), but they do alter the infant's evaluation of the event in context. In general, the more secure the context the more likely the infant is to respond to arousing novel events with smiling and laughter and the less likely to be afraid.

This is not to say that discrepancy (or degree of arousal) is unimportant. Mother with mask is more potent for positive affect than mother alone, and stranger with mask is more potent for negative affect than a stranger without a mask. The novelty of the mask adds to the degree of arousal. Also, in the investigations of stranger reactions discussed in Chapter 6, gradual approaches, allowing the infant control of the pacing, and the use of familiar formats (peekaboo, toy play) were all found to reduce the amount and frequency of distress. One can interpret these factors in terms of a facilitation of the infant's assimilative/accommodative efforts. The infant can anchor the experience within other familiar experiences. Still, these factors may be viewed as operating at the level of evaluation as well.

Evaluation and development

The concept of an evaluation process presents a solution to a fundamental developmental problem. Assume with Piaget that cognitive growth occurs through the failure of assimilation and subsequent renewed accommodative efforts. Fear, as an *inevitable* outcome of the failure to assimilate, would pose a major problem for psychological growth. Infants must fail repeatedly in their assimilative/accommodative efforts. Were such failure routinely to lead to fear and disengagement, rather than continued effort, cognitive structures would not change. Only if failure leads to persistence does change occur. This would, in fact, describe the sequence of neutral responses followed by smiling on subsequent presentations of a novel event, as described in Chapter 5. It is of great importance that infants be able to cope with the very high arousal often associated with novelty and failures to assimilate and not routinely become disorganized by negative affect. Maintaining engagement in such circumstances, which can be done in certain contexts, promotes cognitive growth (Sroufe & Waters, 1976).

The capacity to maintain organized behavior in the face of emotional arousal also represents an important dimension of individual differences, a theme that will be developed throughout the final chapters of the book. Perhaps the central task in all early development is the progressive growth of emotional regulation (Thompson, 1990), which takes the form of a sequential transfer of responsibility from caregiver to dyad to child (Sroufe, 1989). As will be presented in detail, young infants have limited capacities for self-soothing and self-regulation and must frequently be on (and past) the edge of overwhelming arousal (Fogel, 1982). At first, caregivers have almost total responsibility for keeping arousal tolerable. In time, infants play an increasingly active role in a dyadic regulation process, responding to caregivers and, ultimately, instigating regulatory assistance through intentional bids. Gradually, over the early years of life, these regulatory processes are taken over (internalized) by the child (Chapters 10 to 12). By the second half year one may see this process underway in the centrality of the caregiver's presence and availability to the infant's evaluation of novel events. For all infants familiarity of context increases arousal tolerance. For many, the known potential of the caregiver's behavior, and their own effectiveness in eliciting it, are part of that familiarity. These infants are much more likely to evaluate novel situations as benign when the caregiver is accessible to them. The capacity to evaluate is available to all infants by late in the first year; the nature of such evaluations varies with individual history.

The term *evaluation* may seem to imply too much cognitive sophistication for the 8- to 12-month-old infant (though no more so than "appraisal" or "activation of hypotheses" used by others). The term may be defended, both with respect to the complexity of behavior during this age period and its aptness for describing observable phenomena. Developmentally, some such concept seems appropriate. Six-month-olds show none of the subtle, context-differentiated responding of the 10-month-old. With neutral affect they will reach for the brightly colored mask whether it is on mother or a stranger, at home or in the laboratory (Sroufe et al., 1974).

Moreover, the preceding set of results cannot be interpreted in terms of some simple state variable. Behavioral observation (being settled, even content) and concurrent HR recordings suggest that infants in our studies have comparable levels of resting arousal at home and in the laboratory. There is greater HR acceleration to the events in the laboratory, but similar pre-stress levels. Also, in our studies of sequential effects, infants recover between events. Still, the setting or the preceding noxious event (e.g., mother separating briefly) produce their negative consequences. The negative state may temporarily vanish, but with the 10-month-old the affective experience remains in memory and becomes part of a continually updated evaluation of the situation and events that occur within it.

Changing "set points" for threat, to use Bowlby's (1969/1982) term, are a function of a variety of *internal* as well as external parameters. For this reason the term *evaluation* is preferable to the term *appraisal*, which can imply too much of an emphasis on external information, a coldly cognitive process. External information – for example, changes in the event or the mother drawing closer – are of obvious importance, but so are the feelings engendered by preceding events and even the feelings/memories associated with the general situation and the infant's confidence regarding it. When our experimenters at one time wore white lab coats, 10- to 12-month-old infants who had recently visited the doctor for shots were often immediately distressed. This association was highly reliable and made it clear that a very specific and personal meaning, based on experience, was being imported into the situation. This is a subjective process. The term *evaluation* conveys such subjectivity. This is intended, given the centrality of subjectivity to the basic definition of emotion. Again, it is the fact of this subjectivity that will open the way for the fruitful study of individual differences. By the end of the first year, dramatic and stable individual differences are present.

The nature of the evaluation process

Is the evaluation concept we are discussing a cognitive process or an affective process? The answer, of course, is both, and the term was selected deliberately to convey this idea. The infant's evaluation of an unfamiliar event occurring in its context is not a cold calculation concerning possibilities and probabilities. The infant, however sophisticated by 10 to 12 months of age, does not think: "The last time a large man I didn't know came at me some pain resulted. On the other hand, that wasn't at home, and mother was holding me tensely, as though she herself had a sense of foreboding." The infant does not even simply think "this is safe" or "this is dangerous." Rather, he or she *feels* safe or apprehensive. These feelings, which are central to evaluation, depend both on current circumstances (familiarity of the setting, presence and accessibility of the caregiver) and on general as well as specific experiential history. This would include past actions of strangers and caregivers. For example, is the caregiver routinely available and effective when assistance is needed?

Likewise, in widely used laboratory separation and reunion procedures (see Chapter 10), 12-month-olds certainly do not think about their vulnerability to predation when the caregiver leaves or even about the caregiver's unavailability should some threat arise. Rather, the infant *feels anxiety* and that mediates interpretations of events and the overall situation.

Affective as well as cognitive aspects of evaluation are also reflected in toddlers' behavior in social referencing situations. Toddlers do not likely think about the fact that the caregiver is reading or not reading a magazine; they simply feel more confident if he or she is attentive, and such feelings mediate their evaluation of available objects and events that occur. Similarly, in the visual cliff situation toddlers do not likely use an analytical process to reach a logical conclusion (e.g., "Mother is smiling, therefore she has judged this situation to be safe, and since she has vastly more experience than I do in these situations I will accept her judgment"). Information about the situation, as can be gathered by attending to the caregiver, is of course important. But beyond the pure information value, there is the affective value of the caregiver's behavior. The caregiver's smile may lead the infant to feel more secure and confident, which changes the infant's evaluation of the situation. Similarly, when the caregiver is alarmed, this alarms the toddler, again changing the evaluation. An interesting experiment would be to have the caregiver's alarm expressions precede the toddler's approach to the cliff (calling to the child in advance to assure attention). One might obtain similar (though perhaps not identical) hesitancy to cross the deep side with such a procedure, because the toddler's threshold for threat may be altered in advance. (This is similar to an explanation based on mood induction versus interpretation of social signals; Hornik, Risenhoover, & Gunnar, 1987. It seems likely that both are in effect.)

Evaluation and tension

The position being developed is somewhat distinctive in the way that cognition is treated. In other positions, events are often treated as objective and their information value is emphasized. The cognitive process is invoked only after the event has occurred. For example, for Mandler events (that disrupt plans) lead to arousal, and this arousal is cognitively appraised (and is then emotion). For Lazarus it is the event that is appraised, and this appraisal determines the subsequent emotions. While individuals may appraise an event differently because of their unique histories or circumstances, the threat (or benignity) still lies in the event itself. In the current view the infant's engagement of the event in context is emphasized. It is the engagement that produces arousal ("tension"). Moreover, the context, in which events are always nested, includes both the infant's general evaluation of the situation (and therefore felt security) and evaluation based on particular experiences with such events. Thus, the cognitive/ affective process is in operation from the inception. The novelty or saliency (engagingness) of the event has much to do with the degree of tension generated, but the tolerance level for tension is set in advance by the infant's evaluation-based comfort in the situation. Here, cognitive/affective engagement leads to tension, which leads to positive or negative emotion, based on an evaluation of the event in context. The tension and emotion, of course, subsequently enter into ongoing evaluation. But it is not the tension that is solely evaluated (vs. Mandler), and the event and the evaluation are not viewed as independent (as implied by Lazarus).

In summary, context does not include only peripheral events in the situation. It includes just-preceding events, past events, and expected outcomes. Moreover, it includes affect that is being carried forward (ongoing mood), as well as the history of experiences with affect regulation, in this kind of situation and in general. It includes not only the presence and attentiveness of the caregiver, but the expectations of the infant concerning caregiver responsiveness built over the course of their interactive history.

Because of their central importance for the infant's transactions with novel and other critically important environmental events, our discussion focuses on joy and fear. However, evaluative processes also underlie other emotions, such as anger. For all infants, what we define as anger involves recognition of an obstacle to a goal. But, for example, only some infants perceive a caregiver who is physically present as an obstacle to the goal of desired contact when they are highly aroused; that is, their repeated experience of not being comforted when distressed enters into their evaluation of the caregiver when they later desperately need comforting, and anger results.

The dynamic tension model

Tension, as I use the term, is closer in meaning to "arousal" than it is to the psychoanalytic concept of drive. That is, it is not a Freudian concept of energy, striving continually to seek release (or impelling behavior). Rather, the tension is a natural by-product of actively engaging the environment. Tension is not necessarily aversive and so does not need to be maintained at low levels. In fact, it seems rather to be the case that organisms are drawn toward some degree of environmental engagement and thereby tension (as, e.g., in the infant's endless encouragement of peekaboo games; Parrott & Gleitman, 1989).

Despite the possibility of some unwanted surplus meaning, I prefer the metaphorical concept of tension to arousal precisely because it does imply a psychological process. Physiological arousal changes merely in moving from sleep to wakefulness, and it is heavily influenced by the physical parameters of stimulation (loudness of tones, etc., Graham & Clifton, 1966). It is important to distinguish between such physically produced arousal and arousal that is due to meaning. It is when the latter is included that I use the term *tension*. There would be no direct one-to-one correspondence between tension and autonomic arousal. Rather, it refers to the degree of psychological engagement and is closely related to the meaningfulness of the event, which is both affective and cognitive. The heuristic value of the tension concept – that is, its role in explaining emotional development – should become more clear in subsequent discussion.

The tension model, as developed thus far, is illustrated in Figure 8.1. Basically, a dynamic threshold range for affective response is hypothesized. As I have suggested previously:

For positive affect to occur the level of tension must exceed Threshold 1, but not remain above that threshold. Smiling has been interpreted as oscillations around the threshold, laughter as a steeper tension fluctuation . . . Negative affect would occur only when the tension remains above Threshold 1 or exceeds Threshold 2. *The critical feature of the model, however, is that neither threshold is stationary.* (Sroufe, 1982, p. 577, emphasis added)

Thus, no fixed amount of arousal (tension) is necessarily aversive. In certain circumstances (those that promote feelings of security) great amounts of arousal can be experienced without fear or distress and disorganization. This is what accounts for the squeals of laughter when infants are tossed up in the air by their caregivers. Such exuberant laughter cannot occur without a great amount of tension. And in circumstances evaluated as benign, infants may encourage tension-producing stimulation, for example, by signaling caregivers to repeat stimulating events.

Changes from laughter to crying, following prolonged stimulation (or as the infant becomes fatigued over the course of a session), can also be accounted for with this model (Figure 8.1d), as can crying at an event that had been positive just moments before, due to the interpolation of a threat (Figure 8.1e). Not a greater amount of tension, but an altered evaluation, a shifting threshold of aversion, is assumed here.

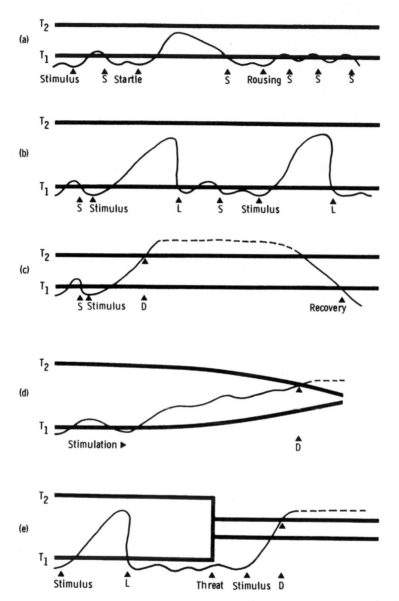

Figure 8.1. Hypothetical tension thresholds, illustrating the occurrence of smiling (S), laughter (L), and distress (D). Both thresholds may shift due to the infant's changing evaluation, changing state, or changing capacities with development. (a) The case of the endogenous sleep smile of the newborn; (b) an older infant; (c) the same infant in a threatening context; (d), (e) the consequences of changing thresholds within an observational session.

Thus, in contrast to the discrepancy model discussed earlier, in the tension model there is more emphasis on internal parameters – that is, not merely the novelty or unfamiliarity of the event, but the individual's threshold for threat. This depends on many factors, including state, immediately preceding events, and constitutionally as well as experientially based individual differences. Individuals will show meaningful differences in their thresholds for threat within and across contexts. Moreover, the exact same event may produce fear or positive affect in the same individuals on different occasions or in different circumstances. (Of course, one may argue that the "event" is not the same when thresholds for threat are altered, but this really is another version of the argument being developed.)

Such a scheme also is important for pointing up critical developmental achievements. Infants show not only changes in the available response repertoire and specific circumstances potent for elicitng various affective reactions, but also marked changes in the capacity for managing tension. Over the course of the first year, there seems to be an increasing capacity to tolerate high levels of arousal, perhaps due in part to a kind of central habituation or adaptation effect in response to repeated experiences of high arousal (Fogel, 1982). Thus, the average level of the upper (fear) threshold increases with development. In addition, there is an expansion of arousal modulation capacities. As will be discussed, caregivers play a vital role in both achievements. With development infants can maintain organized behavior and even positive affect in the face of increasingly greater arousal.

Implications for the role of the caregiver–infant relationship

The preceding emphases on the role of evaluation in determining affective response and on the capacity to maintain organized behavior in the face of high tension make clear the critical importance of the caregiver–infant relationship. Caregivers are potentially great sources of familiarity and security – sources that are highly portable. Without doubt, the most powerful manipulation of the evaluation component that the experimenter can carry out with infants concerns the presence and availability of caregivers. The engagement of novel events and the hedonic tone of affective responses are strongly determined by such manipulations. As we have discussed, the presence or absence of caregivers produces dramatic differences in stranger reactions, and even having the infant on the caregiver's lap versus a few feet away produces observable effects (see Sroufe, 1977). Infants free to crawl to caregivers show less fear than those who are restrained, though in fact they generally do not choose to crawl to them. They are reassured by the mere possibility of doing so. With older infants and toddlers the expression on the caregiver's face (his or her delight in the situation or friendliness toward the stranger) can make a difference in the infant's reaction (e.g., Hornik, Risenhoover, & Gunnar, 1987; Sorce et al., 1985), as can the possibility of visual contact (whether the caregiver is behind a screen or in view; Carr, Dabbs, & Carr, 1975). Moreover, the caregiver's "emotional availability" (attending to the infant in contrast to reading a magazine) dramatically influences the older infant's exploration of a novel setting (Sorce & Emde, 1981).

Clearly, the availability of the caregiver strongly influences the infant's evaluation of events, and there are several reasons for this. By the second half year infants have had ample opportunity to learn that high arousal (tension) in the context of the caregiver need not necessarily lead to distress and disorganization. In the context of the caregiver, increases in tension have commonly been followed by positive outcomes. The caregiver mediates between infant and surround to keep tension within tolerable limits, and when the degree of tension supercedes the infant's capacities the caregiver takes steps to modify the situation. The infant's affective signals are monitored and actions are taken to modulate the tension. And, should the infant's limits be exceeded nevertheless, the caregiver provides effective comforting to restore equilibrium.

From this analysis one would expect that the characteristic degree of availability and responsivity of a particular caregiver would be a major determinant of individual differences in the capacity of infants to engage novel aspects of the environment with positive affect (and in the tendency to break contact that is associated with negative affect). To the degree that the caregiver is reliable, dependable, and consistent, he or she is "knowable" and therefore a source of security in the midst of novel experiences. And to the degree that the caregiver is alert, "attuned" (Ainsworth, Blehar, Waters, & Wall, 1978; Stern, 1985), responsive, and effective, the infant can engage the novel surround with assurance and confidence. By the end of the first year, with sufficient time for this important learning to have occurred, we would expect great individual differences in dealing with novelty and, especially, with using the caregiver as a base for exploration and mastery.

There is another vital role for the caregiver–infant relationship in shaping early emotional development. As will be described in Chapter 9, the caregiver in a sense trains the infant in tension management. In the course of playful interaction the infant learns, over time, to maintain behavioral organization in the face of increasingly high levels of tension. As caregiver and infant play, tension is escalated and de-escalated, to the edge of overstimulation and back again, commonly ending in the bursts of positive affect that are so rewarding for caregivers. Episode by episode, day by day, the infant's own capacity to modulate (and tolerate) tension is developed, and a reservoir or shared positive affect is created. Thus, in time, the caregiver is not only a beacon of familiarity and security, but a repository of positive feelings as well. And, in time, the infant can be more direct and active in seeking what he or she needs by behaving effectively even in the face of high tension.

Studies with animals have demonstrated how experiences within the caregiving system actually tune the CNS to tolerate high arousal (Hofer, 1990; Kraemer, 1992). Through repeated experiences of arousal increase and modulation, the brain itself becomes better adapted for dampening high arousal and for emotional regulation in general (Schore, 1994). Thus, caregiving history is vital in terms of its impact on the evaluation of experiences and at a more physiological level as well.

Here again, a potential for great individual variation may be seen. In contrast to caregivers who finely tune their interactions to move the infant toward ever greater capacity for tension tolerance and self-modulation, other caregivers chronically overstimulate, fail to stimulate, or are strikingly inconsistent in their interactions (Brazelton & Cramer, 1990; Egeland et al., 1993; Fogel, 1993; Schore, 1994; Stern, 1985; Tronick et al., 1978). The expectable range of outcomes from such inappropriate care would include infants who are chronically wary and easily distressed (impoverished in exploration, overreactive, cranky, and unable to be settled) to infants who are unable to become affectly engaged with the surround (failing to thrive, apathetic, and withdrawing).

This will be the subject of extensive discussion as we turn our attention from the unfolding of the affect systems, and conditions governing the expression of affect, to the study of individual emotional development. In this introduction I merely wish to make the point that in stressing the crucial role for the subjective evaluation process in determining the direction (tone) of expressed affect, one also may see a vital role for the caregiver–infant relationship in emotional development in general.

The issue of inborn differences in emotionality

The discussion of caregiver influences on infant emotional development may raise questions about endogenous individual differences in temperament, or even affect expression in particular (e.g., Campos, Barrett, Lamb, Goldsmith, & Stenberg, 1983). Temperament research has established that by the end of the first year, such characteristics as reactivity as well as positive and negative emotionality are stable and consistent across observers and settings (e.g., Bates, 1989; Matheny, 1989; Rothbart, 1989), though such consistency has been shown only rarely and with difficulty in the newborn period (e.g., Korner et al., 1989). Cross-time and cross-situation consistency are two validity criteria for temperament constructs; however, such individual consistency also could result from particular patterns of care, especially given the observation that individual differences become more stable over time. Genetic/adoption studies (e.g., Plomin,

1990) do suggest that individual differences in such dimensions as negative reactivity and inhibition have at least some inborn component. These studies also suggest an environmental component, since there is much less concordance for identical twins reared apart than for those reared together. (For some characteristics, concordance for dizygotic twins reared together surpasses that for monozygotic twins reared apart; e.g., Clifford, 1984.)

To a large extent, of course, a debate about whether emotionality is based on inborn or environmental factors is fallacious. The nature of the developmental process is such that any inborn differences and early care interact (transact) to create the early adaptation of the infant. Caregivers react to this adapting infant, and in time, the infant also behaves in accord with the history of care and experience (Vaughn et al., 1992). Caregiving may (indeed, should) be influenced by the nature (and changing nature) of the infant, and the infant's basic nature is transformed by the caregiving experience. Temperament and experience are not long separable, even if they are so at the beginning of life (Sroufe & Fleeson, 1986).

Moreover, it seems reasonable to propose that experience and stable features of temperament, if they could be disentangled, might influence different aspects of behavior (Sroufe, 1985). In particular, arousability, reactivity, and related dimensions of behavior would more likely have a temperamental basis than would an ability to maintain organized behavior in the face of arousal, confidence in the caregiver, and ability to seek contact when distressed (Gunnar, Mangelsdorf, Larson, & Hertsgaard, 1989; Sroufe, 1985). Infants may have low "thresholds of responsiveness," be "slow to warm up," and so forth and still not show a compromised quality of behavioral organization. An infant who is slow to warm up may, given responsive care, still draw sufficient security from the caregiver to engage novel experiences positively, though perhaps after some delay. Two infants may be quite reactive, but only one may be readily reassured by the caregiver when threatened or be easily calmed when overstimulated. Two others may both be placid, but only one may ignore the caregiver in times of stress, likely because of a history of unresponsiveness by the caregiver. Such issues will be discussed further in subsequent chapters.

Conclusion: a general developmental approach to individual differences in emotional development

The entire discussion to this point can be summarized in the following points:

  1. In examining the emergence and ontogenesis of any specific affect system (pleasure/joy, wariness/fear, etc.), one discovers a central place for engagement and meaning, both in original manifestations of the emotion and in developmental changes. Developmental changes within an affect system are very much

developmental changes in processes for engendering and modulating arousal or tension (which again relate to meaning). This is a critical clue for approaching individual differences in emotional development.

2. Tension, engendered inevitably in engaging the environment, underlies *all* emotional reactions. Therefore, in explaining why one emotion (e.g., joy) rather than another emotion (fear) is aroused, it is necessary to go beyond factors such as the amount of stimulation and the amount of discrepancy (which are related to the degree of arousal and magnitude, but not the hedonic tone, of the affect aroused). Within broad limits, no fixed amount of tension is associated with negative affect; rather, emotion is dependent on an evaluative process, which influences the child's "set point" for threat. A major determinant of the infant's affective reaction (and thereby the tendency to maintain organized mastery behavior) is his or her subjective evaluation of an event.

3. In addition to being subject to developmental change, these set points for threat are dramatically influenced by context. As the context is more secure, the threshold for threat is more elevated; more tension may be tolerated. By the end of the first year, felt security is influenced by past experiences in that situation, more immediate experiences, state variables, the availability of cues associated with security (familiar procedures or objects, predictability, control), and a generalized expectancy concerning likely outcomes when tension is high.

4. The presence and availability of the infant's caregiver are crucial ingredients in the security of context and have a dramatic influence on the set point for tolerable tension. The caregiver is a source of portable familiarity, and commonly infants have learned that in the caregiver's presence high tension need not lead to aversive experiences or behavioral disorganization, but rather can give rise to quite positive outcomes.

5. The infant–caregiver relationship, important in all aspects of emotional development, is thus seen as a cornerstone of individual differences – that is, differences in both tension tolerance and the flexibility of threshold settings. Some infants can manage high degrees of tension (can cope with large amounts of novelty) when the caregiver is accessible to them. It is assumed that this flexibility, perhaps in contrast to such characteristics as reactivity or arousability, are products of the relationship history.

6. Not only may infants functioning within a responsive relationship system more readily engage novel aspects of the environment and thereby expand their mastery capacities, they may also gain experience in maintaining organized behavior in the face of high tension. They thus are prepared for managing tension on their own in subsequent developmental periods.

Part III

Emotional development and individual adaptation

9 The social nature of emotional development

Each partner then progressively escalates – kicking the other partner into higher orbit . . . The exchange occurs in overlapping waves, where the mother's smile elicits the infant's, reanimating her next smile at an even higher level.

Stern (1990)

All these holding experiences are opportunities for the infant to learn how to contain himself.

Brazelton et al. (1974)

The progress of emotional development is intertwined with advances in social development. This is not only because the emotions unfold in a social context, but because broader aspects of emotional development, including the regulation of affect, take place within the matrix of caregiving relationships. In fact, the general course of emotional development may be described as movement *from dyadic regulation to self-regulation* of emotion. Moreover, dyadic regulation represents a prototype for self-regulation; the roots of individual differences in the self-regulation of emotion lie within the distinctive patterns of dyadic regulation (Sroufe, 1989).

The development of the social individual proceeds through a series of phases, from the first weeks when there is little awareness even that some stimulation emanates from the outside environment, through a dawning awareness of self and others, to reciprocal relationships, to a responsive partnership in the preschool years, wherein the child has internalized social values and the beginnings of self-control. Within this process, one of the most significant aspects of socioemotional development is the transition from the virtually complete dependency of the infant to the later autonomous functioning of the child. The data presented in later discussion will be used to illustrate the seeming paradox that the infant who is effectively dependent – who operates successfully from within the caregiver–infant relationship – later shows more effective functioning outside of this relationship – that is, is more capable of independent functioning.

Stated in more explicitly emotional terminology, many infants participate in

151

well-regulated relationship systems and become effective in explicitly using the caregiver to modulate tension. Such infants are later able to manage impulses and feelings flexibly, as well as to maintain organized behavior in the face of high states of tension, when, as young children, they operate more apart from caregivers.

In our developmental view, the secure infant–caregiver relationship, which promotes the capacity for self-modulated arousal, has its roots in the range of affective exchanges throughout early infancy. This includes the repeated experiences of arousal escalation and de-escalation that occur in dyadic interaction. It also includes the frequent occurrences of distress–relief cycles with which the caregiver is associated (Lamb, 1981) and the continued experiences of shared positive affect. Before the infant can explicitly, intentionally use the caregiver as a "secure base for exploration" (Ainsworth et al., 1978), there has been a history of synchronized affective signaling and responding within the pair and a history of shared affect.

As preparation for discussing the roots of individual differences in infancy, we will begin with some general ideas concerning emotional development in the first year. We are shifting our attention from examining development of emotions per se to the development of emotional regulation, which has been viewed as a distinctive aspect of emotional development (Thompson, 1990). A major premise guiding this book, however, is that understanding normative developmental processes, including the expression of the emotions, is the key to understanding the emotional development of individuals. A unified developmental process underlies all aspects of emotional life. During the second half year of life – at the same time that infants become capable of the meaning-based emotions (such as fear and anger), and the nature (hedonic tone) of the emotion becomes based on subjective evaluation – infants are also assuming an active role in emotional regulation. This is apparent both in their own expanding capacities for arousal management and in their intentional bids for caregiver assistance. The changing repertoire of discrete emotions, the changing basis for the instigation of emotion, and the emerging capacity for emotional regulation are all part of the unfolding emotional being.

Becoming an emotional being

The emphasis in the preceding chapters on subjectivity and meaning precludes considering the newborn as an emotional being. Having no awareness of "objects," the newborn cannot experience emotions as they have been defined. Moreover, affect can have little role in guiding and directing behavior, a key criterion for defining the infant as emotional in the full sense of the term. Indeed, for the newborn, a theory of behavior based on drive and reflexes is fairly adequate. Even in the first weeks of life, however, the infant's behavior is increasingly a matter of seeking stimulation, rather than always seeking relief from discomfort, and a matter of synchrony with the caretaking environment, rather than mere need gratification (Sander, 1975, in press).

It has been argued that by about 3 months the infant exhibits the first true emotional reactions, which reflect some awareness of the surround. As discussed, these are subjective experiences (cf. Arnold, 1960), reflecting a *transaction* with the event, in the sense that the effectiveness of the event depends in part on structures within the infant (a psychophysiological as opposed to a simply physiological process). The reaction is not due merely to simple parameters of the stimulus (intensity, rhythm, etc.), but to its content as processed by the infant. As Spitz and colleagues (1970) have suggested, this is the beginning of emotional life, the birth of the self. The infant is moving toward being an emotional being.

Profound changes occur in the next 6 to 8 months, however, such that one may say that the infant in the fourth quarter of the first year is now not merely capable of emotions, but *is* an *emotional being* (Sroufe, 1979a). The infant's emotional life is in many ways more similar to that of an adult than that of a 3-month-old. For example, in stark contrast to the younger infant, the 9- to 12-month-old does not require sustained blocking of behavior, prolonged arrest of attention, or intense stimulation to experience negative affect. The reaction may be almost immediate and may be in response to the event as a member of a category. In a new way the meaning of the event is responsible for the emotional arousal.

Moreover, both positive and negative emotional reactions may be in response to anticipated outcomes or due to remembered associations. The infant may now show distress before a stranger approaches on the second trial of an intrusive procedure. Threat can be experienced even in advance of noxious stimulation. Rather than reacting to the completed response sequence, the 9-month-old laughs in anticipation of the mother's return in peekaboo. Expectation becomes an important part of the event. Anticipation and intention, rather than mere awareness, are part of emotional reactions in the second half year of life.

The remarkable development of memory between 3 and 10 months has dramatic consequences for emotional development (Nelson, 1994; Rovee-Collier, 1989; Younger & Cohen, 1985). Memory development is the foundation for anticipation. In addition, it is the basis for an emotional differentiation of mental images. There is no longer a single class of cognitive schemes; rather, such schemes are categorized and may be affectively toned (Hoffman, 1985). Mental images by this age may carry with them (as part of them) an associated negative or positive affect. It is not coincidental that in this age period integrated, positive greetings to the caregiver also emerge (Vaughn, 1977). After countless episodes of stimulation, visual exploration, and interaction with the caregiver, a reservoir of positive affective feelings has been established, ultimately being tied to the person of the caregiver (or, better stated, partly tying together the person of the caregiver). The bouncing, smiling, arms-raised gestures, which are differential to caregivers, reflect the positive value of the special scheme to which attachment figures are immediately assimilated. This is not a simple smile of recognition or pleasure in anticipated interaction. Neither is it the result of a prolonged inspection of the event. It is feeling happy to see the caregiver, a feeling that is inextricably linked to the visual image. In fact, in usual circumstances, it is not possible for the infant to greet the caregiver without such feelings.

Emotion clearly has a guiding influence on behavior by the end of the first year. Feelings themselves become part of the infant's ongoing evaluation of the event in context; that is, there is an awareness of affect itself. This will be a key point in the discussion of attachment (Chapter 10), for it is necessary to account for the changing thresholds for threat following a separation experience. The experience of the feeling becomes part of the event. The infant can be seen as an emotional being in a new way at this time.

Certainly, by 10 months affective expression does not merely mark the termination of an interaction with the environment. Much more often it "portends" (Emde et al., 1976) behavior as well. It becomes part of the continuing appraisal process. As Gordon Bronson (e.g., Bronson & Pankey, 1977) has suggested, emotions become linked with salient features of the encountered circumstances, then become part of the developing framework within which the infant evaluates further encounters with such events (see also Fiske, 1982).

Finally, in the second half year there are dramatic changes in the dynamics of emotional regulation. In contrast to the early months, infants become more intentional in regulating their emotional states. Primarily, this takes the form of explicit signals to the caregiver in the service of regulation. One consequence of this capacity is that emotional life becomes more fluid; the infant can move to and from states of high arousal with greater ease.

Referring to the infant as an emotional being in the fourth quarter of life is not meant to understate the dramatic changes in emotional development that occur in the second year and beyond. Referring to the 10-month-old as an emotional being may seem arbitrary. During the second year, for example, the infant becomes both capable of moods and more purposeful in communicating affect, and behaves within a prevailing affective state (not simply in response to a discrete affective experience); that is, the infant's mood provides an ongoing context for behavior, rather than fluctuating rapidly in response to external circumstances. Emotions become less tied to immediate events, as, for example, when infants are angry at the caregiver upon return, even though during the separation they have returned somewhat to contented play. By the criterion of subjectivity (personal investment), it is clear that the toddler shows qualitative advances in emotional development beyond the 1-year-old. With the awareness of self come the complex emotions of shame and positive valuation of the self. Such emotions are, of course, quite personal, and well beyond the capacity of the 10-month-old. The emotional being continues to unfold (see Chapter 11).

Still, there is a dramatic turning point after the third quarter of life, with profound implications for normal development and for individual differences. It is for this reason that this period receives emphasis here. This is the period when Schaffer and colleagues (1972) reported the striking shift from immediately reaching for novel objects to attentively studying them, followed by reaching. It is also the period when Campos and colleagues (1975) and Emde (Emde et al., 1976) report a developmental shift to anticipatory HR acceleration based on meaning. Affect is based in past experience and portends subsequent action. It guides interpretation of events and apparently motivates learning. All of this change is revealed in the infant's social behavior, as he or she begins to establish truly reciprocal relationships with caregivers.

That the second half year marks a qualitative turning point in emotional development was suggested by Schaffer and Callender (1959), based on a classic study of infant reactions to hospitalization. Infants younger than 7 months had little difficulty adjusting to the hospital and the hospital staff, and their readjustment when they returned home went smoothly. In sharp contrast, those older than 7 months were quite negative toward hospital staff, were fretful during much of the experience, and had a very difficult period of readjustment when they returned home, showing a great deal of insecurity centered on their mothers. Clearly, for those older than 7 months the hospitalization experience was disruptive of an established emotional relationship; for younger infants this was not the case.

The second half year is also a period of notable brain development, specifically the maturation of the frontal lobes and the elaboration of corticolimbic interconnections (Schore, 1994; see also Chapter 4). Numerous theorists have emphasized the two-way connection between brain maturation and socioemotional development. Brain structural changes not only underlie qualitative advances in socioemotional development, but changes in brain circuitry themselves are dependent on the socioaffective context (e.g., Hofer, 1990; Schore, 1994; Trevarthan, 1990). As Luria (1980) put it, functional brain systems do not arise autonomously "but are formed in the process of social contact" (p. 33).

Early experience and later emotional functioning

The discussion of the infant as an emotional being prior to the end of the first year is far more than academic. If a developmental/organizational perspective is taken seriously, then the roots of healthy emotional development may be laid out even in the first year. This is not to say that early experience is more important than later experience. From an organizational perspective, such an idea makes no sense (Sroufe, 1979b; Sroufe et al., 1990). A tree without water will die however healthy its beginnings. And it is not to say that self-organization is unchangeable. Evidence for change in such organization will be presented in later chapters.

Still, early experience and early emotional development may be of special importance in three closely related ways. First, successful adaptation in the early phases of development means, in part, that the individual is developing the resources to draw on the environment in subsequent phases. While this adaptive advantage may be lost due to experiences in succeeding phases, or due to a lack of the personal resources specifically required there, probabilistically the child with successful early adaptation would be more likely to succeed in later phases. Current development always builds on what was previously present (see Chapter 3). As discussed by Bowlby (1973), earlier development may set the course for later development. To carry forward the earlier metaphor, a tree with a well-elaborated root system is better able later to withstand a poor water supply. If trust in others, positive expectations, and the capacity to maintain organized behavior in the face of high tension are established early, children may be more resilient in coping with later environmental stress. They may show poor adaptation in the face of an overwhelming crisis, but when the crisis has passed and the environment is again positive, they may rebound quickly. Even when floundering some children may not lose the sense that they can affect the environment and that, ultimately, they will be all right. These ideas are supported by accumulating empirical data that will be presented in Chapters 11 and 12 (e.g., Egeland, Kalkoske, Gottesman, & Erickson, 1990; Sroufe et al., 1990).

Second, and related to the first point, children and even toddlers in many ways create their own experiences. As Alfred Adler has suggested, the child is both the artist and the painting. The infant who characteristically retreats from novelty, and cannot engage in mastery of the object world within the context of the infant–caregiver relationship, will be at a disadvantage in the next developmental phase when the issue is facing challenges and solving problems more on one's own. An infant is competent not only to the degree of his or her cognitive or social development, but to the degree that capacities for emotional regulation enable engagement of the available environment (Waters & Sroufe, 1983). To give another example, if preschool children, due to difficulties tolerating arousal or maintaining organized behavior in the face of arousal, isolate themselves from peer contact, they are removed further from positive social experiences. Peer contacts, which could have ameliorative consequences, may not be successfully sought by the very children who need them most. Thus, early emotional development may set the stage for more or less healthy adaptation in subsequent periods by promoting acquisition of the necessary personal resources (and the capacity to draw on them) *and* by ensuring that the child engages opportunities and challenges during subsequent transactions with the environment.

Third, current experiences are interpreted within previously created frameworks. A great deal of research is in progress on what are called "internal working models," representations of salient experience that guide current interpretations (see Chapter 10 and beyond). Just as the memory of particular experiences influences the evaluation of a new, similar experience, broad interpretive frameworks also influence ongoing transactions with the environment. As just one example, children that have experienced chronic rebuff within their primary caregiving relationship later exhibit general doubts about the availability of others and often presume malevalent intent of peers, even when such intent is not present (Dodge & Somberg, 1987; Sroufe, 1983; Suess, Grossmann, & Sroufe, 1992).

Working models are not most fruitfully thought of as only cognitive. Early working models are founded on basic experiences of emotional arousal and regulation. "At their core, the complementary working models of self and others have to do not so much with particular actions or thoughts as with expectations concerning the maintenance of basic regulation and positive affect even in the face of environmental challenge" (Sroufe, 1989). When, for example, conflict arouses strong feelings, not just one's appraisal of the likely reactions of others, but one's habitual patterns of emotional response are activated. The visceral and psychic, cognitive and emotional levels are all part of the same coordinated developmental process.

As was the case with the unfolding of the specific emotions, there is an inherent logic in individual emotional development. The negotiation by the young child of each phase of development provides the framework for negotiating subsequent phases. As is the case with all development, it is not that adaptation in the earlier phase determines later adaptation. But subsequent adaptation grows from (embodies) what was there before, however transformed it might be by current experience.

The developmental issues framework

In studying individual differences there are several advantages to viewing development in terms of a series of issues. Of foremost importance, issues salient for the particular developmental period provide a flexible referent for assessing the quality of individual adaptation. Within this developmental issues approach, in contrast to milestone conceptions or even rigid stage conceptions, no premium is placed on age of acquisition, and there is no idea of a *critical* age (although the concept of sensitive periods of development is still retained). All infants and children are viewed as dealing with the entire set of issues; there is no concept of fixation. Moreover, not age of onset, but quality of adaptation with respect to the issues is of utmost importance. For example, not the age at which the infant first shows signs of attachment, but the effectiveness of this relationship in service of exploration and emotional regulation would be emphasized. In this way, the quality of adaptation is broadened beyond achieved developmental level and, in the case of infant assessment, gains considerable predictive power. Also, since the issues are viewed as ongoing, one is brought to the study of process and organization. This is a key for the study of fundamental individual differences.

In previous writings, along with Sander (1975), Spitz (Spitz et al., 1970), and others, I have proposed a series of issues around which early development is organized (e.g., Sroufe, 1979b). One such scheme was presented in Table 4.3, along with parallel formulations of Sander's and Piaget's stages of sensorimotor development. Each of these proposed issues – initial physiological regulation, dyadic regulation of tension, active participation, formation of an effective attachment relationship, movement toward autonomy – has an affective core, although they reflect and foretell aspects of cognitive development as well. There is some arbitrariness to this series. Other salient issues could be cited and a much more dense series could be delineated. These are not meant to represent *the* stages of emotional development, nor are they completed at once and for all; for example, infants are individuating (striving toward autonomy) from the day of birth, and the attachment relationship continues to evolve well after infancy. These issues *are* viewed as a sequence, however, each rising to ascendancy and each having logical ties to former and subsequent issues.

In contrast to most stage theories, transitions, rather than being a problem, are built into the developmental issues framework (see also Sander, 1975). As will be brought out throughout Part III, facing one developmental issue inevitably leads to the ascendancy of the next in the normal course of maturation and development. For example, the regulation of tension within the caregiver–infant interaction is not only an organizing principle for understanding much important behavior during the first 6 months, and for viewing individual differences in adaptation at that time; it also is the precursor from which the infant–caregiver attachment relationship is constructed in the later phases. As will be elaborated, attachment is the product of interaction, and the security of the attachment relationship is related to the regularity with which arousal has historically led or not led to infant behavioral disorganization in the context of the caregiver.

There are a number of ways of bringing unity to the series of issues. All pertain to the emergence and development of the self. All may be viewed in terms of socialization, and all may be viewed in terms of cognitive, developmental stages. But here I would emphasize that the management of tension represents a single, integrating thread that ultimately becomes woven into the fabric of emotional functioning. What begins as built-in physiological mechanisms for the regulation of arousal (the absolute stimulus barrier) becomes the management of tension within the caregiver–infant relationship (first orchestrated by the caregiver, later more truly dyadic), and ultimately becomes self-regulation (see also Sander, 1975). The ability to maintain flexibly organized behavior in the face of high levels of arousal or tension is a central aspect of stable individual differences in personality organization. This concept is closely related to Block and Block's (1980) constructs of ego control (management of impulses, wishes, and desires) and ego resiliency (flexibility of controls), which they have shown to be stable dimensions of individual differences from age 3 to adulthood (e.g., Block, 1987; Block & Gjerde, 1993). The proposition that such individual differences may be set in train in the first years of life is significant and commands thorough investigation.

Issues for infant and caregiver in infancy

The first phase

Despite the fact that maturation is of such great importance in early development (Chapters 3 to 5), there still are important issues for the caregiver and infant even in the first months of life. Such early experiences are primarily important for the patterns that begin to be established and for the mutual familiarity they provide. It is doubtful that the newborn, without much of a functioning cortex, retains much from his or her early experiences. Thus, studies show that infants adopted in the first half year are just as likely to be secure in their attachments at the end of the year as are birth children (Singer, Brodzinsky, Ramsay, Steir, & Waters, 1985), as are healthy, premature newborns who spent 2 weeks separated from their parents in the prenatal unit (Rode, Chang, Fisch, & Sroufe, 1981). But infants can become familiar with certain qualities of the caregiver and with general patterns of physical contact and holding.

Sander (1975, in press) has provided relevant data on this point. By familiarizing newborns with one nurse over several days and then changing nurses, he showed that these very young infants responded to the change. As evidenced by an immediate and persistent increase over several days in crying and "distress events" (gagging, turning away) during feeding, a specific adaptation between infant and caregiver was shown to be established within the first 10 days of life. This "recognition" is obviously not the same sort as the more specific person recognition that appears much later; rather, it is a general familiarity with the patterns of behavior of the particular caregiver. As Sander put it at the 1977 Society for Research in Child Development conference, "It is to be noted that the hypothesized recognitory processes are not conceptualized in terms of the psychological recognition of the mother. Rather, it is considered to be a biological recognition process, which serves as the *anlage* for the later development of person recognition."

In addition to showing the specificity of infant–caregiver adaptation, Sander (in press) also showed that infants in a contingently responsive environment (rooming-in) more quickly established "synchronization" with the caretaking environment than a group receiving noncontingent care (in the nursery; rigid feeding schedule). In the rooming-in condition, in contrast to the nursery group, crying and motility were decreased. In addition, by day 6 such behavior became predominant during the 12 waking hours as opposed to nighttime hours. Also, there was a synchrony between the periods of activity and crying and the duration and time of occurrence of caregiving interventions. Child behavior was becoming organized around environmental inputs. Effects of the noncontingent caretaking environment, which was terminated at 10 days, persisted over the first 8 weeks of life, as evidenced by an absence of stable individual patterns in this group and increased crying in response to experimentally presented visual stimuli. Stable individual differences were most evident in a third group, with 5 days of rooming-in, followed by home care. For these infants "the interactional idiosyncracies between infant and caretaker for a number of variables (e.g., crying before intervention) were already most strikingly evident by the end of the first 10 days" (Sander, 1975, p. 160). By 8 weeks infants in this group differentially looked at their mother's face compared with a stranger's face. This research and other work (e.g., Condon & Sander, 1974; Papousek, 1977; Papousek, Papousek, & Bornstein, 1985; Prechtl, 1979) suggests that even during the newborn period, infants may be set to detect contingencies in the environment and to synchronize their behavior with a responsive caregiving milieu.

The assigned role for the caregiver during this early phase is providing smooth and harmonious routines (Table 9.1). If the quality of care is responsive and highly reliable, familiarization with the caregiver should be more readily accomplished and a sound basis laid for later interaction. When infants leave the neonatal period, becoming dramatically more outer directed and capable of ongoing, alert transaction with the surround, it remains to be established how much they bring from their experience in the first few weeks. Still, it makes sense that establishing smooth, harmonious routines would provide a good basis for the onset of sustained interaction.

Regardless of how important the early months may be for the infant, they are of clear importance for caregivers. Responding to the emotional states and sig-

Table 9.1. *Issues in development*

Period	Age	Issue	Role for caregiver
1	0–3 mo	Physiological regulation (turning toward)	Smooth routines
2	3–6 mo	Management of tension	Sensitive, cooperative interaction
3	6–12 mo	Establishing an effective attachment relationship	Responsive availability
4	12–18 mo	Exploration and mastery	Secure base
5	18–30 mo	Individuation (autonomy)	Firm support
6	30–54 mo	Management of impulses, sex-role identification, peer relations	Clear roles, values; flexible self-control
7	6–11 yr	Consolidating self-concept, loyal friendships, effective same-gender peer group functioning, real-world competence	Monitoring, supporting activities, co-regulation
8	Adolescence	Personal identity, mixed-gender relationships, intimacy	Available resource, monitor the child's monitoring

nals of the infant is the crucial issue for caregivers in the subsequent period. As will be amply supported in Chapter 10, this responsivity is related to the quality of later infant–caregiver attachment. The first 3 months, then, provide an important opportunity for the caregiver to learn about the infant's particular characteristics and qualities. And even though individual infants may change dramatically, making particular caregiver responses or strategies outdated, something permanent in the way of investment and confidence may be acquired. The caregiver who maintains positive interest and involvement with the infant throughout the early period, which in certain cases may be quite difficult, will emerge with a sense of efficacy and satisfaction. While at times the caregiver may be unsuccessful in comforting or engaging the infant, over the course of the first months more success will come. The reliable social smile and a generally increased social responsiveness emerge at the conclusion of this period, supporting continued caregiver involvement. The caregiver, as well as the infant, is prepared for the upcoming period of more active interaction. As Sander (1975) has summarized in discussing this issue:

One of the features most idiosyncratic during the first three months is the extent to which the infant is helped or compromised in beginning to determine aspects of his own regulation. On the part of the mother trial-and-error learning gives way to ideas of what "works" and to the feeling of confidence that she now knows her baby's needs and can specifically meet them. (p. 137)

The second phase

Caregiver-guided regulation of tension is denoted as the major issue for the next phase (roughly 3 to 6 months). The roots of this issue are, of course, in the preceding phase. The caregiver's ability to respond to signals and cooperate with the infant's actions are, in part, a function of the learning in the earlier phase, as is the motivation to be responsive. Likewise, the infant's ability to maintain engagement with the caregiver here has its origins in the earlier state regulation. Further, the regulation of tension will remain a salient issue through-out the early childhood years. But partly because the infant appears to be for the first time capable of learning characteristic styles of dealing with tension, the issue of tension regulation seems critical in Phase 2. As discussed in Chap-ters 5 and 8, the word *tension* is preferred to *arousal,* because it captures the active role of the infant in creating, as well as responding to, stimulation. At this point the infant can readily become engaged, and it is partly for this reason that he or she is vulnerable to chaotic or unresponsive care.

The regulation of tension involves much more than avoiding overstimulating the infant or providing relief from tension, as emphasized in early psychoanalytic writing (e.g., Fenichel, 1945). These things are, of course, important. Distress–relief cycles (Lamb, 1981), and what Tronick (1989) refers to as "interactive repair" following disruptions of caregiver–infant synchrony, provide critical foundations for basic arousal modulation and the expectation that organization can be reclaimed following organization breakdown. But many critical experi-ences during this phase involve high levels of tension that are associated with smiling and laughter. Beebe and Lachman (1988) describe the high levels of arousal and positive affect that occur in face-to-face "mirroring," and Stern (1990) describes a cyclic escalation of positive affect between caregiver and infant that begins with mutual smiling and ultimately builds to intense joy and "mutual hilarity." Such experiences confirm in a basic way for the infant that even extreme heights of arousal need not be distressing or disorganizing. Face-to-face games, in which excitement builds to positive affective exchanges, are so prominent that this period of life has been labeled the "period of positive affect" (see also Sander, 1975). Such experiences with positive affect are as much a part of the regulation of tension as is the termination of distress.

The caregiver's role is to help the infant remain organized (and affectively positive) in the face of novel stimulation. Cognitive growth comes through mas-tering encounters with novelty. Such mastery involves effort as accommodative and assimilative tendencies are carried out. Tension is the outcome we have inferred to be the inevitable by-product of such effortful engagement. Thus, to the extent that infants can learn to maintain organized and focused behavior in the face of increasing levels of tension, their cognitive and social development will be served. To the extent that tension is disorganizing or leads to withdrawal or behavioral stereotypy, cognitive and social development will be impaired.

Watching infants makes it completely clear that when their physiological needs are met, they are constantly seeking psychological stimulation. The intrinsic motivation to do and to experience is at the base of the infant's development. The capacities to tolerate tension and sustain engagement with caregivers and others in the social world build on this motivation. Sensitive caregivers support this intrinsic motivation by participating with the infant, as well as by allowing the infant the necessary space for mastery.

A number of observers have been impressed with how much learning about (and support of) tension regulation occurs in routine contexts such as feeding, bathing, and play. Helping the infant learn to maintain organized behavior in the face of increasingly high levels of tension is something that caregivers naturally do if they are involved with infants and psychologically available to respond to them (e.g., Fogel, 1993; Tronick, 1989). The system seems to be arranged so that caregivers customarily do what infants need, and infants' responses encourage caregivers to continue or change their behavior appropriately.

Stern (1974) described this in a classic paper entitled "The goal and function of mother–infant play" (see also Brazelton & Cramer, 1990; Gianino & Tronick, 1988; Stern, 1985). In an intricate process of moves, adjustments, arousal increases, and arousal modulation, infant and caregiver wind their way toward positive outcomes of smiling and cooing, which punctuate bouts of interaction. The playful interactions vary greatly, with the infant at times slowing the pace by looking away, for example; or the caregiver may "escalate" and "de-escalate" the stimulation by changing the intensity, variety, or pacing, or by pausing momentarily. An infinite variety of behaviors and behavioral combinations are possible, but all are organized around a common outcome, the affectively positive exchange.

Stern (1985) has also discussed what he calls "matching" or "attunement." The sensitive caregiver responds to the affective state of the infant (as revealed in expressed behavior), behaving in ways that amplify, support, or modulate the infant's response. For example, the infant may coo and smile and the caregiver may shimmy his or her upper body, which promotes repetition of the smile. The caregiver is doing more than simple imitation or even reinforcement, and in many cases interviewing reveals that he or she is unaware of the "matching" behavior.

Consider the following scenario, which portrays a typical example of a brief, playful caregiver–infant interaction:

Hello there pumpkin . . . Mommy's comin' to get you. Yes, she is. [Brief pause.] Momma's gonna get you and tickle you. What do you think of that? [Brief pause.] Come on. Come on, you little sweetie. Let me see that smile. Humm? [Pause.] Yeah, that's right . . . thaaaat's right. [The infant exhibits a big smile with bobbing head, and mother responds in kind, then says,] Oh, well now, are you gonna say somethin'? Are ya? [Pause, mother nodding head, widening eyes.] Come on! [Pause.] Come on! [The baby begins cycling movements of the arms and kicking the feet.] Come on. [Drawn out, then longer pause.] Yeah! [as the baby bursts forth with a gurgling sound, the caregiver then laughs and hugs the baby].

Though a simple, everyday occurrence, such a scenario reflects the intimate social dance that is caregiver–infant interaction. Brazelton (e.g., Brazelton et al., 1974) has described the way the caregiver appropriately escalates and de-escalates the level of tension in the course of such an interaction. The infant is captured with gentle tones, and then the caregiver adds more stimulation with nodding head, changing facial expressions, and voice, so that the infant stays attracted and the excitement builds. No facial expression or voice quality that remains unchanging will maintain an infant's attention. But modulated tones and expression can build excitement. In fact, of course, at any age an infant can become overstimulated, overexcited. It is here that the sensitive caregiver takes cues from the infant. Infants will turn away, look away, or begin to show distress when the level of tension becomes too high. The sensitive response when the infant withdraws or begins to be distressed in this situation is to de-escalate, to reduce the level of stimulation. The infant sometimes needs opportunities to reorganize before continuing. The sensitive caregiver will relax and wait for the infant, realizing that the infant's signals are not a personal rejection. Pursuing the infant when he or she is seeking to break off contact will result in further attempts to avoid stimulation, or to distress.

Understanding that infants need to modulate their own level of tension, the responsive caregiver remains relaxed when they break contact and comes in again when they are ready. Sensing the importance of such interchanges, or simply enjoying them, the responsive caregiver stays involved with the infant, with episodes and the total encounter becoming greater in length and more rich and varied.

The infant derives a great deal from this play. In such play the roots of mutuality are set out. The infant gains a primitive sense of give and take, social participation, and efficacy (e.g., Fogel, 1993). The caregiver *will* respond to him or her, as well as be a source of stimulation. The infant's action has an effect, and what the caregiver does in response further stimulates the infant to behave. When the caregiver skillfully frames such interaction, the infant derives a sense of participation by being fitted into a "dialogue."

The infant also learns to tolerate increasing amounts of tension through this interactive play. As he or she can tolerate more tension without breaking contact and without behavior becoming disorganized, the variety of situations (or sheer amount of stimulation) that can be engaged increases. Increasingly, the infant is not restricted to situations of moderate intensity, novelty, or complexity, but can cope with an increasingly rich and varied experience. A tolerance for tension and sustained attention in the face of challenging complexity are obvious foundations of important transactions with the environment and important learning. Infants and children learn through doing, through action. An increasing ability to maintain organized action in the face of complexity and novelty is of fundamental significance. As Brazelton and colleagues (1974) have summarized:

The mother tends to provide a "holding" framework for her own cues. That is, she holds the infant with her hands, with her eyes, with her voice and smile, and with changes from one modality to another as he habituates to one or another. All these holding experiences are opportunities for the infant to learn how to contain himself, how to control motor responses and how to attend for longer and longer periods. They amount to a kind of learning about organization of behavior in order to attend. (p. 70)

Many investigators have stressed the importance of contingent responsiveness in infants' learning that they are able to affect the world. Lewis and Goldberg (1969) referred to this learning in terms of a "generalized expectancy," the belief that one may have an effect (White's, 1959, "efficacy"). The psychoanalyst Bettelheim (1967) referred to the same idea with his concept of "mutuality" – infants learn not only that the environment affects them, but that they can affect the environment as well. Such contingent responsiveness is undoubtedly of great importance. But, as the preceding discussion suggested, there is more to responsive care than waiting for an appropriate response from the infant and being prompt with a reward. The caregiver also creates a climate and arranges the interaction such that the response can occur. It is much more a matter of synchrony than contingency alone (Bloom, 1975; Fogel, 1993; Tronick, 1989).

So important is the role of the caregiver in the early regulation of arousal and emotion that researchers have used terms like "co-regulation" (Fogel, 1993) or "mutual regulation" (Tronick, 1989) to describe the process (see also Thompson, 1988). Caregivers at first play a dominant role, with that of the infant steadily increasing. Gianino and Tronick (1988) describe the broadening repertoire of infant regulatory skills between 3 and 9 months, which in part arise in response to the inevitable mismatches that at times occur.

When well orchestrated, interactions between infants and caregivers can give the impression of true reciprocity, with each following the lead of the other. In fact, however, it has been shown that in the first half year it is the caregiver that guides the interaction, crafting the mutuality that the infant may then experience. If, for example, one imagines an interaction sequence, such as A,b,C,d,E,f, where capital letters represent infant behavior and lowercase letters caregiver behavior, it appears as though there is turn taking. Careful analysis (using sequential probabilities) reveals, however, that caregiver responses genuinely fit infant responses and call forth the next behavior (e.g., Hayes, 1984). If the infant breaks the sequence, the caregiver follows (e.g., A,b,E,f), but the reverse happens only rarely. This is why during the second quarter we refer to *caregiver-guided dyadic regulation.*

Ainsworth's "sensitivity" scales. Based on such considerations, Ainsworth (e.g., Ainsworth et al., 1978) has argued that caregiver sensitivity is a key focus for assessment during this period, even if one is interested in the growth of infant emotional capacities. Infants, she states, can be competent only to the extent that the caregiver responds to their preadapted behaviors, state changes, and primitive affective signals. In agreement with Sander (1975), one is assessing the "fit" between infant and caregiver, but the caregiver is the one able to make intentional adjustments. Based on participation in caregiver-guided interaction at this time, however, the infant is becoming prepared for an increasingly active role in the interaction in the next phase.

Two of Ainsworth's scales, which have received substantial validation (see Chapter 10), are Sensitivity to the Baby's Communications and Cooperation–Interference. The first entails four essential components: (1) awareness of signals, (2) accurate interpretation, (3) appropriate response, and (4) prompt response. To be aware of the infant's signals the caregiver must be accessible and attentive. He or she must also empathize with the infant and read the signals without distortion; that is, signals must not be interpreted within the caregiver's own needs or fantasies (e.g., "She being in a hurry might perceive any slowing down in feeding as a sign of satiation"). As Ainsworth (1970) puts it:

The sensitive caregiver responds socially to his attempts to initiate social interaction, playfully to his attempts to initiate play. She picks him up when he seems to wish it, and puts him down when he wants to explore. When he is distressed, she knows what kinds and degree of soothing he requires to comfort him – and she knows that sometimes a few words or a distraction will be all that is needed. On the other hand, the mother who responds inappropriately tries to socialize with the baby when he is hungry, play with him when he is tired, or feed him when he is trying to initiate social interaction. (p. 2)

Sensitivity does not require that caregivers always give in to the infant's demands. In accord with Erikson (1963), Ainsworth acknowledges that frustrations are inevitable and a normal part of healthy development; however, such frustrations need not be capricious and arbitrary. Sensitive caregivers acknowledge the infant's wishes even though not unconditionally acceding to them. Further, they participate in reparative interactions when such frustrations do occur (Gianino & Tronick, 1988).

Finally, according to Ainsworth, sensitive care is reflected in interactions that are "well rounded" and "completed." When an infant seeks contact, for example, the sensitive caregiver maintains the contact long enough for the infant to be comforted, so that when the infant is put down he or she does not want to be picked up again immediately. Sander (1975, in press) has also stressed the distinction between thorough and perfunctory ministrations.

The central issue underlying the Cooperation–Interference scale is "the extent to which the mother's interventions and initiations of interaction break into, interrupt or cut across the baby's ongoing activity, rather than being temporally fitted and suitable to the baby's state, mood and current interests." The highly interfering caregiver "has no respect for her baby as a separate, active, and autonomous person whose wishes and activities have a validity of their own." Cooperative caregivers guide, rather than control, their infants.

Responsivity, mutuality, reciprocity, and cooperativeness are all related. When caregivers respond to an infant's signals, they lay the groundwork for a sense of potency. The infant finds that the world (the caregiver) responds to his or her needs; the infant can have an effect. Likewise, such a sense is fostered when caregivers tune their ministrations to the infant's activity (see also Fogel, 1993; Tronick, 1989). The infant is stimulated when open to stimulation. Stimulation and baby-initiated actions are not at cross-purposes. There is a flow in the interaction, with smooth transitions between activities. The cooperative caregiver does not, for example, just jerk the infant away from a toy and plunk the infant into the bath. First, one gets the infant's attention on one's voice and face. To this stimulation one may add some water play – maybe by wiping gently with a lukewarm cloth, then, gradually, the bath. The infant learns that stimulation from (in the context of) the caregiver is not chaotic, not strident. Although during early infancy mutuality and reciprocity refer primarily to the caregiver's consistency and reliability (making room for the infant's needs), the sense of trust and efficacy that comes out of noncapriciousness ultimately will promote a truly mutual interaction.

Sensitive, cooperative care provides an important context for the infant to have experiences in maintaining and modulating high levels of tension, as well as for learning that tension in the context of the caregiver need not be disorganizing. The validity of these propositions lies in the strong associations between sensitive care during the second developmental phase and exploration, limited crying, tolerance of novelty, ability to be comforted, and general security of attachment by 12 months (e.g., Ainsworth et al., 1978; Belsky & Isabella, 1988; Isabella, 1993; see also Chapter 10), as well as in important correlates in both caregiver and child behavior throughout childhood (e.g., Carlson, Jacobvitz, & Sroufe, 1995; Egeland, Pianta, & O'Brien, 1993; Jacobvitz & Sroufe, 1987; see also Chapters 11 and 12).

Sensitive, face-to-face interaction is also of vital importance because it allows the infant to make the transition from a physical basis for security and comforting to a psychological basis. In early infancy, physical contact (ventral–ventral), rocking, patting, and stroking are the basis for comforting. During this second phase, however, the caregiver "holds" the infant with eyes and voice, and the infant is secure within the face-to-face intimacy of this interaction.

To be sure, physical contact remains important, but early caregiver–infant play has a basic role in promoting the transition to an internalized attachment, to a feeling of security based on the expectation that care is available even when there is not immediate physical contact. Both caregiver and infant may express feelings across a distance. An increasing flexibility to engage novel aspects of the environment results, as the infant can derive a sense of security from progressively more distal cues. There is much greater freedom to explore and learn when the infant can range away from the caregiver, rather than sit on the caregiver's lap.

Moving toward attachment

The broad developmental issue in the second half year is the formation of an effective attachment relationship (Table 9.1). While the role for the caregiver remains responsive care, the infant as an emotional being assumes a more active role in the process at this time. Responsive care, of course, changes as the infant's capacities change. Cooperating with the infant increasingly involves allowing the infant more room to initiate interaction and to respond to the caregiver. Sander (1975) has described this transition as being from actions that the caregiver *interprets* as signals to explicit, *directed* signals on the part of the infant. The caregiver remains responsive to these initiations, but now is responding to the intentional bids of the infant.

I have used the analogy of teaching a child the game of table tennis. At first one hits the ball directly to the child's paddle. Holding the paddle rigidly, the pupil's shots fly off in every direction, always being recentered by the teacher. In time, however, the teacher requires the pupil to make minimal adjustments, and little by little, the pupil moves toward a more equal role. Effective teaching involves increasing the pupil's role at a pace that is not disheartening or that does not allow the child to advance. So it is with effective caregiver–infant interaction. What begins with the caregiver rather completely staging the interaction and responding to the infant leads to a more mutual interaction, where each partner initiates and each responds in turn to the other.

In the second half year, the infant is well disposed to play this more active role. Piaget (1952) has written of "procedures for making interesting sights last" and, by the end of the period, imitation of novel acts. I have labeled the period from 7 to 9 months (Table 4.1) the "phase of active participation," mainly due to the dramatic changes in social behavior at this time. Many observers have noted that this is the period when infants make "persistent efforts to elicit social responses" (e.g., Escalona, 1968), even from other infants (Goodenough, 1934). In the first half year infants will look at other infants and perhaps smile, but by 7 to 8 months they will vocalize, cajole, touch, and otherwise try to elicit a response from the baby. Similarly, with their caregiver, clear signs of the deliberate initiation of an interaction appear. If a bid for a response is not successful, not only may it be repeated, but an alternative may be tried. This also is the age at which a dramatic increase in laughter in response to social games appears (Sroufe & Wunsch, 1972; Chapter 5). Infants laugh, for example, at playing tug and at pulling a cloth from mother's mouth, games that clearly require a considerable degree of reciprocity. By 10 months, of course, infants also attempt to hand the yarn back to the mother or stuff the cloth back in mother's mouth, and they laugh uproariously at this.

Sander (1975) has labeled this same 7- to 9-month period as one of "initiative," describing as its salient features infants' initiation of social exchange and their clear goal-directed activity. In agreement with the outline of emotional development presented in this book, he writes of the new capability of experiencing success or interference (and anger) in achieving goals.

The increasingly active role for infants, as well as their increased mobility, leads to visible changes in the organization of their behavior around the caregiver in the subsequent period (10 to 12 months). The caregiver takes on the role of the "home base" (Mahler et al., 1975) or "secure base" (Ainsworth), and infants center their expanding exploratory activities around this base. Sander has aptly described this period as one of "focalization," capturing the way in which the caregiver has moved to the center of an expanding world. There may be a preoccupation with the caregiver, and separation distress reaches an onset peak at this time, but it also is the case that the infant begins moving out into the world. The organization of the infant's world around the caregiver is the crux of the "specific" attachment relationship, which we will discuss in Chapter 10.

Increasingly during this period, the role for the caregiver is to be available rather than initiatory. As the infant begins ranging away from the caregiver and moving more actively toward the novel world, it is important that the caregiver be ready to respond when the infant becomes threatened or distressed. The thesis to be elaborated in subsequent chapters is that it is the infant's historically based confidence in the availability of the caregiver that promotes exploratory behavior. Infants who know the caregiver will take prompt action when they are distressed and who have learned that disorganizing tension is unlikely when the caregiver is nearby, need not be anxious in exploration. Such infants are secure in their attachment relationships.

Caregivers may, of course, be either pleased or threatened by the infant's increased intentionality and goal directedness (an early form of independence) in Phase 3 or the heightened need and demandingness of Phase 4. The continued responsivity and availability of the caregiver is of critical importance. As Sander (1975) concludes:

The successful negotiation of a reasonable set of conditions for, and of limits to, a predictable availability of the mother has appeared from the study of our material to be closely associated with a preservation of the same basic affect of delight that has marked interpersonal "fitting together" since issue II [reciprocal exchange]. Depending on adequate negotiation of the issue of focalization, the same affect becomes available for the next step in the sequence, namely the turning of investment and attention to widening mastery of the world beyond the mother. (p. 140)

Conclusion: the unity of development

A major theme of this book is the unity of development. Thus, processes seen in examining the development of the specific emotions are also found to underlie the growth of emotional regulation. Moreover, physiological, cognitive, and social aspects of development are coordinated in the unfolding of all aspects of emotional life.

In Part II the development of the specific emotions was tied to the growth of meaning. Increasingly over the first year, the expression of emotion was seen to be determined not simply by what events happened *to* the infant, but by what sense the infant made of these events. Similarly, when we now examine emotional regulation more broadly, we find a growing role for evaluative processes across this same period. In the second half year the regulation of arousal and emotion no longer depend simply on what the caregiver does, but on how the infant interprets the caregiver's accessibility and behavior, as well as on the infant's more general expectations concerning the environment and characteristic, history-based thresholds for threat.

These increasingly cognitive processes build on earlier physiological prototypes. There is a basic arousal escalation or arousal modulation core to all mature affects, and there is a physiological *anlage* or root form to basic expectations concerning tension regulation. Such cognitive expectations (e.g., that organized behavior may be maintained even in the face of high arousal) are preceeded by a history of visceral experiences of arousal escalation and de-escalation, in which, typically, a fundamental entrainment of the CNS occurs and leads to a neurophysiological capacity to contain and modulate arousal.

A major reason for the coordination and harmony between the physiological underpinnings of emotional regulation and the cognitive/evaluative components is that both are forged within the caregiving relationship. By engaging the infant with tolerable but increasing levels of stimulation and by protecting the infant from (or helping to repair the consequences of) excessive arousal, caregivers actually help to craft an adaptive, flexible nervous system (Schore, 1994). Furthermore, by responding to the infant's primitive signals and later intentional bids, they promote the infant's expectation that he or she can have an impact on the environment and the belief that, especially in the context of the caregiver, organization can be maintained when arousal is high.

So closely tied are emotional and social development in infancy and early childhood that the term *socioemotional* development is widely used in the field. Ministrations from and interaction with caregivers are critical in shaping emotional development. At the same time, advances in the infant's emotional development make possible new levels of social relatedness and participation. From state and arousal regulation, wherein the caregiver provides stable routines and a reliable patterning of care, to caregiver-guided regulation of tension, to intentional use of the caregiver by the infant for the purposes of tension regulation, the child moves toward establishing the first emotional relationship. This is the specific attachment relationship that we will discuss in Chapter 10.

10   Attachment: the dyadic regulation of emotion

> In stable environments in which mothers allow infants to move from them when the infant feels secure enough to do so and . . . allow infants to return to them freely, the infants are able to modulate their arousal levels.
>
> Rosenblum (1987)

> The varied expectations of the accessibility and responsiveness of attachment figures that different individuals develop during the years of immaturity are tolerably accurate reflections of the experiences those individuals have actually had.
>
> Bowlby (1973)

Attachment, which refers to a special relationship between infant and caregiver that evolves over the first year of life and beyond, is inherently an emotional construct. Not only does it imply an "affective bond" between parent and infant, it also is properly characterized in terms of the regulation of infant emotion. In fact, it is the apex of dyadic emotional regulation, a culmination of all development in the first year and a harbinger of the self-regulation that is to come.

In particular, the emergence of specific attachment relationships refers to that phase in development when the infant assumes a more active role in dyadic regulation; that is, there is movement from regulation orchestrated by the caregiver to what is more truly dyadic. In the first half year, emotional regulation is accomplished through built-in regulatory capacities of the infant and a responsive caregiving environment. The caregiver reads the infant's signs of distress and other affective communications, imbues them with meaning, and responds to them – dyadic regulation being accomplished without intentionality on the part of the infant. But in the second half year the infant specifically and intentionally directs communications to the caregiver, takes purposive action to achieve contact, and flexibly selects and alters behaviors from an expanded repertoire until the goal of interaction or contact (and emotional restabilization) is achieved. It is when one sees such active behavior, corrected with respect to the goal of emotional regulation and directed preferentially to a particular other, that one may speak of attachment.

Clear signs that an attachment relationship with a specific caregiver has emerged are universally present by the end of the first year in normal infants. The first of these signs, all of which are emotional, is separation distress, which shows a strikingly similar course across cultures with a peak onset commonly seen at about 9 months (e.g., Kagan et al., 1978; Schaffer & Emerson, 1964). Even when emerging somewhat earlier, as in Ainsworth's (1967) classic study in Uganda, it is presumed to reflect the same developmental process of discrimination learning and formation of a scheme of the caregiver (person permanence), moved forward by the particular patterns of care (the infant always having access to the mother in the Ugandan study). The emergence of separation distress is paralleled by the development of the integrated greeting reactions, which also are differential to caregivers.

Another important sign of the emergence of attachment is "secure base" behavior. The infant ranges around the caregiver, keeping him or her at the center of explorations. Infants are more confident exploring when the caregiver is nearby and attentive, and they retreat to the caregiver when threatened. Closely related to the secure base phenomenon is the preferential treatment shown to caregivers in particular circumstances. Infants are very engaging of others in general by the end of the first year, but when threatened or distressed they seek out the caregiver in particular (Tracy, Lamb, & Ainsworth, 1976).

The attachment relationship consolidates in the second half year, but it is based on the interactive history in the prior months. The infant repeatedly experiences in the first half year that, in the context of the caregiver, arousal need not lead to disorganization (see Chapters 8 and 9), and that when arousal does exceed the infant's modulation capacities, the caregiver will take action to recapture equilibrium. Based on this cumulative experience and their expanding cognitive abilities, infants can now recognize the caregiver's role in affect modulation and their own role with respect to eliciting caregiver availability and assistance. Infants may now seek to have caregivers nearby, may signal their intentions at a distance, and may *actively* seek contact when threatened. Should such actions consistently achieve the goal of emotional regulation, the infant will develop expanded confidence in the relationship and will therefore tolerate greater amounts of tension in engaging the environment (novelty, physical distance, etc.). The infant will also develop a continually expanding and more flexibly organized repertoire of behaviors to be used in the dyadic regulation process.

At the same time, positive affective sharing, the other side of dyadic emotional regulation, also becomes more intentional. "Affective sharing" refers to the routine, automatic sharing of pleasurable discoveries with the caregiver, complete with broad smiles and vocalization (as in the example of the infant with the puzzle piece in Chapter 1). An aspect of such sharing is communicative pointing or "joint visual attention," which increases dramatically between 10 and 13 months (Butterworth, 1991). Such affective sharing is a core part of the attachment relationship, the reservoire of positive experiences that underlies the affective bond between most infants and their caregivers (Waters, Wippman, & Sroufe, 1979). The broadening means of communication also supports the child's exploration of the surrounding world.

Attachment as an organizational construct

Bowlby's behavioral systems model

It was Bowlby (e.g., 1969/1982) who first defined attachment in terms of a dyadic, behavioral system. Previously, psychologists had defined attachment as a trait of the infant, in terms of frequencies of particular behaviors (e.g., crying or clinging). Just as a child could be too dependent, an infant could be *too* attached. Great difficulties arose from this pre-Bowlbian conceptualization. For example, infants would become less attached with age (because toddlers sought proximity less than infants); yet common observation made it obvious that attachment doesn't wane, but merely changes its manifestation. Children, as well as infants, are attached to their parents. Likewise, "index" behaviors for attachment proved to be unstable across time and even across situations, leading to the paradoxical conclusion that attachment was invalid as an individual differences construct (Masters & Wellman, 1974).

Before the rise of Bowlby's conceptualization, even the formation of attachment was seen in terms of drive- or reinforcement-based traits. One view was that attachment was a secondary drive, derived from more primary motives. Since the mother fed the infant, and in other ways reduced tension, she became the object of attachment through association. Other views emphasized contiguity or reinforcement; the caregiver became a discriminative stimulus for reinforcement because he or she was present so often when rewards occurred, or the caregiver rewarded certain behaviors, making them prominent in the repertoire. Abundant evidence ran counter to these views (see Ainsworth, 1969), including Harlow's classic studies with cloth or wire "surrogate mothers" for rhesus monkeys (e.g., Harlow & Harlow, 1966). The animals clearly seemed more "attached" to the cloth surrogate (e.g., running to it when frightened), even though the wire surrogate was the source of food, both were present at all times, and neither contingently reinforced behavior. A modern interpretation of this study, following Bowlby, is that cloth surrogates allowed more opportunity for the operation of the attachment behavioral system of the monkeys.

Bowlby's theory was distinct from the preceding positions. As part of its evolutionary heritage as a social species, the human (primate) is viewed as having a set of preadapted behaviors that unfold with development. In the early months these include looking, smiling, crying, and (especially in nonhuman primates) clinging. Later, following, proximity seeking, and signaling emerge. Such behaviors were built into the repertoire through evolution because of their role in promoting survival. Human infants, like any organism, will naturally express behaviors in their repertoire when supported by a suitable context. These behaviors will emerge and be directed at the most available and appropriate target. No secondary drive concept is invoked. In natural circumstances, it is the tendency of the infant to organize these behaviors around one or "a small hierarchy" of adults. The adult does not need to teach or reinforce such behaviors, but merely be available and interactive for them to occur. Again, in usual circumstances one or more adults will be especially disposed to respond to the preadapted behaviors and will nurture, touch, talk to, and in general interact with the infant. This interactive presence facilitates the ultimate organization of the infant's behavior around the caregiver and the dyadic regulation of infant emotion – that is, the attachment relationship. In the mature, 12-month-old infant, any or all of the attachment behaviors can be used with respect to the "set goal" of maintaining or reachieving contact with the caregiver. They are activated when increased contact is required, because of increased physical distance or increased threat, and they are terminated when the increased contact is achieved.

The attachment relationship was distinguished from attachment behaviors by Bowlby. Various behaviors may be used in the service of attachment, but no behavior is exclusively an attachment behavior. Smiling, vocalizing, and even proximity seeking may serve systems other than attachment. For example, each of these is directed to total strangers at times and may be seen to serve affiliation or exploration. It is for this reason that the presence, or sheer frequency, of particular behaviors cannot "index" attachment. When infants smile after several presentations of a toy clown (Chapter 5), we do not speak of the growth of attachment (or its waning on later trials without smiling).

Attachment, in contrast to attachment behaviors, refers to the particular organization of behaviors with respect to a caregiver, and to the special role of this dyadic organization for emotional regulation. Attached infants do not at all times cling to and exclusively direct their attention to caregivers; rather, they separate to explore the environment. In so doing, they direct their looking and smiling elsewhere and adjust their proximity. In the absence of threat, this may be most of the time. The balance between attachment and exploration is as much a part of human survival as attachment itself, given the role of environmental mastery in human adaptation. Bowlby's evolution-based theory does require, however, that under conditions of threat infants immediately seek haven with the caregiver, either by locomotion, signaling, or both, and that they are sufficiently alert to the caregiver's whereabouts that this is possible. Bowlby has discussed the essential survival value of this state of affairs; thus, the importance of the study cited earlier (Tracy et al., 1976), empirically documenting that infants do specifically seek caregivers when they are threatened or otherwise in need of assistance for emotional regulation. It is not amount of proximity, but its organization with other behaviors and with context that defines the attachment relationship.

Bowlby's position has important implications for studying individual differences. Important individual variation would *not* be in terms of amount or intensity of particular attachment behaviors or age first shown (which would be influenced by cognitive/developmental factors). By the end of the first year, virtually all normal infants will become attached, so biased is the primate nervous system to form such attachments (Schore, 1994). The *quality* of the attachment, however, will vary greatly, depending on the responsivity of the caregiver and degree of reciprocity possible between infant and caregiver. To the extent that the infant's signals elicit appropriate responses, and to the extent that infant behaviors can be coordinated in exchanges with the attachment figure to achieve ongoing emotional regulation, a good-quality attachment relationship is to be expected. Poor-quality, anxious attachment will be manifest in dysfunctional dyadic emotional regulation.

Extending Bowlby's organizational conceptualization of attachment

Bowlby's conceptualization is the starting point for an organizational view of attachment and remains the definitive work on the topic. By casting attachment in systems theory terms of set goals, goal correction, and function, he distinguished his construct from concepts of causal traits. Attachment is not a thing the infant has. It is not a need or a motive. Therefore, it does not cause the infant to do something. Rather, attachment refers to a behavioral system, selected for its effect on the reproductive success of individuals in the environment in which they evolved. Viewing protection from predation as the biological function and proximity as the set goal of the system, Bowlby argued that diverse attachment behaviors (crying, following, etc.) were functionally related; all may lead to the same predictable outcome, caregiver–infant proximity. Moreover, the set goal, goal correction concept implied that such behaviors would be activated *automatically* when information reached the infant that a (context-influenced) proximity–distance threshold had been exceeded. In the manner of a feedback loop, such behaviors would remain operative until (and only until) proximity was reestablished. In this way Bowlby removed drive considerations and the need to posit an attachment motive. Birds don't stop building nests because their nest-building drive is expended (they keep going if a researcher dissembles it) but because it is finished. Likewise, infants seek proximity until it is achieved.

However, to yield a truly viable developmental construct, Bowlby's control systems model (as distinguished from his broader theoretical perspective) requires elaboration. Bowlby discarded drive reduction in his working model of attachment at the expense of motivational and affective components, which are central to the organizational view presented here and which are not tied to drive reduction except by tradition (Engel, 1971). Emotion and motivation are downplayed despite the fact that Bowlby's observations led him to describe attachment as an "affective bond" and despite the fact that the position outlined here is clearly anticipated in his work. The cybernetic model does not do justice to some of his more important observations, especially in neglecting the mediating role of affect.

With attachment tied to the set goal of proximity, and external information as the major determinant of behavior, the infant's tendency to be more readily upset when one separation follows a preceding separation–reunion experience cannot be explained. (The same distance threshold is crossed, so why should the reaction be stronger unless it is mediated by the preceding affective experience.) Likewise, the effectiveness of developmentally advanced alternatives to contact (e.g., showing toys) cannot be encompassed. Inappropriate analogies to imprinting and fixed behavior patterns are drawn. It may be appropriate to say that a duckling, seeing its mother move away, automatically follows. But human behavior is much more flexible and complex than this.

When, on the other hand, the set goal of the attachment system is viewed as "felt security," and affect is seen as mediating adaptive behavior, these problems can be resolved (Sroufe & Waters, 1977a). Proximity seeking is not automatically activated, but depends on the infant's evaluation of a variety of external *and* internal cues, resulting in a subjective experience of security–insecurity (Bischof, 1975). Because of their impact on the infant's emotional experience, setting, preceding events, and other aspects of context (Chapters 6 and 8), as well as the infant's mood and developmental level, influence the initiation of bids for contact or closeness. With development there are increasingly varied means of maintaining contact, and there is decreasing proximity to caregivers in the absence of stress (e.g., Feldman & Ingham, 1975).

Proximity seeking clearly is not triggered automatically when some fixed distance threshold is crossed. For example, infants may require more proximity when first entering a new situation. As they feel more comfortable in the setting they allow greater distance. Should the caregiver leave briefly, they may then be sensitive to even the slightest movements after he or she returns. Bowlby would speak of changing set points, but without a role for emotional experience the dynamics of such changes are left unexplained.

Further, with an older infant or toddler, a reassuring word from the caregiver may moderate feelings of separation anxiety and therefore subsequent protest behavior. Upon the caregiver's return, showing a toy or otherwise interacting across a distance may be sufficient to reinstate feelings of security and to circumvent the need for proximity entirely. Other infants, because of interfering affect, may fail to approach caregivers and even (pathognomically) actively avoid them despite being distressed (discussed later). Clearly, proximity seeking is not automatically activated in human infants.

Bowlby's account of the function of attachment also requires broadening. While protection may be a sufficient function for explaining the evolution of attachment behavior in many species, a role in support of exploration is also of importance in human adaptation, since environmental mastery and opportunism are advantages of our species. Consequently, the concept of the attachment figure as a secure base for exploration (e.g., Ainsworth, 1973) may be added to the protection function, again making attachment a more viable developmental construct. The caregiver, as a mobile source of security who can be referenced across a distance, supports engagement of the unknown and therefore potentially threatening world. In the caregiver's presence the balance between attraction to and wariness of novelty is commonly tipped in favor of exploration. When this exploration leads to stress, the caregiver is available for comforting, supporting the return to play.

Attachment as a relationship construct

Attachment refers not to a set of behaviors or to a trait of the infant, but to a special, emotional relationship between infant and caregiver. Like other relationships, an attachment relationship evolves over time and is the product of the interactional history of the particular dyad (even varying, though with some modest concordance, with different parents; Fox, Kimmerly, & Shafer, 1991; Main & Weston, 1981). There is no such thing as instant attachment. It is distinct from the concept of ''bonding'' (Klaus & Kennell, 1976), which usually refers to the caregiver's tie to the infant and is presumed to occur quite rapidly in the first hours or days of life. Attachment refers to an evolving dyadic process and to a mutual relationship. Caregivers *are* tied to their infants – alert to their signals, waking when they stir in the night, anxious should they come to harm, and, for mothers, lactating when they cry. But infants, too, are emotionally tied to caregivers. The pair is ''psychobiologically attuned'' (Field, 1985).

That the infant is emotionally ''tied'' to the caregiver, as well as the caregiver to the infant, is supported by a variety of evidence. The use of the caregiver as a secure base for exploration and preferential treatment of the caregiver by the infant when threatened or distressed were mentioned earlier. Infants monitor caregivers when wary and are differentially comforted by them when upset. When the attachment relationship is newly consolidated at the end of the first year, even brief separations (a few minutes) are often upsetting (presumably because of a threat to the affective bond), and reunions are special even when the infant had not been upset.

Most profound, however, are the infant's or toddler's reactions to more pronounced separations (e.g., weeks). A characteristic sequence is seen in which there is a period of protest, followed by a period of dispair, and then detachment (Bowlby, 1973; Robertson & Robertson, 1971). The sequence cannot, of course, be explained by the behavior of the absent caregiver and therefore testifies to organizing processes within the infant. It is testimony to the enduring quality of the affective bond. Upon reunion, following prolonged separation, another sequence characteristically unfolds (Heinicke & Westheimer, 1966). Infants first ignore the caregiver, as though there is no recognition, although they do recognize and respond to less significant figures after such absences. A period of angry ambivalence follows and then, finally, rapprochement. This sequence again suggests the affective core and special quality of the attachment relationship. With prolonged separation the emotional upheaval is so great, the experienced vulnerability so profound, that the infant's behavioral organization is dissembled and cannot be instantly put back together. In clinical terms, one could speak of the infant as at first defending against the possibility of renewed pain and vulnerability by not acknowledging the presence of the caregiver.

Further evidence for the heuristic value of defining attachment as an emotional relationship construct comes from research on the stability of individual differences in attachment. With development there are dramatic changes in the manifestation of attachment behaviors. Wariness in a novel setting and distress when left with a stranger decline markedly between 12 and 18 months. As a consequence, greeting and distant interaction replace proximity seeking. When sought, physical contact is brief and settling when distressed occurs rapidly for most 18-month-olds (Sroufe & Waters, 1977a). Given such developmental changes, it is not surprising that individuals show little stability over this period in terms of frequencies of discrete behaviors (vocalizing, looking, amount of proximity; e.g., Waters, 1978). Still, individual differences in the patterning and organization of behavior – the quality of the emotional relationship – can be quite stable in ordinary environments. Infants distressed by separation at 12 months, who strongly and effectively sought contact upon reunion (which promoted a return to play), as a group tended to show quite different but functionally similar behavior at 18 months. Not being distressed, they might exuberantly greet and interact with the caregiver across a distance, but they were not nonchalant or petulant. Physical contact was transformed to psychological contact, but the relationship still served exploration, and the affective bond remained undiminished.

Viewing attachment as a relationship construct has clear implications for assessing individual differences. While such assessments must be anchored in individual behavior, the focus is on the dynamics of the relationship – namely, its effectiveness for serving exploration and emotional regulation of the infant. Such effectiveness may be manifest in numerous ways, and infants and caregivers of greatly varying behavioral styles may have effective relationships in common.

Assessing individual differences in the quality of attachment

Assessing the quality of attachment relationships entails considerable complexity. No simple index or frequency count procedure will likely yield valid measures. The procedure must take into account context and, above all, must tap into the organization of behavior with regard to the dyadic regulation of emotion. Establishing the validity of an assessment procedure would also be complex. Security (quality) of attachment is a construct, and the procedures of construct validation require establishing a network of relations with antecedent, contemporary, and outcome correlates. If the quality of attachment has been captured, assessments should be tied to an unfolding developmental process and related to important developmental consequences.

The Ainsworth paradigm

Ainsworth developed an assessment procedure that was explicitly targeted at the organization of behavior, with a focus on emotional expression and emotional regulation (e.g., Ainsworth et al., 1978). Moreover, it results in a classification system having as its core dimension the effectiveness of the relationship in serving arousal modulation and exploration. The system is exquisitely behavioral, and yet avoided the simplistic operationism of preceding decades. Moreover, the variations in patterns of attachment she discovered have stood the test of more than 25 years of research.

In the course of a detailed longitudinal study of home behavior in the first year of life, Ainsworth developed a laboratory procedure that has been widely used. The initial validation of the procedure and scoring method rested in its relation to exploration, crying, and proximity seeking in the home. This was absolutely critical. Any procedure claiming to assess attachment (even variations or new applications of the Ainsworth procedure) must be anchored to observations of the attachment–exploration balance in the natural environment. That is the crucial criterion.

The procedure consists of eight episodes: (1) Caregiver and infant enter a novel, sparsely furnished room containing a variety of attractive, age-appropriate toys (1 minute); (2) the infant is allowed to play with the caregiver present but seated in a chair (3 minutes); (3) a stranger enters, sits quietly for 1 minute, chats with the caregiver for 1 minute, then engages the infant in play, taking cues from the baby; (4) the caregiver leaves (3 minutes, unless the infant is unduly distressed and cannot be settled by the stranger); (5) the caregiver returns and stranger leaves unobtrusively (3-minute reunion); (6) the caregiver leaves infant alone (3 minutes or less); (7) the stranger enters, attempts to comfort the infant if needed (3 minutes or less); and (8) the caregiver returns (3-minute reunion).

Deliberately, this procedure represents a cumulative (and in Western cultures moderate) stress situation for the infant. The order of events was purposefully arranged. A novel environment is mildly stressful, but in the caregiver's presence the attractiveness of the toys should overbalance any wariness. The stranger represents an additional stress, but her chatting with the mother and allowing the infant considerable control in pacing their interaction makes this stress mild. Again, in the caregiver's presence most infants would soon warm up to the stranger. The caregiver's departure is a clear increment in stress, and many 12-month-olds become distressed in this episode. The second separation is more stressful, both because it is a second arousal of alarm and because this time the infant is left alone. Nearly all infants from middle-class samples cry in this episode. Still a clear majority but somewhat fewer infants from poverty samples cry, perhaps because of more experience with a variety of people. Still, the episode is stressful, even for those who don't cry (as witnessed by subdued play or autonomic arousal; e.g., Sroufe & Waters, 1977b).

In this system, the quality of attachment is assessed primarily by how well the achieved dyadic emotional regulation serves exploration and mastery. These are the salient developmental issues for the 12- to 18-month-old. The ease of separating from the caregiver to explore (security derived from mere availability) partly defines an effective attachment relationship, and so does the ease of deriving comfort from the caregiver when distressed, which promotes a return to play. As the procedure continues, there is increasing stress and, typically, increasing need for contact. Most infants require comforting in Episode 8; yet, for the majority such comforting should be effective. When infants can't separate to explore or don't seek or derive comfort when distressed, the relationship with this caregiver is judged to be ineffective (an "anxious" attachment).

Reunion episodes are emphasized in the assessment because they tap the capacity of the dyad to manage the stress of separation, the threat to the affective bond. The separation–reunion sequence places a maximal load on the dyadic affect regulation capacity. Given a closed door, infants cannot do much during separation, and many factors influence the degree of distress experienced (e.g., illness, fatigue, extent of engagement with the stranger, and, with older toddlers but apparently not 12-month-olds, the caregiver's departure style; Weinraub & Lewis, 1977). Thus, the presence and degree of separation distress cannot be crucial in determining the quality of attachment. What the infant does upon reunion, however, whether distressed or not, is of great importance.

Schore (1994), drawing on the work of Field (1985), Frijda (1988), Thelen (1989), and others, stresses the importance of separation–reunion experiences for infant development. They provide key experiences of dramatic "psychobiological state transition," a shifting from strong negative affect to positive affect and/or from a low-energy to a high-energy state. Such experiences not only are the basis for the expectation that organization may be reclaimed in the face of distress, but, according to Schore, actually affect the formation of dynamic brain systems (sympathetic–parasympathetic balance). "By promoting symbiotic entrainment of her [caregiver] mature and his [infant] immature nervous system, the child shifts from a parasympathetic dominant . . . into . . . a sympathetic dominant energy-expanding mode" (p. 112). Further, this "externally" activated sympathetic activity leads to increased arousal, "regenerated positive affects," and increased mobility, "which enable the reenergized toddler to go back out into the world" (p. 113). In time, such sympathetic–parasympathetic balancing will be a capability of the child. Such experiences are therefore critical on both a physiological and a psychological level.

Four categorical scales are used in examining the effectiveness of reunion behavior in the Ainsworth system (proximity seeking, contact maintenance, contact resistance, and avoidance). All are concerned with the effective use of caregivers for emotional regulation, having to do with the directness, thoroughness, and ease of deriving comfort from them. The scales are a compromise between subjective ratings, which lack precision, and measures based on frequency counts, which fail to capture the meaning of behavior. For each point on the scale, various examples of actual behavior are provided, which, while diverse, represent equivalent scalar positions based on the rating assignments of a group of judges. The researcher's task is to find the best match between observed behavior and scale examples. (For details of the scales, see Ainsworth et al., 1978.)

Basic patterns of attachment

Based on ratings of reunion behavior and observations throughout the procedure, attachment relationships are classified into one of three major groups, based upon the patterning of behavior.

Group B (secure attachment relationships). Typically, these infants readily separate from the caregiver and become absorbed in toy play, perhaps sharing discoveries across a distance. They rarely are unduly wary of the stranger, though they may visually check back with the caregiver when the stranger enters or approaches. They may or may not be distressed in the separations, though if not distressed one often sees subdued play and looks to the door or to the caregiver's chair. If distressed, upon reunion they go *directly* to the caregiver, *actively* seek contact, and maintain it until settled. They often cling, sink in, mold, or otherwise clearly show their desire for contact and its effectiveness in providing comfort. Their recovery from an overly aroused, disorganized state is smooth, steady, and carried to completion. If not distressed, they typically do not seek physical contact on reunion; rather, they smile, bounce, vocalize, or show a toy, actively seeking interaction (psychological contact). They are happy to see the caregiver. Whether distressed or not they show a clear preference for the caregiver. They may accept contact from the stranger, even settling some, but they immediately leave the stranger upon the caregiver's return and treat the caregiver in a qualitatively different manner. They show no reluctance to re-engage the caregiver and no mixture of anger, petulance, or rejection with contact seeking (though they may show these behaviors with the stranger).

Group C (anxious/resistant attachment). These infants exhibit a poverty of exploration and wariness of the stranger, perhaps needing contact even prior to separation. They are quite distressed by separation and unable to be settled by the stranger. Crucially, upon reunion with the caregiver they still show great difficulty settling. They may stiffen the body, kick, push away, bat away offered toys, and squirm to get down only to cry for pickup again. Although they seek contact, in some way they also resist it (showing clear ambivalence), or they simply cry and fuss in a passive way. In any event, they cannot effectively use the caregiver for emotional regulation. They do not get thoroughly settled and as a result do not return to involved exploration and play.

Group A (anxious/avoidant attachment). Members of this group separate readily to play (though their play may be superficial), and they generally show little wariness of the stranger. They are upset only if left alone and commonly settle when the stranger returns in Episode 7. Most significantly, upon reunion with the caregiver, they show no more than a casual greeting and may ignore or pointedly look away from, turn away from, or move away from the caregiver. They do not initiate interaction and they are not responsive to the caregiver's attempts at interaction. Such *avoidance* (which is not shown to the stranger) tends to be greater in the second reunion. Thus, the relation between stress and contact seeking is turned around; as the stress increases, the avoidance increases. While often not overtly distressed during reunions, these infants nonetheless are autonomically aroused during separation and reunion and show a compromised ability to explore (Sroufe & Waters, 1977b).

The resistant group's attachments are obviously anxious, with a clear ambivalence and failure to explore. The anxious attachment of the avoidant group is more inferred from the apparent interference with attachment behavior that they experience under stress. It is believed that they too are doubtful about the caregiver's availability. It is presumed that the desire to seek contact is present, but is not expressed due to some kind of interference. Main (1977) has suggested that incompatible anger, as well as a desire for contact, is aroused, leading to ignoring or other displacement behavior. Alternatively, a history of rejection when contact has been sought, which routinely produced a disorganizing affect, may lead the infant to suppress approach behavior when aroused. To approach is to risk disorganizing affect (including anger). In either case, emotional experience, either historical or current, is inferred even without affective expression, due to the absence of expectable behavior and in keeping with the organizational perspective. Even ignoring is referred to as avoidance in this context. (The validity of these propositions will be supported in the next section.)

As with Ainsworth's rating scales, classification is a matter of template matching. There are subgroups under each major category. Some securely attached infants, for example, appear wary of both the novel surroundings and the stranger; they cry a great deal at separation and require considerable contact (Group B4). They are classed as secure because they actively, effectively, and smoothly seek contact, with little sign of contact resistance, and the contact is effective in terminating their distress. Other securely attached infants may not cry at all and may seek little or no physical contact (Group B1). Their security is manifest by strong greeting behavior and the active initiation of interaction at a distance. Another subgroup of secure cases shows some avoidance on the first reunion, which gives way to proximity seeking in the second reunion (B2). (It is noteworthy that avoidance and resistance are not attachment behaviors at all; yet their *absence* is critical in defining secure attachment.)

Ainsworth's discovery of the three basic patterns of attachment was based on a small sample; yet others have found that 90% of large samples usually may be readily classified. Those unfamiliar with attachment assessment may not appreciate Ainsworth's accomplishment, believing that the three patterns (eight subtypes) are simply all possible patterns. But they are not. In our original middle-class sample, for example, we saw no infants who avoided the caregiver *and* who were wary of the stranger or cried when left with the stranger, and no infants avoided both mother and stranger (Sroufe & Waters, 1977a). Such patterns might be expected based on the concept of an "avoidance trait" or generalization of avoidance; yet they were, predictably, not observed. Moreover, there were virtually no infants who exhibited contact resistance upon reunion *and* who did not cry when left with the stranger.

Subsequent research has shown that even cases that fail to fit Ainsworth's system often represent meaningful variations. Main and her colleagues (e.g., Main & Hesse, 1990) have argued that cases fitting the Ainsworth system, even the Group A and Group C patterns, reflect coherent strategies for dealing with attachment feelings when aroused. Avoidance, for example, may be thought of as a strategy for keeping a routinely rejecting caregiver near at hand (rather than leading to further alienation). This leaves open the possibility of responsiveness should an extreme threat arise. But in certain cases no coherent strategy may be evolved. The infant may exhibit disorganized sequences of behavior or odd behaviors such as freezing or stereotypies or lying prone on the floor when the caregiver returns. Main argues that these infants have not been able to form coherent strategies because the behavior of the caregiver has itself been incoherent or threatening. Thus, the very figure that would be the target of attachment behavior is also the source of disorganization or threat. Such cases, comprising Group D (anxiously attached, disorganized), have been associated with histories of abuse or with caregivers having histories of unresolved trauma (Carlson, Cicchetti, Barrett, & Braunwald, 1989; Main & Hesse, 1990).

Research support for attachment as an organizational construct

Following Bowlby, the essential hypotheses of the organizational position are (1) that differences in quality of care will lead to differences in the quality of attachment (i.e., early caregiver regulation will forecast the pattern of later dyadic regulation) and (2) that such differences in attachment will have a profound impact on the infant's later self-regulation of emotion.

Central to the first hypothesis is the idea that based on the interactive history, the child will form expectations concerning the responsiveness of the caregiver and, in time and in a complementary manner, his or her own degree of effectiveness in eliciting responses (what Bowlby calls "inner working models"). Commonly, from coordinated exchanges orchestrated by the caregiver in the first half year, and from the caregiver's responsiveness to the infant's explicit signals in the second half year, infants learn that the caregiver is most likely available and that when available emotional regulation may be maintained or reachieved if lost. Such expectations are revealed in the organization of attachment behavior. Infants that expect the caregiver to be responsive explore with confidence, signal needs intentionally or actively seek contact when needed, and respond quickly to caregiver interventions (expecting that they will be effective).

The second hypothesis centers on the idea that the experience of dyadic regulation, with an ever more active role for the infant, provides a necessary foundation for self-regulation. As the caregiver is responsive, the child acquires confidence in his or her own causality. The infant is indeed having an impact on the environment. The movement to self-regulation need not be accomplished at once, but through a series of phases as the child's unfolding capacities allow less frequent, less pronounced, and more distal use of the caregiver as an aid in regulation. Confidence in the caregiver becomes confidence in the self with the caregiver and, ultimately, confidence in the self.

Quality of care and quality of attachment

Ainsworth's original study provided the initial confirmation of Bowlby's first hypothesis (e.g., Ainsworth et al., 1978). She found that in cases when caregivers had been rated high on her "sensitivity" scales (see Chapter 9) at several points over the first year, attachment relationships at 12 months were more likely classified as secure. Both the avoidant and resistant groups had caregivers who had been rated low on sensitivity, despite the fact that nothing was distinctive about the infants' behavior early in the first year (Blehar, Lieberman, & Ainsworth, 1977). The avoidant cases were distinguished by one particular feature; the caregivers showed an especially strong tendency to rebuff the infant precisely when the infant sought to be picked up. (Although they did not in general have less physical contact with them, they did not seem to enjoy physical contact.) Thus, those ultimately assessed to have secure attachments indeed had histories that would foster expectations of caregiver responsiveness. Those who became anxiously attached had histories that would lead to uncertainty about the caregiver's availability or effectiveness or, especially for the avoidant cases, to profound doubts about caregiver responsiveness, especially in times of need.

One specific finding in Ainsworth's research concerned the relation between prompt, reliable responding to crying in the first year and attachment at 12 months (Bell & Ainsworth, 1972). Such responsiveness was associated with later secure attachment and, paradoxically from a narrow reinforcement point of view, with reduced crying. This finding is consistent with the broader learning postulated to occur by Bowlby. Crying is not a randomly occurring operant; it is a signal, at first automatic, in response to overarousal (much as we shiver when we are cold). Later, it is more directed. After infancy, of course, it can become manipulative and can be inappropriately reinforced. But young infants do not become spoiled by responsiveness. Instead, they learn that the caregiver is responsive to their signals, which differentiate with development. Having learned that the caregiver will be reliably responsive to their distress (having experienced effective dyadic regulation of emotion), older infants may be reassured simply by the presence of the caregiver or the caregiver's response to a vocalization, smile, or some other signal across a distance. They need not use the less differentiated signal of crying.

Ainsworth's basic finding has been replicated by a number of investigators (Bates et al., 1985; Belsky & Isabella, 1988; Egeland & Farber, 1984; Grossmann, Grossmann, Spanger, Suess & Unzer, 1985; Isabella, 1993; Isabella & Belsky, 1991; Kiser, Bates, Muslin, & Bayles, 1986). In each case, Ainsworth's sensitivity scale ratings at 4 or 6 months (and sometimes at other ages as well) were related to attachment classifications at 12 months, always done by independent coders. The relationship between caregiver rejection and avoidance has also been replicated (Isabella, 1993). The Grossmann study was especially interesting because sensitivity ratings at 2 and 6 months were predictive of attachment, but ratings at 10 months were not. This was because in their North German sample, caregivers in general begin to push for "proper" deportment late in the first year. The variance in sensitivity disappears and mean sensitivity moves down. This is a remarkable confirmation of Ainsworth because the predictiveness of the early sensivity ratings for later quality of attachment held despite later changes in caregiver behavior over time due to the general cultural standard.

Other studies, too, have shown that various aspects of caregiver-guided emotional regulation in the first year, including caregiver "emotional availability" and quality of emotional communication, have been related to the later security of attachment (e.g., Egeland & Sroufe, 1981; Tronick, 1989). In all, the hypothesis that the quality of attachment is related to earlier quality of care is amply supported by developmental studies.

Intervention studies, often involving training and other efforts to enhance sensitivity, offer some additional support for Bowlby's hypothesis. While not always showing effects, results from well-done studies have at times been quite powerful and lasting (e.g., van den Boom, in press). Sensitivity training can dramatically increase the proportion of secure attachments, especially when one works with groups of challenging infants or dyads already showing difficulty (Lieberman, Weston, & Pawl, 1991).

It bears repeating that temperamental variation in different dimensions of behavior is not invalidated or disallowed by these considerations (see Chapter 9). In fact, sensitivity by its very definition embodies differences in behavioral style. Being sensitive means being responsive to the particular nature, moods, and manner of signaling of the specific child. Also, attachment variation and temperamental variation may be viewed as orthogonal for two reasons. First, they represent different levels of analysis. Assessments of attachment are at the level of the organization of behavior. Thus, it is not how much an infant cries and squirms, but in what context and sequenced with what other behavior and in what manner that are critical. (Infants who cry a great deal during separation, even early in reunions, and who squirm mightily with the stranger are still judged to be securely attached if they are comforted by caregiver contact and return to play.) Second, as described earlier, securely attached infants (and anxiously attached infants) show great differences of behavioral style, from slow to arouse and noncuddly (B1) to slow to warm up and easily overaroused (B4).

In examining separation–reunion behavior, Thompson (1990) has argued that temperamental differences may influence primarily *what infants require* upon reunion. Security of attachment "derives from how well this assistance is provided" (p. 386). Those, for example, who respond to separation with imperative, high-intensity distress require an immediate and thorough response from the caregiver, and in the case of some secure attachment relationships this is how it goes. Others, not so distressed, need only distant interaction, and this can also be done effectively in secure cases.

Research supports the distinction between the quality of attachment relationships, based on history of care, and variations in temperament. First, assessments of temperament in the first year, either from behavioral observation or parental report, consistently fail to predict attachment security (Ainsworth et al., 1978; Bates et al., 1985; Blehar, Lieberman, & Ainsworth, 1977; Bohlin, Hagekull, Germer, Andersson, & Lindberg, 1990; Egeland & Farber, 1984; Vaughn, Lefever, Seifer, & Barglow, 1989). Second, studies have shown that temperament assessments (both parental report and assays of cortisol reactivity to stress) do predict the amount of crying during separation episodes of Ainsworth's procedure (i.e., proneness to distress in general), but do not predict the amount of crying during reunions; nor do they predict the amount of avoidance or resistance (Gunnar et al., 1989; Vaughn et al., 1989). It is the latter that are critical for determining attachment security and that reflect the degree of confidence in the caregiver and expectations regarding one's own actions based on the history of care.

While infant temperament has not been shown to affect attachment directly, there is an interaction between temperament or newborn neurological status and other factors. For example, Crockenberg (1981) found that only in combination with low levels of social and emotional support for caregivers did nonoptimal newborn status predict anxious attachment. In more recent work, Mangelsdorf and colleagues (Mangelsdorf, Gunnar, Kestenbaum, Lang, & Andreas, 1991) found that infant proneness to distress interacted with a maternal controllingness trait to predict anxious attachment. Proneness to distress did not predict anxious attachment independently, but only in combination with highly controlling mothers. These findings suggest that in some cases temperament factors may contribute to caregiver sensitivity or insensitivity.

Quality of attachment and later emotional development

There are numerous bases for expecting links between the quality of infant–caregiver attachment and later development of the child. Some of these would emphasize positive expectations concerning social relationships that may derive from a secure attachment history or the sense of agency that comes from responsive care. These and other propositions are relevant for testing organizational theory and will be taken up in the following chapters. Here we will briefly consider the developmental implications that derive from the particular viewpoint of attachment as the dyadic regulation of emotion. How might differences in the dyadic regulation of emotion influence subsequent differences in the course individual development? Put more precisely, what differential developmental pathways might be initiated by emerging variations in the organization of dyadic regulation?

The effective dyadic regulation of emotion in infancy (secure attachment) is predicted to have consequences for emerging expectations concerning emotional arousal and, at the behavioral level, consequences for the expression, modulation, and flexible control of emotions by the child. Those infants participating in a smoothly functioning, well-regulated relationship have repeatedly experienced (1) that others are available and respond when they are emotionally aroused, (2) that emotional arousal is rarely disorganizing, and (3) that, should such arousal be disorganizing, restabilization commonly is quickly achieved. Based on such expectations, children with secure attachment histories should readily engage situations having the potential for emotional arousal and should directly express emotions, since emotions themselves are not threatening and are expected to be treated as communications by others. Thus, children with histories of secure attachment would be predicted to exhibit a notable curiosity, zest for exploration, and affective expressiveness, especially in social situations. Likewise, when even strong affect is aroused, these children typically should remain organized, should manifest efforts to modulate arousal, and should effectively turn to others if their own capacities fail. They should be emotionally flexible or "resilient" (see Chapter 12), with the expression of impulses and emotion varying with context (e.g., exuberant on the playground, contained during reading time), and with the capacity to rebound following experiences of high threat and/or emotional arousal.

One particular prediction, which perhaps summarizes all of the preceding behavior, is that children with secure histories should later be more emotionally independent (self-reliant in Bowlby's terms; 1973) than children with histories of anxious attachment. Being deeply assured of the availability of others, knowing that others can be approached when needed, and believing in their own capacities for eliciting care, such children have the confidence to exercise emerging capacities for autonomous coping with arousal. One's actions have been effective in the past (though with reliance on caregiver response), so one expects newly developing capabilities to be effective as well. Should one's own efforts fail, others can always be called on for assistance. From some points of view this is the most paradoxical of all predictions based on the organizational perspective derived from Bowlby. Securely attached infants directly express their dependency on caregivers, consistently turning to them when threatened or needy and often engaging in full and complete physical contact at such times. In contrast, some with anxious attachment, members of the avoidant group, fail to seek contact when moderately threatened and at times appear indifferent to the caregiver. Thus, it is the effectively dependent infants, rather than those some have called (inappropriately) "precociously independent," who are predicted to be more emotionally independent later.

As will be detailed in subsequent chapters, each of the predictions outlined here has been amply supported by longitudinal research. Support has been especially strong for the predictions regarding dependence–independence. Assessments of anxious attachment in infancy are strongly associated with assessments of dependency during the preschool years, middle childhood, and on into adolescence (e.g., Elicker, England, & Sroufe, 1992; Sroufe, Carlson, & Shulman, 1993; Sroufe, Fox, & Pancake, 1983).

Conclusion: causality in an organizational perspective

The preceding discussion should not be taken to imply a simple, linear model of causality. Anxious attachment in infancy, for example, does not inevitably lead to later emotional dependency; nor does it in a simple sense cause later dependency. In keeping with Bowlby (1973), behavior is always a complex product of past experience and current circumstances. All routes of development are thought to start close together so that, initially, an individual has access to a large range of pathways along any one of which he or she might travel. The one chosen, it is held, "turns at each and every stage of the journey on an interaction between the organism as it has developed up to that moment and the environment in which it then finds itself" (p. 364).

Thus, in a new context or in the presence of new supports fundamental change in behavior may occur (Pettit & Bates, 1989; Vaughn, Egeland, Waters, & Sroufe, 1979). One useful model for considering pathways of individual development is the division of tracks in a train yard or the branching of a tree (Bowlby, 1973; Waddington, 1957; see Figure 10.1). Any pathway enjoined early (e.g., a pattern of attachment) has multiple possibilities that may be followed based on later contingencies. Two individuals may begin similarly and diverge or begin on different major pathways and ultimately have similar pat-

Figure 10.1. Illustration of Bowlby's (1973) developmental pathways concept.

terns of adaptation due to subsequent turnings in development. The model does imply, however, that early adaptation exercises constraints on later development. The past is not simply erased; it too remains a force in individual adaptation, especially as patterns are repeatedly supported over time. One view of the predictive power of assessments of infant attachment is that one has tapped into a significant developmental process and identified nascent developmental pathways. The focus, then, becomes moving beyond the predictive power of early assessments to an understanding of the processes that maintain and deflect individuals from pathways initially enjoined. We will further discuss continuity, change, and models of causality in the final three chapters.

11   The emergence of the autonomous self: caregiver-guided self-regulation

A positive, reciprocal interpersonal set between parent and child, which renders the child ready, receptive, and positively motivated to respond to parental socialization . . . and internalize parental standards and values may be the result of a long-term positive relationship.

Kochanska (1993)

The psychobiological state of shame distress represents a sudden shift from sympathetic-predominant . . . to parasympathetic-dominant trophotropic arousal . . . The caregiver influences the parcellation of the two limbic circuits . . . and thereby the permanent excitation–inhibition (autonomic) balance of his prefrontolimbic regulatory system.

Schore (1994)

Impressive development occurs in the years just after infancy, development that again is characterized by qualitative change and transformation. Major changes include the advent of symbolic representation and language, self-awareness, and the beginnings of self-control. Yet despite the profound changes that occur during this period, the same principles that governed development in infancy are again apparent. Development is unified and orderly, building on what was previously present yet moving to progressively new levels of complexity.

The overarching socioemotional task for the preschool years is the movement from dyadic regulation toward the self-regulation of emotion. In keeping with the nature of all development, there is a succession of phases in accomplishing this task. As regulation orchestrated by the caregiver prepared the way for more truly dyadic regulation in infancy, so too there is a transition here, wherein self-regulation supported and guided by caregivers precedes regulation by the child outside of the caregiving matrix. In the period just after infancy, known in Western culture as the toddler phase of development, the young child at times is able to regulate arousal and behavior successfully without caregiver intervention. But at times disorganization is avoided only by falling back on the greater capacities of the caregiver or through the caregiver's anticipatory actions, and in most cases a supportive emotional presence of the caregiver enables and

192

bolsters the child's own self-regulation activities. Caregivers will step in during periods of high arousal, and they are heavily involved in the control of aggression and impulse expression. The caregiver's task is to anticipate frustration and to intercede should the child begin losing control, while at the same time allowing the child as much self-direction as possible (see Wertsch, 1979, drawing on Vygotsky, 1978). Thus, the child gains increased experience in managing arousal on his or her own, while still being under the protective guidance of the caregiver. In parallel, the child is learning to inhibit impulses, even those strongly impelled by affect. Although few caregivers expect complete inhibition in their absence, they do expect compliance to their direct prohibitions. So the task for the toddler is to learn to inhibit impulses under the guidance, tutelage, and enforcement of the caregiver. All of this paves the way for later self-regulation.

As was the case in infancy, various aspects of development proceed in a unified, integrated manner during the toddler period. Developments in cognition, social behavior, and physical maturation converge to issue in both new emotional experiences and new capacities for regulating emotion, and these new experiences and capacities, in turn, promote cognitive growth, including advances in self-awareness. CNS development supports all of these advances, and experiences based on new capacities influence the further development of the brain (Schore, 1994; see later). Because of motoric and cognitive advances, affective states arise more as a result of the child's own actions, leading to a sense of self as agent. As a result, certain new affects arise, such as shame and "positive self-evaluation," which exercise a powerful influence on the child's social behavior and inner experience. The new sense of agency, as well as the recognition of self versus other as the cause of powerful, new affective experiences, motivates the child to engage in ever more autonomous regulation.

Development in the toddler and later preschool period is also characterized by increasing complexity. During the toddler period the child not only appraises and responds to events in context (including the context of feelings), but now also evaluates his or her own behavior in relation to standards – at first external standards but ultimately (by the preschool period) internal standards (e.g., Kochanska, 1993; Lewis, Alessandri, & Sullivan, 1992). Such a capacity and the new emotions attendant upon it represent profound and qualitative changes in development.

As will be discussed, changes in emotional life are also characterized by differentiation. When new emotions first arise they are often triggered by broad classes of events. In time, there is both an increasing specificity of context in the instigation of emotion and a differentiation of emotional reactions from more global and unspecified arousal toward specific emotional reactions (Kochanska, 1993).

Finally, normative and individual development will again be seen as mutually informative as we consider the toddler and preschool periods. Processes governing the emergence and transformation of emotions during this period, and the regulation of their expression, are also key to conceptualizing meaningful individual differences. The emerging sense of self and the advancing capacities to regulate behavior with respect to standards are the central features of normative development, as well as core aspects of individual differences. Individuals who are ill-prepared for or unsupported in self-regulation, who are not guided in establishing realistic standards for behavior, or who are punished for even the slightest deviation of behavior from a standard are vulnerable to overwhelming feelings of rage and shame (and later despondency and guilt).

As always, individual differences have their roots both in developmental history and in contemporary circumstances. Developmental history especially involves the degree to which responsive care has been given to the particular child, but it includes inborn variations as well. Temperamental characteristics, emphasized by others in accounting for the development of self-regulation (e.g., Kochanska, 1993), are thus seen as part of one's developmental history. Such temperamental differences are viewed as complex constructions, with inborn variation transformed in the context of caregiving relationships, rather than as freestanding, relatively immutable characteristics of the child. In agreement with temperament researchers, however, in this developmental view the child under construction is nonetheless seen as a strong force in his or her development by the toddler period. Toddlers influence the reactions of others and, in part, create their own environments. Having expectations concerning the environment and themselves in it, children evolve more characteristic ways of coping with situations and are not as changeable in the face of varying patterns of care. What are often referred to as temperament characteristics have become more stable aspects of personality (Schore, 1994).

The twin tasks of emotional life during this phase are to directly *express* affect and yet to *control and modulate* it when necessary. Direct expression requires having free access to feelings, as well as the freedom to express them. Control and modulation require positive expectations regarding one's safety in expressing affect and one's capacity to stay organized in the face of high arousal, as well as the belief that one can recoup following strong affective expression (e.g., that one can be angry without obliterating or being obliterated, i.e., be fully angry and recover). Although such issues come to fruition here, it can be seen that the basis for individual differences in such characteristics have been under construction since early infancy. The groundwork for modulated self-expression can be seen in the "holding framework" in caregiver–infant face-to-face contact in the early months (Chapter 9) and in the security–exploration balance of the attachment relationship described in Chapter 10. An abiding confidence in regulation predates the child's own autonomous actions in this regard. In Erikson's

(1963) terms, trust is the foundation for autonomy. During the toddler period the child builds on this background, learning not only that strong feelings are acceptable, but that they must be bounded and can be contained, albeit with guidance from the caregiver.

Normative development in the toddler period

Emergence of the autonomous, aware self

Major theorists such as Erikson, Spitz, Mahler, and Sander, though using diverse terms including *autonomy, will, individuation*, and *self-constancy*, are in accord in suggesting qualitative advances in the sense of self during the toddler period, in parallel with advances in cognitive and linguistic functioning. Spitz (1957), for example, in his book *No and Yes*, proposes that the "I" experience derives from the toddler's increased awareness of his or her own intentions, coupled with the restraints inherent in increased socialization pressure during this time. Sander (1975), Mahler and colleagues (1975), and Erikson (1963), as well, point to a constellation of changes, which include both awareness of the self as an actor and a motivation for action determined by the self.

A complex of developments conspire to propel toddlers toward more autonomous functioning. Some of the more obvious are the development of motor skills (walking, climbing, fine motor manipulation) and representation, including language. Infants move out from the caregiver in a literal way (Rheingold & Eckerman, 1971) and have a new capacity for representing experiences and their own place at the center of this experience (e.g., Bretherton & Bates, 1985). Observers have also described a tendency for toddlers to overcompensate in pulling away from the dependency of infancy in accord with a dialectic principle of development. Such phrases as "I do it" and "do it myself" in the toddler's language are early exemplars, and even before that toddlers can be quite clear in making their wishes known. As Breger (1974) has put it:

As the toddler pushes his independence to its limits, he is forced to rely on those techniques within his capabilities. Since parents frustrate his wishes by saying "no" to him, and since (the toddler's) thought rests largely on the imitation of gestures, it is only natural that he turn their "no's" against them. This is part of the negativistic behavior that is so typical of the period. (p. 135)

Toward more independent functioning. Numerous investigations of exploratory behavior support the idea of a growing independence or "executive competence" (Wenar, 1976) during the toddler period. In the course of exploration, toddlers may even range out of sight of caregivers (e.g., Rheingold & Eckerman, 1971). Moreover, they generally seek less physical contact, relying instead on vocalization and other means of distance interaction (Feldman & Ingham, 1975; Sorce & Emde, 1981; Sroufe & Waters, 1977a) or affective signals across a distance. In situations of uncertainty toddlers look to their caregivers and take cues from their expressions of positive or negative affect. This has been referred to as "social referencing" (e.g., Boccia & Campos, 1989; Gunnar & Stone, 1984). Moreover, they may be reassured by even the *opportunity* for visual or physical contact. Thus, Carr and colleagues (1975) found that toddlers whose caregivers were present but on the other side of a screen played and explored less and vocalized more than toddlers who had visual access to their mothers. The toddlers with free access to their caregivers did not go to them or even look at them very often. By this age the mere possibility of doing so was sufficient.

The emergence of self-recognition. In parallel to these behavioral reflections of the emerging autonomous self, there also is direct evidence for the emergence of self-awareness at this time. Most pertinent are the studies of mirror self-recognition. Drawing from the paradigm developed by Gallup (e.g., 1977) in studying chimpanzees, Amsterdam (1972) was the first to demonstrate that by 22 months most human infants showed evidence of self-recognition. When rouge is unobtrusively smeared on the infant's forehead (or nose in later studies), infants at this age, in contrast to infants before 16 months, reach to their forehead rather than to the image in the mirror. They know the smudge is on *them.* Infants in the first year smile and laugh at the image in the mirror, but by 12 months they are commonly sober, attentive, and even curious (Sroufe & Wunsch, 1972). Coy reactions and "embarrassment" emerge somewhat later (Amsterdam & Leavitt, 1980; Lewis and Brooks-Gunn, 1979). Reactions late in the second year, however, are qualitatively different, with verbally precocious infants even naming themselves. Lewis & Brooks-Gunn (1979) replicated Amsterdam's findings, and Bertenthal and Fischer (1978) presented an elaborated stage theory, along with a series of scaling procedures that reveal the development of self-recognition.

Our own research (e.g., Mans, Cicchetti, & Sroufe, 1978) involved Down syndrome subjects in order to illustrate the ties between self-recognition and cognitive development. The general retardation and heterogeneity of these children were perfectly reflected in the self-recognition data. While, as a group, children with Down syndrome showed mirror self-recognition significantly later than nonretarded children, this was completely a function of cognitive developmental level. Children showing markedly later recognition showed a parallel lag in mental development, while those showing near normal onset of recognition had normal development quotients (DQs). (One child with a Bayley DQ of 125 showed mirror self-recognition at 16 months.) Clearly, self-recognition has intimate ties to advances in cognitive growth.

Understanding of self and other as agents. Self-awareness and an understanding of the self and other as agents proceed in parallel, with three phases described during the toddler period (Wolf, 1982, 1990). At 12 months children recognize that others can do things that they cannot, but they don't seem to grasp that others are agents in their own right. Infants may mimic parents who cover their own faces with their hands; then, when lifting their hands away infants seem surprised to find the parents' face still covered. The distinction between the two sets of hands and two faces is not clear.

Later in the second year children seem able to understand the boundaries between their own and other's actions, allowing them to engage in genuine turn taking. An understanding of the "other" is still limited, however. They may know that the parent's hands must be removed, but infants may not wait for the parent to do it, instead assuming both roles and removing the parent's hands themselves.

Then, by the end of the second year, there emerges a genuine understanding that self and others are independent agents; that is, both actors in the social exchange are playing separate roles. Now toddlers can, for example, play a real game of hide-and-seek. At a younger age they will most likely jump out of hiding before being found, as though the distinction between hider and seeker is blurred. By age 2, however, waiting to be found may still be hard, but at least they run in the opposite direction when the seeker comes near. They recognize the separateness of people's roles and intentions.

Some of the best evidence that toddlers recognize their own agency (responsibility for acts) derives from emotional reactions that occur during this period. Toddlers show obvious pleasure when a puzzle is completed or a problem is solved, and more so when *they* complete the task than when it is done by an experimenter (Stipek, Recchia, & McClintic, 1992). Likewise, they are ashamed when scolded for a wrongdoing (see the next section).

Awareness of standards and the beginnings of self-regulation

The process of acquiring a set of rules, values, and, ultimately, principles, as well as using such standards as guides for behavior, takes place over the entire course of childhood and adolescence. Still, major advances toward standard-governed behavior occur during the preschool period, with precursors apparent even in the second year of life. Standard-governed behavior evolves in a logical manner from these precursors. The beginnings of behavioral control, which are consequent to the dawning awareness of standards for behavior, is considered a hallmark of the toddler period (Maccoby, 1980).

Even by the middle of the second year, toddlers show a sensitivity to social demands – for example, understanding that certain activities are forbidden (Kochanska, 1993; Kopp, 1989). They may hesitate, start and then stop the behavior, or, at times, do the behavior while looking at the caregiver. They also show an awareness of things not being as they should be (Emde, Biringen, Clyman, & Oppenheim, 1991; Stipek et al., 1992). This is seen in expressions of uncertainty or distress regarding a flawed object or distress when an external standard is violated or cannot be met (as when they cannot do something they are told to do). Moreover, they are sensitive to the distress of others (Zahn-Waxler, Radke-Yarrow, Wagner, & Chapman, 1992), as well as to others' transgressions (Dunn & Munn, 1985). Such reactions are critical for what they reveal and portend about development, especially with regard to the child's own actions as a major basis of such emotions as shame, guilt, and pride. These reactions remain quite primitive in the toddler period, however; for example, such reactions show no distinctiveness with regard to whether a performance standard or a parental rule was violated. They have been interpreted as perhaps reflecting a generalized reaction to adult disapproval and are best characterized as generalized arousal, often having a strong quality of uncertainty (Kochanska, 1993), and may be mixtures of interest, upset, and amusement (e.g., Dunn & Munn, 1985). Only in subsequent years do they become more differentiated.

By the end of the second year, toddlers are responsive to negative affective signals (Emde, 1992) and show specific negative emotional reactions to their own transgressions. They show distress or "deviation anxiety" when they commit or are about to commit a forbidden behavior (Dienstbier, 1984; Hoffman, 1985; Kochanska, 1993). In experimental studies involving staged mishaps (juice spilled on a new shirt, a doll breaking while the toddler plays with it), a variety of negative emotions are displayed along with verbalized concern and even attempts at reparation (Cole et al., 1992). In more naturalistic research situations, toddlers also show spontaneous self-corrections, often mediated by language (Londerville & Main, 1981), perhaps, for example, saying, "No, can't," and getting back down from a place they were told not to be. Still, even by this age standards remain externally based, and the adherence to standards almost always requires an adult presence.

Developmental changes in emotional experience

From an integrative, organizational view of development, coordinated advances in the affective domain necessarily occur during this same toddler period. Self-awareness, a differentiation of self and others, and an increasing capacity to tolerate arousal all have inevitable consequences for the unfolding of the emotions, both the further differentiation and transformation of already present emotions and the emergence of new ones.

The transformation of existing emotions occurs both because there is an increased capacity to remain organized in the face of high arousal and because of the differentiation of self and others. Thus, the toddler can express *rage*, which has the intensity and all-involving character of very early frustration reactions yet the directedness characteristic of later anger. Similarly, toddlers can experience terror and glee at levels that would have been totally disorganizing earlier. Such tolerance of tension supports the toddler in initiating and sustaining raucous games. Uproarious laughter now occurs when the toddler is the agent in covering and uncovering the caregiver's face, for example.

The differentiation of self and other allows anger and joy to be expressed in new ways toward caregivers, resulting in the emergence of defiance and affection (the prototype of love). Toddlers are aware not only that the caregiver is separate (as 10-month-olds knew), but also that they themselves are separate from other people. As such, they can oppose others or experience feelings of positive regard that are no longer in reaction to specific events. For example, 18-month-olds can become excited in anticipation of the caregiver's return following a brief separation or maintain an angry mood over a period of time. Two-year-olds can initiate affectionate contact when not distressed and can resist control (at times for its own sake) with a strength that is testimony to the human spirit.

Important new emotions also arise during this phase, including shame and what may be termed "positive self-evaluation." Shame, for example, is the sense of the self exposed and vulnerable – the bad self (Erikson, 1963). Tomkins (1963) has contrasted shame with other negative emotions in the following way:

While terror and distress hurt, they are wounds inflicted from the outside . . . shame is felt as an inner torment, a sickness of the soul . . . the humiliated one . . . feels himself naked, defeated, alienated, lacking in dignity or worth. (p. 118)

It is, of course, the toddler's new understanding of self that makes possible such an emotional reaction. Given a fragile and rather undifferentiated self at this time, the toddler is vunerable to a global feeling of dissolution when being punished for a specific behavior (especially if done harshly or in a degrading way). On the other side, shame is paralleled by the capacity to feel globally pleased with oneself (the well-known cockiness of the toddler), which is qualitatively different from anything seen in the first year. When praised for some behavior there is a global swelling of the self. These affective experiences both reflect *and* define the emerging sense of self.

Michael Lewis (e.g., 1992; Lewis et al., 1992) has also argued that many emotions arising in this and the following developmental period are qualitatively different from the fundamental emotions of infancy. He refers to these emotions – which are not possible prior to the emergence of some objective sense of self (including self as agent), as well as some understanding of standards for behavior – as the "self-conscious" emotions or, to distinguish them from the fundamental emotions that emerge in infancy, the "secondary" emotions. He includes among these embarrassment, shame, pride, and guilt. All of these emotions, he argues, are clear indicators of an emerging self and, at the same time, are critical for consolidating the self that is emerging. Experiencing connections between one's acts and resulting feelings, as well as overt consequences, is central to the very sense of self.

Lewis argues that in contrast to the basic emotions of infancy, the self-conscious emotions are manifest in an array of postural, bodily, and verbal reactions rather than solely in a stereotyped facial response. Citing the work of others, for the emotion of shame he describes a lowering of the head and/or eyes, "collapsing bodies," tense posture with a stilling of one's behavior, and disingenuous smiles. In pride, by contrast, which is readily apparent by age 3, one sees an upright posture, perhaps with both arms and eyes raised, and "triumphant" expressions with broad smiles.

Within the present developmental perspective a further distinction and differentiation among the set of self-conscious emotions is proposed. In contrast to Lewis's analysis, here shame, guilt, and pride are not viewed as arising at the same age. Emotions such as pride and guilt do not emerge until the preschool years, building on precursors and prototypes in preceding periods. In contrast to toddler emotions such as shame, those of pride and guilt require both a more separated sense of self and the acquisition of *internal* standards of behavior, rather than simply sensitivity to external standards. As was the case in the analysis of primary emotions in infancy, guilt and pride are nonetheless conceptualized as evolving from emotions that have preceded them. These are shame (for guilt) and (for pride) what I have termed "positive self-evaluation" (Sroufe, 1979a). The toddler's emotions may be thought of as prototypes in that they involve the core essence of the more mature emotions – a diminution or a swelling of the self. Yet compared with the later emotions, feelings of shame and positive self-evaluation require only a rudimentary sense of good and bad conduct. They are more global, less specific reactions (feeling globally bad or good about the self) that go beyond the boundaries of a particular action and often entail an inexact appreciation of what one has done (Lewis, 1992). Moreover, the reactions of others are overwhelmingly influential to such feeling states. Guilt and pride, by contrast, can be readily experienced even when no one else is present.

The context of toddler emotional development

The developmental changes in psychological functioning described on the preceding pages unfold within a supportive context. Two critical and interrelated aspects of this context are the child's developing CNS and the child's ongoing attachment relationships, both of which support emotional changes in many ways. At the same time, changes in the child and in the child's experience have an impact on relationships and on the forming brain itself.

Normative changes in brain development and functioning

Remarkable changes in the CNS continue to occur in the second year of life (Schore, 1994). For survival purposes, excitatory subcortical structures are active from birth, and certain cortical structures related to the sympathetic nervous system mature rapidly in the first year. But many more finely tuned inhibitory processes, including those associated with the parasympathetic nervous system mature more slowly (Thompson, 1990). One critical development is the further maturation of the frontal lobes, such that by 15 months all layers of the cortex achieve a similar state of maturity. Beyond this, there are notable changes in brain organization. Perhaps most salient for our consideration is the maturation and hierarchical integration of two limbic circuits (Schore, 1994). There is expanded development of the lateral tegmental (inhibitory) limbic circuit in the orbitofrontal cortex that brings this system to the state of maturation earlier achieved by the ventral tegmental (excitatory) circuit. This allows for delayed response capacities, as well as more varied and more rapid shifts between emotional states.

These two systems are in balance and are mediated by different catecholamines. Such an organization allows for a rapid shift from sympathetic to parasympathetic responding. Schore and others argue that such a state transition is the neurophysiological prerequisite of the experience of shame, a rapid shift from sympathetic excitation to an inhibited, low-arousal state. (Likewise, they argue for the importance of recovery from the state of inhibition to a more positive state once again).

Socialization and emotional development

During the toddler period parents often begin to shift from rather uniform acceptance of behavior to more differential responses, with an increase in directiveness, instruction, and prohibition (Sroufe et al., in press). In one study it was estimated that parents of 11- to 17-month-olds express prohibitions once every 9 minutes (Power & Chapieski, 1986). Such prohibitions are often accompanied by disapproving affect and lead to complementary affective experiences in the toddler. In this and in other ways parents convey to toddlers the expectation that they are to begin controlling certain behaviors.

A number of investigators have emphasized the role of shame in the socialization of the toddler (see Schore, 1994, for a review). Such experiences are highly salient. Shame often occurs when the toddler is experiencing high levels of excitement and positive affect, perhaps in bringing some discovery to the caregiver (Izard, 1991). When the caregiver reacts with strong displeasure or disgust, the child experiences a sudden and dramatic disregulation of relationship attunement and a deflation or "decrescendo" of affect, along with a marked inhibition of motor behavior (Stern, 1985). Shame powerfully underscores the importance of the act in question.

The child's own development also plays an important role. This includes the emerging capacity to recognize emotional expressions of the caregiver and to represent experience. By the toddler period the child also has the capacity to sustain states of high, positive arousal, which is critical for experiencing the affective swing that marks shame.

That shame plays an important role in socialization and, ultimately, the movement toward self-regulation in no way suggests that parents should deliberately try to shame toddlers. Such experiences will occur inevitably, and they are only one facet of socialization. In fact, as we will pursue when discussing individual differences, it is critical that such experiences are relatively rare and are routinely followed by reestablished harmony in the parent–child relationship. Such a consequence will help the child learn that only certain behaviors must be inhibited, not positive affect itself, as well as that strong negative affect need not permanently disrupt the relationship (Malatesta-Magai, 1991).

The interaction of brain development and socialization

The maturing brain, of course, supports the process of socialization. It does so in a general way by sustaining the child's motor and cognitive advances (e.g., emerging language), which guide encounters with the social environment and make the child open to new social inputs. Moreover, postnatal developmental changes in brain structure and functioning support the emergence of new emotions in the toddler period and the beginnings of emotional regulation.

At the same time, socialization experiences within the caregiving relationship, along with attendant affect, influence the development of the brain itself. This is the central thesis of Alan Schore (1994). Schore argues that affective transactions in the toddler period, especially those associated with shame, produce neurohormonal changes in the developing brain. Such experiences activate the lateral tegmental noradrenergic (inhibitory) circuits of the dual limbic system and deactivate the ventral tegmental dopaminergic circuit. In time such experiences lead to differential elaboration of these circuits. For example, the "sprouting" of the "parasympathetic terminals into the overlying cortex allows for delivery of noradrenaline, and this bioamine acts to trophically induce a further maturation of the orbitofrontal regions" (p. 230). In this way differential experience can lead to individual differences in the balance between the two limbic circuits and, ultimately, variations in the autoregulation of affect and self-regulation more generally. Such observations underscore the critical importance of the toddler period in the development of individual patterns of emotional regulation.

Individual differences in the toddler period

The critical importance of individual differences during the toddler period has both empirical and theoretical support. Empirically, research shows that many characteristics become notably stable by this age, in sharp contrast to the infancy period. Such stability makes possible greater predictiveness of later child behavior. For example, stability in measures of emotional tone has been demonstrated in the toddler period, including various measures of both positive and negative affectivity (e.g., Bates, 1989; Rothbart, 1989). Some children are consistently rated as more cheerful, more sociable, and less irritable, characteristics that have a dramatic influence on emerging social relationships. Other investigators have shown that individual differences in physiological reactivity, fearfulness, anxiety, or inhibition in the face of novelty are stable by the toddler period and on into childhood (e.g., Broberg, Lamb, & Hwang, 1990; Gunnar, 1991; Kagan, Reznick, & Gibbons, 1989). Furthermore, some evidence has been found that in interaction with patterns of socialization, such individual differences are related to aspects of later self-regulation – for example, that fearful children react more strongly to power-assertive parenting techniques than do nonfearful children (Kochanska, 1991). In general, emerging differences in individual characteristics provide varied contexts for ongoing socialization.

Theoretically also, developmental accounts of the toddler period point to its profound importance. At every level of analysis, one may see critical roots of later patterns of adaptation. Neopsychoanalytic theorists, such as Erikson, Mahler, and Sander, have stressed the level of the self or consciousness. According to such thinkers, the newly emerging self is seen as malleable and vulnerable. In a sense, this period represents the initial framing of the personality. The first conscious experiences of the self occur during this phase, and as a consequence early, and perhaps prototypic, representations of the self are established, having as core features an individually varying sense of basic self-worth. Thus, in a context of emotional abandonment, chronic derrogation, or harsh treatment by the caregiver, the toddler is vulnerable to developing pervasive doubts about the capacity for self-regulation. Such a proposed vulnerability is in accord with the empirical findings on toddlers' acute sensitivity to adult approval and disapproval (e.g., Stipek et al., 1992).

At a more behavioral level the roots of impulse control are proposed to be laid out during this phase (Kochanska, 1993; Maccoby, 1980). In the face of clear, firm, and reasonable external limits, in contrast to relatively lacking, inconsistent, or unrealistically stringent limits, the basis for flexible self-regulation of behavior is established.

Finally, during the toddler period individual patterns of basic neurophysiological regulation may be acquired (Schore, 1994). Appropriate socialization experiences lead to a dynamic balancing of excitatory and inhibitory systems, such that excitation may be dampened and that there may be a recovery from inhibition. Affective arousal states may be modulated and the child may with some flexibility shift from one state to another. The experience of other children will lead to a truncated or overelaborated inhibitory system, or to lability and a lack of balancing between excitatory and inhibitory systems. It is argued that through experiences of repeated and differential caregiver-guided arousal modulation during the toddler period, there may be a basic entrainment of underlying physiological systems. For example, a child that is repeatedly provoked to states of high arousal, then shamed for misbehaving, may develop a vulnerability to dramatic overswings in emotion and physiological arousal.

The next chapter presents evidence indicating that stability of self-regulation, *as an individual characteristic*, emerges in the preschool period (e.g., Kopp, Krakow, & Vaughn, 1983). However, building blocks for such a stable self-structure are apparent in the toddler period. In complying with adult demands and in staying within boundaries provided by them in the toddler period, the child not only receives valuable experiences in modulating arousal and controlling behavior, but becomes confident in his or her own control abilities, as well as able to enhance a positive valuation of the self (a sense of basic goodness). Alternatively, during this phase the child is easily shamed and easily made to doubt, in a basic way, his or her ability to control impulses or, on the other hand, is easily driven into a pattern of unresponsivity to feeling or of a rigid control of impulses.

The developmental dynamics of the toddler transition

The movement toward autonomy and self-regulation is viewed as rooted in the quality of the earlier infant–caregiver relationship. In attachment relationship theory, for example, the security derived from the history of responsive care, and repeated experiences of using the caregiver as a base for exploration and comfort when threatened or distressed, support toddlers' positive expectations concerning autonomous activities now (e.g., Sroufe, 1990). Secure in their attachment relationships, that is, confident in the availability of the caregiver, toddlers are free to move out more on their own into the world of objects and to engender and express the range of consequent feelings. Should emotional disregulation occur, regulation may readily be reachieved by utilizing support available from the caregiver. Patterns of arousal modulation and expectations concerning encounters with novelty have already been established and are simply carried forward in a new way as the child's own capacities expand. Active participation in the dyadic regulation of emotion leads inevitably to an expanded role for the self in regulation.

Margaret Mahler (e.g., Mahler et al., 1975) has provided one detailed description of the way earlier care supports the transition toward autonomous regulation. In Mahler's terms (but quite parallel to Ainsworth's), a "symbiotic" (close) relationship in infancy paradoxically supports the movement toward autonomy or "individuation." Because the infant has confidence in the caregiver and because the caregiver is available for "checking back," the toddler may move out into the world, which Mahler refers to as "practicing." The toddler relies on the caregiver even when at times not utilizing literal physical support. When in the course of exploration some mild threat is encountered, the child may look to the caregiver, but because dyadic arousal modulation patterns are so well established, emotional equilibrium is reachieved without the need for physical comforting. Within certain boundaries the child is self-regulating, with the caregiver in a more auxiliary role. By allowing the child such autonomy and at the same time protecting the child from overwhelming stress and aiding him or her in restoring equilibrium when necessary, the caregiver promotes the growth of self-regulation.

The child achieves a degree of autonomy without at first even recognizing the separateness involved. An enchanting description by Søren Kierkegaard (1938) captures this process exquisitely:

The loving mother teaches her child to walk alone. She is far enough from him so that she cannot actually support him, but she holds out her arms to him. She imitates his movements, and if he totters she swiftly bends as if to seize him, so that the child might believe that he is not walking alone . . . And yet, she does more.
Her face beckons like a reward, an encouragement. Thus, the child walks alone with his eyes fixed on his mother's face, not on the difficulties in his way. He supports himself by the arms that do not hold him and constantly strives towards the refuge in his mother's embrace, little suspecting that in the very same moment that he is emphasizing his need of her, he is proving that he can do without her, because he is walking alone. (p. 85)

Mahler goes on to say that such autonomous functioning, supported by emotional closeness, does in time inevitably lead the child to recognize separateness from the caregiver and creates a potential crisis in the second year. The infantile closeness with, and ready accessibility of, the caregiver is a great deal to leave behind. Moreover, as part of their expanding autonomy and moving toward self-regulation, infants must at times maintain their own inner aims even when these are contrary to those of the caregiver. Thus, a certain degree of conflict is an inevitable part of development during this phase and potentially threatens the child's feelings of security and harmony with the caregiver. As Sander (1975) has argued, this relationship conflict is important. Especially in the historical context of stable dyadic regulation, taking such a contrary position allows the child to

> begin dimly to recognize his own role in determining action, i.e., that he is pursuing his *own* intention rather than reacting to a lead. The emergence of autonomy as here proposed is based on the further differentiation of awareness – especially that of inner perception, which sets the stage for the "disjoin" of the self-regulatory core. (p. 141)

The self cannot emerge without recognition of one's own inner aims. Moreover, resolving such conflicts is an important building block of the child's emerging sense of competence at problem solving, and as Erikson argues, it also deepens the child's trust in the caregiving relationship. Such prototypical conflict experiences within the security of the caregiving relationship can also represent a model for later close relationships, providing an abiding confidence that relationships may be sustained despite strife, which allows the person to risk conflict in relationships and, ultimately, to even see its value.

Normally, several factors conspire to help the child resolve the crisis of the second year and achieve a rapprochement with the caregiver. First, given a history of responsiveness, the child may be confident that the caregiver will remain available even now should strong need arise. Second, the infant evolves new ways of remaining in contact with the caregiver when operating in relative separation. Through countless experiences of showing discoveries and sharing affect at a distance, the child retains *psychological* contact even while moving away from *physical* contact; the connectedness is not dissolved but transformed. Also, the toddler period is not characterized merely by willfulness, expressions of autonomy, and negativism. As Sander (1975) has pointed out, not all of the toddler's initiative is directed away from the caregiver, but "is balanced by bids for reciprocation with her" (p. 140). Finally, the motive to explore and master the environment is its own strong impetus for development. Children show pleasure in discovery and problem solving even in the absence of praise (Stipek et al., 1992). If, during Mahler's practicing phase, exploratory activities have been interesting, gratifying, and relatively nonthreatening, the pull of the external world will more than overbalance the need for the former symbiotic closeness.

For most toddlers, then, the issue for this period is not autonomy *or* connectedness, but autonomy *with* connectedness (Emde & Buchsbaum, 1990). From the infancy period the child brings forward an investment in participating in a harmonious, affectively close relationship. New capacities and initiatives raise fresh challenges for the child–caregiver relationship but also provide new ways to maintain connectedness. Children do not need to be forced to comply with alien parental standards. They need to be shown the standards, through clear affective expressions and in other ways, and they need to be supported when their own capacities for behavioral control and arousal modulation are exceeded, but generally they will wish to comply with parental desires (Ainsworth, Bell, & Slayton, 1974; Kochanska, 1993; Maccoby, 1980; Rheingold, 1983; Waters, Kondo-Ikemura, & Richters, 1990). The child is already invested in the relationship system. As more is learned about its ways and rules in the course of development, the child naturally seeks to adapt to these standards (Waters et al., 1990), because parental goals and demands are part of "a history of joint activity in the pursuit of mutual goals" (Maccoby & Martin, 1983, p. 69). Following Ainsworth and colleagues (1974), this might be termed a view of "socialization from the inside" (Sroufe et al., in press).

A strong prediction emerges from these considerations – namely, that the quality of the emotional relationship between infants and caregivers should forecast patterns of adaptation in the toddler period. For example, infants that bring forward a history of secure attachment should show a smoother transition to effective autonomous functioning, having evolved positive expectations concerning their exploratory competence and a capacity to modulate arousal and communicate affectively within the relationship, as well as confidence in the ongoing availability of the caregiver. They will enthusiastically engage opportunities and challenges in the environment up to the limits of their capacities and will also flexibly draw on caregiver resources when needed, commonly cooperating with the parent with reference to joint goals. On the other hand, anxiously attached infants should be more likely to function poorly as toddlers, either because of their insecurity concerning separation and their related poverty of exploration or because of their difficulty maintaining emotional closeness as the period of separation and individuation unfolds. Both a continued preoccupation with the caregiver – often manifest in such behavior as tantrums and frustration, having as their goal caregiver involvement – and a precocious independence (withholding of affective involvement in play, indirect negativism, and/or inability to draw on the caregiver when their own resources are exhausted) would be viewed as maladaptations, with notable consequences for later development.

Assessment and validation of individual differences

Individual differences in the toddler phase of development have been approached in two ways. The first, often followed by those working within a temperament perspective, has been to focus on particular dimensions of behavior. This research (discussed earlier) has been important for showing that there is a degree of consistency and stability in emotional experience and emotional expressiveness by the toddler period, and that such individual differences have implications for future behavior. But such research on specific characteristics has seldom been concerned with descriptions of the *development* of such differences (beyond looking at earlier measures of the same trait) or with the organization of such characteristics into an individual personality.

The second approach, that embraced and presented in detail here, is to reference assessments to the overall pattern and quality of toddler behavior with respect to the salient issues of the period – that is, to assess how well the toddler is negotiating the transition to self-regulation of emotion under the guidance of the caregiver. Such a complex level of assessment seems appropriate, given the integrative nature of the self-regulation issue, and this multivariate, organizational approach has proved quite powerful.

Within an organizational/adaptational perspective, children are viewed as negotiating the issues of the toddler transition period in different ways. Variations of interest lie in the different patterns and behavioral organizations that characterize individual transitions – that is, the quality of guided self-regulation achieved. This is a different level of analysis than that focused on specific traits. Children who are highly active or low-keyed, bold or reserved, may be moving toward self-regulation smoothly or with great difficulty. Even when the focus is on such complex, organizational differences, individual variation may be reliably described.

Assessment efforts begin with a consideration of the behavioral organization of the well-functioning toddler, based on the theoretical issues outlined earlier. While there is much room for stylistic variations, certain patterns of behavior seem optimal for allowing positive experiences in parent-guided regulation and movement toward self-regulation itself. At the least, it is important for toddlers to engage in new experiences and problems in the environment with some consistency and persistence and to engage them as much as possible relying on their own inner resources. This entails generating enthusiasm for mastery or at least a degree of interest and curiosity. For engagement to be sustained and repeated, positive affect must overbalance negative affect, and a degree of arousal modulation is involved. Mastery experiences will be compromised for the child who cannot become engaged or who is easily frustrated. To move toward self-regulation the child must stretch the developing capacity to maintain organized behavior in the face of arousal (while still having the parental relationship as a directly supporting context). At the same time, in the face of limited capabilities, the child must at times draw on the greater resources of the parent. Children who can directly and clearly signal needs, and who have parents who respond to and even anticipate such needs, have the freedom to probe the limits of their own capacities and yet routinely have positive mastery experiences, as well as practice in smooth, ongoing emotional regulation. Using parents as a resource when needed, and complying with their directives and support when required, also helps the child move toward an internalization of control, which is the hallmark of the next period.

Many arenas and diverse measures could serve the goals of an organizational assessment. They would have the following in common: that they be broadly based (at the level of behavioral organization rather than at the level of specific skills); that they be integrative, that is, call on the organization of affect, cognition, and social behavior with respect to context; that they center on real-life tasks, taxing the affect regulation capacities of the child (i.e., have a variable degree of challenge); and that they, of course, be keyed to the salient developmental issues of the period. In this way, while not requiring separation and reunion experiences, such assessments would be parallel to Ainsworth's paradigmatic attachment assessments. Our own approach, now used widely by others (e.g., Bates et al., 1985; Spiker, Ferguson, & Brooks-Gunn, 1993), involved a free-play period, a toy cleanup session, and a graded series of problems, all with a caregiver present (e.g., Matas, Arend, & Sroufe, 1978). Each situation involved a different "load." The play session was minimally taxing for both toddler and parent and normally should have posed no problem for independent functioning. The cleanup session placed a maximal load on the parents who, at a prearranged signal, were instructed to interrupt the child's play and get the child to put the toys on shelves. Some conflict of wills seemed unavoidable. The graded series of four problems (the simplest being to push a toy out of a slot with a stick; the hardest being to weight down a board with a block in order to get candy up through a hole in a large box) ensured that each child would progress from problems that he or she *could* solve alone to at least one problem that was beyond the child's abilities. It was ideal for assessing the flexibility of both child and parent with respect to the goals of the child's emotional regulation and guided self-control.

Within this procedure it was possible not only to examine all of the various dimensions of behavior relevant to the movement toward self-regulation, but also to assess the overall organization of behavior across changing contexts. The play session afforded a view of toddlers' ability to become positively and creatively involved in exploration and play under their own initiative. The cleanup session, followed by the tool problems, allowed an analysis and comparison of compliance with parental directives across situations where the children would most likely wish to comply (the tools) and a situation where their goals and parental goals might well be at cross-purposes. Such a comparison reveals much more than a simple frequency count of noncompliance in a single situation and without regard to context. The tool problems also allowed assessment of children's enthusiasm, affectivity, frustration tolerance, and flexibility in utilizing resources.

Our approach has been to rely heavily on rating scales because they can be readily designed to be sensitive to context, but these are supported by more straightforward behavioral measures (e.g., the persistence rating and a measure of actual time spent working on the problems; a negative affect rating and the frequency of crying and fussing). To capture the overall organization of behavior, the diverse rating scales were factor analyzed, cluster analyzed, and/or assembled into rational profiles (e.g., Gove, 1983), and in later studies we also made molar ratings of the overall quality of the child's behavior and experience in the session. Factor analysis revealed a coherent broad-band "competence" factor, which included most major variables but was loaded most heavily with measures of enthusiasm, positive affect, persistence, and compliance. Interestingly, this factor was orthogonal to a second factor that could be viewed as more temperament based (frustration behavior, negative affect) and was relatively independent of Bayley DQ (which itself loaded on a third factor), all implying that the first factor captured unique aspects of the quality of adaptation.

Validity data for these assessments were impressive in our original study and in two follow-up studies at the University of Minnesota with a different sample (Erickson, Egeland, & Sroufe, 1985; Gove, 1983). In each case, the quality of toddler adaptation was strongly related to attachment security in infancy. Those with secure histories were more persistent, flexible, compliant, enthusiastic, and affectively positive than those with histories of anxious attachment. Moreover, the toddler assessments, especially at the most molar level, predicted functioning into later childhood, including broad aspects of competence, such as curiosity, self-esteem, independence, and positive peer behavior, but also flexible self-regulation specifically (Sroufe, 1983).

The individual differences captured by these assessments appeared to be at the level of behavioral and emotional organization (and toddler and parent as a regulatory system), rather than being attributable to underlying temperamental dimensions. The temperament factor was not significantly related to attachment security, for example; and where certain specific characteristics were differentiated, they were so in terms of their organization, not mere presence or frequency. Thus, in the toy cleanup situation those with secure histories were just as likely as those with anxious histories to exhibit oppositional behavior (though ultimately complying as their caregivers maintained limits). However, on the tool problems, especially when the child sought help, those with anxious histories showed far more noncompliance with parental directives.

There was also a meaningful variation in caregiver behavior during the toddler assessments. It is noteworthy that such differences were strongly predicted by

attachment history, even though in the attachment assessments only infant behavior was the focus. Caregivers whose infants showed effective, secure base
behavior in infancy now encouraged their toddlers, shared their joy in mastery,
anticipated frustration, and comforted them when needed (reflected in a rating
of "supportive presence"), as well as provided clear, appropriate, well-timed
cues that neither left the children to struggle too much nor robbed them of a
mastery experience by prematurely solving the problem for them ("quality of
assistance"). Furthermore, these caregiver ratings likewise predicted child behavior in the preschool when the caregiver was not present (Arend, Gove, &
Sroufe, 1979; Sroufe, 1983) and even the attachment classifications of second-
born siblings an average of 3 years later (Ward et al., 1990).

These findings in total suggest that in carrying out assessments of early caregiver regulation of infant arousal and affect, subsequent attachment assessments
(dyadic regulation), and the follow-up toddler assessments in this way, one is,
in fact, capturing individual differences in the process of moving from dyadic
regulation toward self-regulation. It is the case that the single best outcome
criterion (with respect to attachment) and the best predictor of later self-
regulation in the preschool years from the toddler assessment was the overall
rating of the effectiveness of the pair in providing the child with a positive
experience of mastery, with capacities stretched but not strained. It is also the
case that attachment and toddler assessments taken together more strongly predict later flexible self-control and other aspects of individual competence than
does either assessment alone (Erickson et al., 1985; Sroufe et al., 1990).

In subsequent studies distinctions among maladaptive patterns of toddler adaptation were underscored (e.g., Gove, 1983). Both cluster analysis and a priori
rating scale profiles distinguished those who had histories of avoidant and resistant attachment in terms of patterns of behavioral and emotional regulation.
Across the tool problems, as difficulty increased, the resistant group became
increasingly oppositional, highly frustrated, angry, and distressed. While they
sought more contact with caregivers, the contact became more negative and they
became increasingly oppositional. Their caregivers, in complement, became
more active in directing the child, but the quality of their assistance deteriorated.
A common result was for these pairs to become embroiled in conflict, with the
tool problem seemingly fading into the background. Unlike the resistant group,
those with avoidant histories did not often directly confront or direct frustration
at the caregiver but showed anger out of context, as well as indirect or passive
noncompliance (perhaps going on as though they didn't hear the caregiver or
hitting the caregiver with one of the tools, apparently without immediate prov-
ocation). In fact, these partners often seemed emotionally uninvolved throughout, even when the problems became too difficult for the child. The children
did not increase contact seeking and the parents did not increase directives. Both

groups with histories of anxious attachment behaved in sharp contrast to those with secure histories. These children effectively sought increased help as the problems became harder and the caregiver provided more clear and direct cues, resulting in greatly reduced negative affect, a positive problem solving experience, and shared joy in mastery.

Continuity and change in adaptation

The position just outlined maintains strongly that patterns of toddler adaptation are best conceived as evolving from qualitative differences in dyadic emotional regulation that preceded them. They are reflective of a relationship system in the process of being carried forward and internalized by the child. Yet nothing in this relationship perspective denies a role for endogenous child variation (which necessarily enters into and is transformed by the relationship system) or imputes blame to caregivers. The most dramatic evidence for the transforming power of relationships and for the inappropriateness of blaming parents comes from the data on change. Despite significant and at times dramatic continuity, a substantial change in individual adaptation has also been demonstrated, especially in the toddler and early childhood periods. And the most strongly supported mediators of transformation are changes in life stress, social support, and the quality of adult relationships available to parents (e.g., Belsky & Isabella, 1988; Erickson et al., 1985; Carlson et al., in press; Vaughn et al., 1979). Child adaptation, with respect to the movement toward effective self-regulation, is enhanced or hampered (with respect to previous adaptation) to the degree that parental resources and challenges change. Intervention studies also show (though with some inconsistency) that both dyadic regulation and guided self-regulation in the toddler period may be enhanced through experimenter-provided support of caregivers (e.g., Lieberman et al., 1991; Spiker et al., 1993; van den Boom, in press). This is congruent with a relationship systems view of the process of individual development.

Conclusion

During the infancy period there were important developments both in the range of affective experiences and in the regulation of affect within the infant–caregiver system. The regulation of emotion at that time was due to the presence and actions of the caregiver, as well as to the infant's increasingly intentional bids and expectations based on the reliability and predictability of care. But in the toddler period the child moves toward self-regulation of affect, based on greatly increased intentionality and self-determination. Toddlers seek to carry out their own aims and to remain autonomous even in the face of challenges and frustrations. Affect is less tied to immediate circumstances and is more often due to the actions and desires of the child than to environmental events per se, and parents may be recognized as a source of interference, as well as support.

Such is the movement toward autonomy in the toddler. Recognizing the self as the origin of action, the toddler can experience both shame and positive self-evaluation and can engage in purposeful, even angry, struggles with caregivers that persist beyond some specific cause. Within certain boundaries the toddler is much more able than the infant to regulate affect – for example, fighting down tears or meting out angry feelings in subtle and indirect ways. But as stronger feelings, impulses, or desires arise, the toddler's emerging capacities for self-regulation are easily overwhelmed. An important issue becomes whether the caregiver can continue to provide guidance and support. Despite the intentionality and willfulness often characteristic of the period, toddlers do not yet have the capacity of self-management in a wide range of circumstances. Even though now outside the "symbiotic orbit" (Mahler), the toddler at times remains reliant on the caregiver for limits and boundaries. As will be discussed in the next chapter, only if such external control remains dependable can the child develop flexible self-regulation of feelings, impulses, and desires.

Theorists writing primarily about the realm of cognitive development have introduced concepts such as the "zone of proximal development" (Vygotsky, 1978) and "scaffolding" (Bruner, 1975) to refer to the way that more competent others (e.g., parents) can provide frameworks within which children can operate at the limits of their capacities, even stretching them. Thus, within the guidance, boundaries, and support provided by caregivers, toddlers can achieve a substantial level of self-regulation, which prepares the way for the more true self-regulation that is to emerge. Vygotsky (1978) summarized this as a general characteristic of development in the following way: "Every function in the child's cultural development appears twice: first, on the social level, and later, on the individual level; first *between* people (*interpsychologically*), and then *inside* the child (*intrapsychologically*)" (p. 57). So it is with the development of self-regulation.

12 The growth of self-regulation

In becoming internalized, adopted strategies which first characterized regulatory relationships with the interpersonal surround will now function as features of self-regulation and eventually characterize personality idiosyncrasy.

Sander (1976)

A psychological function . . . which is externally regulated in one phase of infancy is internalized and autoregulated in the succeeding phase.

Schore (1994)

In contrast to the situation for the toddler, which is paradoxically referred to as "*guided* self-regulation," the preschool-age child in Western culture is expected to assume a much larger role in the self-regulation of emotions and impulses. The task becomes to contain, modify, and redirect impulses even when briefly not under immediate adult supervision. While still requiring adult monitoring, reinforcement, and support, children must to a large extent follow rules and prohibitions without direct adult input; that is, they are to internalize the standards for behavioral control and conduct themselves in accordance with these standards, even inhibiting strong impulses on their own. Also, to an increasing extent they must protect *themselves* from being overwhelmed by stimulation or the disorganizing influences of their own feelings. In psychoanalytic terms such protective processes are referred to as "defenses," which are a part of normative development but which may also become pathological.

The child is now expected to manage frustration and generally to modulate emotional expression. Children must delay, defer, and accept substitutions without becoming aggressive or disorganized by frustration, and they are expected to cope well with high arousal, whether due to environmental challenge or fatigue. At the same time they are to be spontaneous and exuberant when circumstances permit. Children, of course, continue to require some direction from adults, and occasional breakdowns in emotional control, especially when taxed, fatigued, or ill, are an expected part of healthy emotional development. Still, progress is remarkable during this period.

Another aspect of the growth of emotional control has been studied under the label of dependency. While preschool children often show "instrumental dependency" (seeking assistance with problems or tasks beyond one's abilities), they are seen to be far less "emotionally dependent" than toddlers (Hartup, 1963; Maccoby, 1980; Sroufe et al., 1983). Emotional independence includes being able to operate in the environment without constant attention, guidance, and nurturance from adults. The world of peers and objects, not caregivers or teachers, should command the preschool child's attention. The preschool child who cannot separate from parents, who chronically hovers near the teacher, or who routinely acts out or performs antics to receive attention or praise is viewed as unduly emotionally dependent. Well-functioning preschoolers still rely on adults when injured, ill, or disappointed, and they share discoveries with them and enjoy interchanges. Such behavior, in fact, will generally promote expanded commerce with the environment. It is when the need for adult contact or attention interferes with mastery that emotional growth is seen to be compromised (Sroufe et al., 1983; Urban, Carlson, Egeland, & Sroufe, 1991).

As part of this increasing self-sufficiency, the preschool child develops certain aids to emotional control (Maccoby, 1980). Many of these, of course, derive from cognitive advances, including the ability to understand (primarily through language) that a desired outcome will occur after a delay, that negative consequences will follow certain acts while positive consequences will follow others, that different actions will make others feel badly or well, and so forth. Another important capacity, perhaps not sufficiently appreciated, is the development of fantasy play. Through such play children can express vital feelings in a controlled context and by repeating experiences in varied symbolic ways can work through conflict and painful feelings (Breger, 1974). Fantasy play is a major tool for emotional regulation, available primarily to the preschool child, being poorly developed before this time (Sroufe et al., in press), and declining as the child moves into Piaget's phase of concrete operations (Doyle et al., 1985). Individual differences in such play may be an important indication of emotional regulation during this period.

All of these capacities may be seen to converge in establishing relationships with peers, a central issue for the preschool child. Adequate peer relationships involve not only an understanding of the rules of give-and-take, but the ability to be emotionally engaged and to find and share fun, the capacity to understand and respond to the feelings of others, and the capacity to regulate the tension that is invitable in complex social interactions (Sroufe et al., 1984). In a sense, peer relationships complete the cycle, from dyadic regulation to self-regulation and back to dyadic regulation again, though in a qualitatively different way since it is now among equals. Given how the interaction with peers calls on all of the preschool child's capacities for emotional regulation, it is easy to see how assessments of peer functioning may represent one of the best overall indicators of individual adaptation during this period, predicting functioning throughout the childhood years and into adulthood (Parker & Asher, 1987; Sroufe et al., in press).

Individual styles of adaptation with respect to these issues are quite distinctive at this time. Moreover, there is a remarkable coherence to the organization of the various aspects of adaptation. Flexible self-control, emotional independence, curiosity, rich fantasy play, empathy, and effective, warm relationships with peers and adults tend to co-occur, and there is patterning to maladaptation as well (Eder & Mangelsdorf, in press; Magnusson & Torestad, 1993; Sroufe et al., in press). For example, children rated high on aggression do not show much prosocial behavior or rich social fantasy play, and children who are overtly dependent on teachers are neglected by peers and are rated low on expressed curiosity (Henderson & Moore, 1980; Sroufe, 1983). In general, this is the age when unique styles of emotional regulation seem to become consolidated, with some children characteristically withholding engagement, avoiding emotionally arousing situations, and disowning feelings of anger or fear, other children showing chronic dysregulation, diffuse anxiety, an absence of interpersonal boundaries, and so forth. Such coherence of behavioral organization, as well as strongly evolved expectations regarding the self and the social world by this age, allow one to speak of the emergence of "personality." As will be discussed further after considering issues of normative development, coherent and stable individual differences have been clearly documented in the preschool period.

Normative aspects of emotional development in the preschool years

The growth of self-control

Numerous aspects of self-control develop rapidly in the preschool years, having dramatic implications for emotional expression and regulation. By this age children show a much improved capacity to direct and even to monitor their own behavior (Kopp et al., 1983). They also show a noted advance in the ability to inhibit actions (Arend, 1983; Kopp et al., 1983). For example, the Russian investigator A. R. Luria (1980) required children to press a bulb held in the hand when a green light appeared, but not to press it when a red light appeared. Two-year-olds pressed repeatedly for both lights, but by age 4 children were able to inhibit responses to the red light. Such inhibitory capacities would also apply to emotional expression, which may at times be masked by this age (Izard & Malatesta, 1987). A third capacity is that of remaining organized in the face of frustration. Two-year-olds show greatly reduced tantrum behavior and other signs of frustration in the face of unsolveable problems compared with 18-

month-olds (van Lieshout, 1975), but by age 3½ years even distress in such a situation is greatly reduced, with children often directing themselves to alternative creative activities (Arend, 1983; Sroufe et al., in press). In keeping with this and other capacities, children also show more self-control in their relationships with parents. Direct defiance and passive noncompliance decline notably between ages 2 and 5 years, being replaced by negotiation and increased simple refusal (Kuczynski & Kochanska, 1990).

The internalization of standards

Congruent with and as part of the emerging capacity for self-control, the preschool child also shows clear signs of having internalized standards for behavior. This is revealed in the shift from external control to internal control cited earlier (e.g., Power & Manire, 1992). In particular, there is a notable increase in the capacity to delay and to comply in the absence of the caregiver (Kopp et al., 1983).

The internalization of standards is also manifested in advancing reactions to success and failure. This is shown not only in clear negative emotional responses to task failure (pouts and frowns), which appear after 30 months of age and increase through the preschool years (Stipek et al., 1992), but in changed responses to successes as well. In the series of experiments by Stipek and colleagues, children were observed in competitive situations and in situations in which either they or an experimenter completed a task. Only after the toddler period did they respond differentially, showing more pleasure to their own successes. Moreover, their clearly positive reactions to such completions became less dependent on the adult reactions, occurring before or even in the absence of seeking feedback from the experimenter. Such behavior indicates the advent of performance evaluation.

Another manifestation of developing internalization lies in the concern shown for others. In the third year children not only respond emotionally to mishaps they cause or witness, but also seek to make reparations (Cole, Barrett, & Zahn-Waxler, 1992). They often refuse to violate parental prohibitions and show signs of affective distress, even in the absence of the parent, and they may confess to parents upon their return when violations did occur (Emde & Buchsbaum, 1990). All of this has led Emde et al. (1991) to conclude that by age 3 years there is the rise of the "moral self."

Indirect evidence of the child's internalization of standards and, reciprocally, one major factor promoting such internalization, are the changing socialization practices of parents during the preschool period (Power & Manire, 1992; Sears, Maccoby, & Levin, 1957). Parental control practices shift from direct, at times strong controls (e.g., explicit prohibitions, direct intervention, demonstration) to indirect external controls (e.g., praise) and finally to the encouragement of internal controls. The latter is revealed in the increased use of reasoning and persuasion. Based on a review of the literature and their own research, Power and Manire (1992) conclude that when parents provide information concerning rules and values, as well as underscore them through consistent behavior, children are more likely to show socially responsible behavior in the parents' absence.

Emotions based on internalized standards

The cognitive and social changes of the preschool period have important consequences for emotional life. The basis for emotional reactions changes. In contrast to infancy and the early toddler period, when reactions are dependent on the presence and affective responses of parents, and the later toddler period, when the reaction may be based on an explicit prohibition, emotional reactions of preschoolers are based on internalized standards. A guilt reaction occurs, for example, not because of what parents do, or even what they say, but because the behavior is "wrong." Such reactions are also more organized (as opposed to, e.g., global anxiety) and more context specific, being in response to particular wrong behavior, which therefore allows reparation (Kochanska, 1993; Lewis, 1992). Negative emotions are now not so much due to a fear of being punished as to an undermining of self-esteem (Kochanska, 1993).

Likewise, true pride is distinguished from earlier joy in mastery or global positive feelings about the self because it is dependent on self-evaluative, internalized standards. Thus, preschoolers show more pleasure and other signs of pride (see Chapter 11) when they have solved a problem than when the experimenter solves it (Stipek et al., 1992). Moreover, such signs are more common and stronger when the problem solved is difficult than when it is easy (Lewis et al., 1992). Such a change reveals that children not only evaluate task complexity, but have their own standards for performance.

Individual differences in the preschool period

The process of self-organization

Self (or personality) is best conceived not as a set of traits that individuals "have" to various degrees, but as an inner organization of attitudes, beliefs, and values (Sroufe, 1990). Key features of such an organization include individuals' degree of openness to the range of emotional experience, unique styles of regulating arousal and emotion, confidence in their own regulation capacities, and their expectations about others and relationships in this process. Such beliefs and expectations define the affective core of the self. And it is by the preschool period that a coherent and stable self in this sense may be said to be present.

One of the most intriguing of all developmental questions concerns the emergence of the self. As defined in Chapter 1, the self is truly an emergent entity. Clearly, one may not speak of a self in the newborn, whose cortex is hardly functional (see Chapter 2) and who has not a single belief, much less an organization of expectations and attitudes. Nor is any observation of newborn behavior sufficient to predict the remarkable, complex, and self-regulating organization that we call the individual self. Yet from a developmental perspective one cannot simply postulate the self as springing into existence (something arising from nothing). How then is the emergence of this unique organization to be explained?

As forecasted in previous chapters, and as clearly articulated by Louis Sander (e.g., 1975), the resolution of this problem lies in the fact that there is present from the beginning a self-regulating organization, sufficiently complex to provide the basis for the evolving of the self. This organization, however, resides not in the newborn alone, but in the infant–caregiving system, which at first may be described in terms of the caregiver's synchronization with the infant. The emerging self, then, reflects the incorporation of this systemic or dyadic organization into the developing psyche of the child through a series of phases in the course of development. In the preceding chapters a process was described wherein the growth of intention and awareness led to increasingly active participation by the child in the regulation process, first participating in chains of behavior orchestrated by the caregiver, then initiating familiar sequences, then enacting novel procedures adjusted in terms of goals for caregiver behavior, and at the same time progressing from inborn reflexive behaviors that automatically elicited caregiver ministration to explicit, intentional signals that called for regulatory assistance. It was argued that at each stage the nature and quality of the dyadic organization in a basic sense recapitulated that which preceded. Thus, the infant's role became more active, but the organization remained the same. The infant's emerging capacities fit into the already existing framework. Then, in the toddler period, as the child moved toward self-regulation, playing an ever larger role in emotional regulation, his or her own regulatory efforts were guided by patterns of arousal and affect modulation repeatedly experienced in the earlier phases. Such patterns are physiologically entrained (Schore, 1994) and are also supported by strong cognitive expectations concerning the likely consequences of emotional experiences and states of heightened arousal, as well as the availability of support for maintaining organization. Further, at this stage the boundaries of arousal and affect expression continue to be monitored and guided by the caregiver, in keeping with the organizational goals that have been present from the beginning.

Sander describes a final phase of the emergence of the self in terms of a "disjoin" of the self-regulatory core from the infant–caregiver system, along with a new level of awareness. Congruent with the ideas presented in Chapter 11, there is no need to postulate a specific motive for separation. Rather, as children acquire self-regulatory capacities they will naturally exercise them, drawn forward simply by the motive for expanded autonomous functioning. Sander's description of the normative process of this disjoin has clear implications for investigating individual differences. He draws on Piaget's ideas of "operations" and "reversibility" to explain the acquisition of *self-constancy*. During the third year the child can perturb the relationship with the caregiver, not only deliberately and with foreknowledge, but also with an awareness that the caregiver is aware of this intent (shared awareness). Repeated perturbing operations represent a threat to harmonious regulation within the system. But when such perturbations are continually reversed and harmony with the caregiver is re-created, through reparative actions by either child or parent, a new sense of the durability and trustworthiness of the relationship and the self in it emerges, a sense of constancy even in the midst of profound change.

The emergence of such a stable and serviceable self-regulatory core is based on the entire history of harmonious regulation, with the gradual transfer of regulatory functions to the child, as well as on the caregiver's acceptance at this time of greater independence for the child. Should the caregiver be threatened by this independence or punitive of the child's expressions of autonomy and need to experiment with a contrary position, important features of the inner self may be compromised. Relaxed acceptance by the caregiver of the child's explorations (confidence that the relationship will remain intact) and continued availability for closeness following the child's lead promote flexible self-regulation by the child.

In terms of attachment theory, confidence in the relationship (on the part of both caregiver and child) becomes self-confidence; security within the attachment relationship leads to self-reliance. In contrast, children who have experienced chaotic, inconsistent care have neither the reservoir of positive regulatory experiences to guide their own efforts nor the confidence in the caregiver (and consequently themselves) required for flexible experimentation with regulation. Likewise, children who have been forced toward independence precociously due to emotional unavailability or harsh care on the part of the caregiver will tend to adopt rigid regulatory strategies, often carried out in isolation or at least without making use of social resources.

Attachment theory can be combined with the work of Sander, Mahler, Erikson, and others (described in Chapter 11) to yield a developmental view of the emergence of unique, individual selves. In the normative case the individual's sense of security may be thought of as the core or innermost layer of this self

– that is, the individual's fundamental sense of others as caring, the self as worthy, and the world as safe. All of these are inevitable outcomes of a history of responsive care within the attachment relationship. Beyond this core, attitudinal base, actual experiences in pursuit of one's own inner aims and with guided self-regulation in the toddler period provide a second fundamental layer of the self. Often this builds on an earlier experience of agency within the caregiving relationship (derived from the contingent responsiveness of the caregiver), but the agency here concerns efforts to achieve intentional goals and to maintain some degree of emotional regulation through one's autonomous efforts. The child may learn in this phase that his or her inner aims and impulses are acceptable and valued (and, by extention, that the self is valued and valuable), and also evolve a sense of confidence in his or her own regulatory capacities. Success at guided self-regulation deepens the attitudinal bases for later competence, as well as providing experiences in regulation through one's own actions that may be drawn on in the future. An actual sense of instrumentality, competence and pride emerges in the preschool years and beyond as the child actually assumes self-regulatory responsibility and functions in the world of peers and other arenas that are at times outside of adult purview. These experiences are, of course, deeply important (and therefore require continued monitoring and guidance by adults), but they build on the attitudinal and experiential base of earlier history. In sum, the distillates of responsive care are *security, acceptability*, and *instrumentality*.

Variations or distortions in this process can occur in different ways and at different steps, leading to fundamental variations among individuals. While each history and each individual is unique, and complexities are substantial, certain general patterns of adaptation (or "coping strategies") may be described and related to fundamental emotions in each period.

In the first period, when responsive care is unavailable or inconsistently available infants are vulnerable to pervasive fearfulness, and anger becomes not a signal but a chronic experience. Two possible strategies for adaptation in such circumstances (associated with the two primary patterns of anxious attachment) are, on the one hand, to treat a wide array of situations as threatening and to perpetually signal to the caregiver and/or seek continual contact, and, on the other hand, to in a primitive way cut oneself off from affective experience and, especially, the need for tender care when aroused. (The "disorganized" attachment category of Main [e.g., Main & Hesse, 1990] will not be discussed. In these extreme cases, it is argued, children are faced with a confusing or threatening caregiver and are unable to form a coherent strategy for coping with attachment feelings at all. They thus lie outside the range of usual variation discussed here.)

Similar but more advanced patterns are observed in the second period. If during the movement toward self-regulation children are not given proper guidance or are required too soon to attempt genuine self-regulation, they will experience pervasive failure, with associated feelings of rage and shame (cf. Erikson, 1963). Common individual patterns include chronic dysregulation (and associated overstimulation) and the adoption of rigid self-regulation strategies. Adaptations in the first two phases, whether congruent (which is often the case) or interacting in complex ways, are carried forward to the issue of self-regulation in the preschool period.

If children are not able to regulate emotion flexibly and achieve a degree of instrumentality and social effectiveness at that time, they are vulnerable to low self-esteem and a sense of incompetence, with associated feelings of worthlessness, guilt, and depression. Defenses, which can normally serve young children, can become ingrained defensive strategies. Some children are characteristically (1) easily frustrated, overstimulated, tense, and anxious; (2) dependent, passive, and helpless; (3) hostile, aggressive, and antisocial; (4) emotionally insulated; or (5) profoundly disconnected from experience. The first two of these, reminiscent of resistant attachment, are defensive in postponing actual autonomous coping and in calling for continual adult care. The latter three serve to keep people and feelings at a distance. All tend to foreclose on the development of flexible strategies of emotional regulation.

Hypotheses regarding individual adaptation in the preschool years

The major hypothesis that emerges from these theoretical considerations is that qualitative aspects of individual styles of emotional regulation and environmental engagement in the preschool period will be forecasted by the quality of dyadic regulation that came before. The discussion that follows will center specifically on predictions from patterns of infant–caregiver attachment as the cumulation of regulation experiences in the infant period.

When considering the preschool period, this general hypothesis has many specific aspects. Flexible emotional regulation, or what Block and Block (e.g., 1980) have called "ego-resiliency," itself is multifaceted. Well-regulated children can contain affect and impulses when required, as well as fully and flexibly express feelings when appropriate, drawing on a history of acceptance and flexible containment. As part of this regulation, those with secure histories are expected to exhibit the full range of emotional experiences and to have an emotionally rich fantasy life as revealed in play. They are able to become emotionally invested in activities, as revealed by curiosity and personal agency (exploring the new, trying hard at tasks, flexibly persisting toward the achievement of goals).

Closely related to these capacities is the fact that well-regulated children are self-directed. Bowlby (1973) specifically predicted that children with histories of secure attachment should be more emotionally self-reliant, even as compared with those with avoidant histories who have been pushed toward early independence. Genuine self-reliance (as opposed to aloofness) derives from a history of effective emotional regulation within the caregiving system and an abiding sense of trust that things will be alright even in the face of challenge or stress. Thus, these children, deeply believing in their capacity to affect the world, will draw on their own resources first and will flexibly seek adult assistance when their efforts are exhausted or when special needs arise.

Feelings of high self-esteem are expectable concomitants of flexible self-regulation. This is both because of the genuine effectiveness of the child in the environment and because such children carry forward deep feelings of self-worth. Having been cared for, one inevitably evolves a model of the self as worthy of care and as valued.

Finally, social relationships are of particular relevance. For example, not only do relationships call on (and therefore manifest) the child's capacity for regulation (engaging others, sustaining interaction in the face of high arousal, expressing affect, modulating affect, etc.), but they reveal expectations concerning the patterning of interaction derived from the history of dyadic regulation. As one strong hypothesis from the perspective of internalizing relationship patterns, children with secure histories are expected to be empathic with others. Having participated in responsive relationships, such children see relationships in these terms. In a relationship, when one is needy the other expresses care. All that is required, then, for the development of empathy and prosocial behavior are the emerging capacities of interpersonal perception and instrumentality in the preschool period (e.g., Sroufe & Fleeson, 1986).

Observed patterns of adaptation

The continuity of adaptation from infancy to the preschool years has been the subject of many studies. Here the discussion will focus on the relationship between patterns of attachment in infancy and functioning in the nursery school and kindergarten (three separate studies). Such contexts reveal functioning with respect to the whole range of issues pertinent to self-regulation and therefore allow a direct test of propositions concerning the internalization of earlier dyadic regulation. Since infant attachment figures are not present, child behavior cannot be said to be directly stimulated by, or conditional upon, parent behavior. Results of these studies have been reviewed previously (e.g., Sroufe, 1983, 1988, 1990), so only an overview will be presented here.

Self-regulation, self-reliance, and self-esteem. Abundant data are available on the various capacities of preschool children to direct and regulate themselves and the associated feelings of self-esteem. With respect to links to attachment history, results have often been quite powerful. For example, in the central nursery school study (two classes, 40 children), the dependency ratings and rankings of three independent teachers showed virtually no overlap between those with secure versus anxious histories (including those in the avoidant group thought to be pushed toward early independence). Moreover, these judgments of greater self-reliance in those with secure histories were corroborated by independent observations of the nature and frequency of child-to-teacher and teacher-to-child contact during playtime and the frequency of sitting next to a teacher in circle time (Sroufe, 1983; Sroufe et al., 1983). Those with histories of avoidant attachment, as well as those with resistant histories, were more often leaning against a teacher or on a teacher's lap than were those with secure histories.

Likewise, both rankings and a Q-sort-derived index of ego-resiliency strongly discriminated attachment groups. In the Q-sort procedure teachers do a forced-choice sort of a set of 100 items along a 9-point continuum, according to how closely they describe the particular child, with two to three teacher sorts then being combined. These descriptions are then correlated for each child with an ideal Q-sort of the "highly ego-resilient child" made by expert judges. This correlation becomes a score. The average correlation with the ideal for the groups with histories of resistant, avoidant, and secure attachment, respectively, were .07, $-.13$, and .50, with no overlap between the latter two groups. Even individual items were also discriminating, with, for example, the secure group described as more expressive, more curious about the new, and better able to delay, but as less likely to "fall to pieces under stress." Independent observation supported these teacher descriptions. Detailed recording revealed a greater range of affective expression, more full expression, and a faster recovery following emotional upheaval for those with secure histories (Sroufe, Schork, Motti, Lawroski, & LaFrenier, 1984). The capacity of these children to invest in activities and in relationships, as well as their ability to tap resources inside themselves in order to make a strong effort in the face of challenge, was also confirmed by independent laboratory studies of barrier behavior (Arend, 1983), as was their greater curiosity when observed with Banta's Curiosity Box (Nezworsky, 1983).

Children with secure histories were seen to be well managed in other ways as well. They were observed less often to be aggressive or to pose disciplinary problems in the classroom, and indeed, they were less often disciplined by the teachers. Ratings made of teacher–child relationships from videotaped interactions revealed that teachers (all without a knowledge of child history) held up high standards of behavior for those with secure histories and had high expectations for compliance with their directives, in general relating to such children in a warm, matter-of-fact, age-appropriate manner (e.g., Sroufe & Fleeson, 1988). With both anxious groups, the teachers were highly controlling and had low expectations for compliance (as revealed, for example, by following up a directive with another action before the child really could have complied, in contrast to going on about their business with confidence as they did with those having secure histories). Moreover, with the resistant group teachers were quite nurturant, showing high tolerance for rule infractions and generally treating the children as though they were younger. The avoidant group did not receive such nurturance, and indeed, children in this group were the only ones to elicit anger from the teachers. But neither the avoidant nor the resistant group was seen as well managed.

In accord with external aspects of emotional regulation, the play of those with secure histories revealed a richness in the quality of their inner fantasy lives (Rosenberg, 1984). Those with secure histories showed not only more investment but also greater flexibility and complexity in their play, with a broader range of emotional themes. The play of the other groups was relatively impoverished, and in the case of the avoidant group, virtually unpeopled, a striking absence in the play of preschoolers. Moreover, it may be argued that the play of those with secure histories was more serviceable; when a conflict theme was introduced, as was frequent with all three groups, the conflict was more routinely brought to a successful resolution. (For example: "Oh no! He got hit by the truck! He broke his leg. Here come the ambilens . . . Take him to the hospital. They fixed it!")

Finally, the greater self-confidence and feelings of self-worth of those children with secure attachment histories are manifest in many ways – engaging new experiences, flexibly persisting in the face of challenge, going to adults when injured or ill, sticking up for themselves in disputes, and not tolerating ill-treatment from others. Laboratory observations revealed that when faced with an extremely difficult problem and left to their own resources, those with secure histories were more flexibly persistent, remained creative in dealing with the situation, were able to renew efforts when ultimately provided with new leads, and, in general, were able to regroup following frustrated efforts. They showed the capacity to enjoy even a difficult experience and to keep "expecting well," which culminated in a global rating of high self-esteem made by pairs of independent coders (Arend, 1983). In the preschool, global rankings of self-esteem made by the teachers again strongly distinguished secure and anxious attachment groups, with all of the very bottom ranks going to those with anxious histories and the top ranks to those with secure histories (Sroufe, 1983). Similarly, a Q-sort-based index stongly discriminated the groups, and in addition, targeted individual items (e.g., "appears to feel worthy") also yielded dramatic differences. (Such differences were also found in two other studies of preschool groups;

Arend et al., 1979; Waters et al., 1979.) On the other side, teacher judgments and observational measures of affect identified only those with avoidant histories (about half) and a minority of those with resistant histories as showing signs of depression (Garber, Cohen, Bacon, Egeland, & Sroufe, 1985).

All of this data converges to suggest that those children with histories of effective dyadic regulation show a capacity for flexible, effective *self-regulation* in the preschool period, along with the attendant feelings of positive self-esteem and efficacy. Because of this they are able to exploit the opportunities and face the challenges present in the world of the preschool. This is reflected not only in their curiosity and powerful sense of agency with respect to the world of things, but in their relationships with peers as well.

Relationships with others: dyadic patterns carried forward. Emotions are central in relationships in two senses: first, because the very core of close relationships is the affective connection between individuals and the feelings they share (J. Sroufe, 1991) and, second, because the give-and-take, negotiation and management of conflict that are a part of all close relationships are based on the emotional regulation capacities of the individuals involved. Thus, one clear hypothesis from our organizational perspective is that the quality and nature of the preschool child's relationships will reflect and, in a sense, recapitulate the patterning of the earlier dyadic organization. This hypothesis has been strongly confirmed.

Those with secure histories, having experienced responsive care and unwavering affection, value relationships with other children, enjoy being with them, and show concern and regard for their well-being. They more often are observed to initiate interactions and respond to the bids of others with enthusiasm and positive affect (and less often with negative affect) than are those with anxious histories (Sroufe et al., 1984). Ratings by independent, "blind" judges, based on repeated dyadic play sessions, revealed that these children's relationships showed more commitment and emotional closeness (Pancake, 1988), and that they were nurturant with less able partners and self-assertive with aggressive partners (Troy & Sroufe, 1987). Valuing themselves they will not tolerate exploitation; caring for others they do not exploit. This is supported both by teacher assessments of empathy (based on Q-sorts) and by videotaped records of empathic/prosocial behavior when another child was injured or distressed (Kestenbaum et al., 1989; Sroufe, 1983).

In contrast, those with histories of anxious attachment tend to have difficulties managing the emotional challenges of peer relationships. Those with avoidant histories were often emotionally distant from or hostile toward other children. They exhibited the most frequent unprovoked aggression and at times behaved in exploitative or hurtful ways toward others. In the study of empathy (Kestenbaum et al., 1989), they forced the creation of a new category, "anti-empathy." In response to another's distress they were significantly more likely to do that which would precisely further distress the child (e.g., scaring a child with the very mask that had been frightening, taunting a crying child and calling him or her a "crybaby," punching a child with a stomachache in the stomach). In the play pair study (Troy & Sroufe, 1987), 5 pairs of 19 total pairs were observed to show a systematic pattern of exploitation, where one child took advantage of and mistreated the other. In each case the "exploiter" was always a child with an avoidant history.

Those with resistant histories tend to show other problems. Often immature and easily frustrated or overstimulated, they had difficulty sustaining the give-and-take of relationships, though they were oriented toward social contact. They might hover on the fringes of the group or engage only to retreat when upset. Sometimes they had difficulty maintaining personal boundaries. In the empathy observations they often would become upset themselves when another was distressed (e.g., holding their own lip and seeking a teacher's lap when another child had fallen). They were perfect fodder for the bullying child, always becoming upset when targeted and never taking firm or effective action. In fact, those with avoidant histories exploited only children with resistant histories or another avoidant child who had some special vulnerability (e.g., being mentally slow).

Because the teachers in the nursery school study may be thought of as a constant, the differences in teacher–child relationships mentioned earlier must in some way be due to differences in the children. Thus, teachers nurtured, controlled, and infantalized those with resistant histories because of their immature and obviously needy behavior. They at times were angry at and felt like rejecting (and isolating) those with avoidant histories because of their cool defiance toward adults and their hurtful behavior toward other children.

Patterns of maladaptation. As theorized the behavior of these preschool children revealed a coherent inner organization of expectations and attitudes about themselves, others, and relationships. The five patterns outlined earlier (in the section on the process of self-organization) were indeed observed, and as expected, those with resistant histories were probabilistically more likely to be classified (by independent judges using teacher Q-sort descriptions) into the (1) tense, anxious, easily frustrated and (2) passive, weak, adult-oriented patterns, while those with avoidant histories were more likely classified into the (3) hostile, aggressive, antisocial and (4) aloof, emotionally insulated patterns. As another specific example, both groups of children with histories of anxious attachment were seen as highly dependent, but they manifested their dependency in distinct ways. Those with avoidant histories revealed their dependency in very indirect ways. They explicitly did not seek contact when upset or disappointed, but drew near the teachers (often in subtle and barely noticeable ways) during quiet times. One child, for example, sought out one teacher every day at the beginning of class, but he did so through an elaborate series of oblique angles, much like a sailboat tacking into the wind. Those with resistant histories, in contrast, "wore their hearts on their sleeves," often showing immature behavior and eliciting a great deal of nurturance and support from teachers.

Outcomes in middle childhood and adolescence. Follow-up data on these children show that major aspects of self-regulation and personality organization continue to be predictable throughout the years of immaturity. For example, data from a series of summer camps and weekend camp reunions showed considerable continuity not only from the preschool period, but from infant attachment history as well (Elicker et al., 1992; Sroufe et al., 1993; Urban et al., 1991). The differences between those with secure and those with anxious histories in ego- resiliency, self-confidence, self-esteem, and social competence were highly significant in both middle childhood and adolescence. Data on dependency were especially strong, with very little overlap between groups and with correlations in the .50s and .60s over this time span. In middle childhood those with secure histories were more likely to form a close friendship (based on teacher judgments, observed frequency of interaction, and reciprocated sociometric choices) and to be able to balance the challenges of close friendship and effective group functioning. Others could be incorporated into their play with friends, and their close friendship kept them in commerce with the group. Pairs of resistant children (somewhat rare) were unable to sustain the complexity of this balance and alternated between being with their friend and being in the group. A single avoidant pair observed showed a very exclusive relationship, playing at all times separate from groups, being jealous of another's approach (see Freud & Dann, 1951), and being at a loss when their friend was absent. Similarly, in adolescence, those with secure histories were better able to coordinate the additional complexity of functioning in the adolescent crowd. Related to this, those with secure histories were given significantly higher ratings by their counselors on a scale created just for the adolescent period, called Capacity for Vulnerability. This scale tapped the capacity of the teenager to fully engage the range of camp experiences, including those that were affectively charged and in which the self would be to some degree exposed.

Coherence over time. The preceding findings focused on prediction from the end of infancy to later childhood; yet other research has shown lawful relations across each step of the proposed developmental sequence. Thus, in general, early patterns of caregiver-guided regulation predict to dyadic regulation (attachment patterns) and to later parental acceptance of autonomy and promotion of instrumentality (e.g., Matas et al., 1978; Pianta, Egeland, & Sroufe, 1989). Moreover, assessments of caregiver-guided regulation, made prior to the emergence of infant intentionality and the formation of the specific attachment, have also proved to be powerful predictors of later child regulation. In particular, a measure of "intrusiveness," from Ainsworth's Cooperation–Interference scale (see Chapter 9), has been shown to be a predictor of frustration behavior, hyperactivity, and attention problems throughout the preschool years, as well as a variety of academic and emotional problems in the early elementary school period (Carlson et al., in press; Egeland et al., 1993; Jacobvitz & Sroufe, 1987). Thus, an over-stimulating, dysregulating pattern of care forecasted later problems of self-regulation, especially the modulation of impulses and affect.

While these group data provide impressive general confirmation of our key hypothesis, they cannot do full justice to the coherence of individual emotional life as it emerges step by step over the course of early development. Detailed case studies from this project are being presented by others (Egeland, Pianta, & Dodds, in preparation). Here, two examples must suffice.

One child alluded to earlier, who upon seeing another with a cut lip climbed up on a teacher's lap and held his own lip, was prototypically passive and teacher-oriented. He almost never initiated play with other children and was essentially unnoticed by them. From early infancy the care he experienced was uncommonly intrusive and parentifying, his mother responding in terms of her needs for affection and not his signals. In the lever tool problem at age 2, she literally taunted him (lifting the candy out and then dropping it when he came to reach for it). She mocked him when he then got frustrated, then pleaded with him to kiss her. Then she told him that this time she would let him have the candy, only to thwart him again and repeat the cycle. Granted, other preschool manifestations would have seemed possible (e.g., hyperactivity); nonetheless, this child's total inability to be self-directed and self-regulated, his passivity, and his craving for adult care seem quite understandable in light of this history, as does his inability to separate his emotional experiences from those of others.

As another example, the child who "tacked" toward his teacher on arrival and went off by himself when disappointed or injured, was prototypically emotionally insulated. Once, being highly attracted to a simulated space capsule in the classroom, he was observed to hastily retreat upon discovering the presence of other children inside. He was also quietly cruel to other children when they were injured or vulnerable. With his play partner, he was once observed to disdainfully reject 137 bids for contact, saying, for example, "That's dumb," when the partner suggested they play with a car. (The partner had a resistant history.) In infancy this child's caregiver was a classic example of what we came to call "emotionally unavailable" (Egeland & Sroufe, 1981). She was stiff and undemonstrative and seemed to disdain physical contact, especially if initiated by him. Their attachment relationship was classified as avoidant at both 12 and 18 months. He was totally unsupported emotionally in the tool problems, his mother sitting back and occasionally snickering even when he was completely stuck. His avoidance of emotionally engaging social situations and his subtle cruelty seem to be no mystery in light of this history.

Continuity and change in individual adaptation

Individual adaptation is characterized by both continuity and change. Even though the preceding data demonstrate substantial continuity, they embody change as well, for the continuity lies not in a stability of particular behaviors over time, but in the coherent patterns of behavioral organization despite a continually expanding repertoire and the ascendancy of ever new issues as development proceeds. Of course, there is also change in the basic quality of individual adaptation in some cases, with the preceding results being generalizations relying on group data, and not every case shows such graphic continuity as the two just presented. Both continuity and fundamental change are to be understood and explained.

The coherence of individual adaptation over time has several bases (Sroufe, 1988). First, the quality of care often shows a degree of continuity, and parents who are supportive with respect to early developmental issues often remain supportive later (e.g., Hiester, 1993; Pianta et al., 1989). Second, the nature of development is such that capacities acquired at one phase often represent important foundations for subsequent phases; thus, for example, the child with a history of secure attachment has affect regulation capacities, object mastery skills, and positive social expectations that promote successful interactions with preschool peers. Third, and related, based on their expectations children in many ways increasingly create their own environments. While experiences with children and teachers could have ameliorative influences for children with unsupportive backgrounds, it tends to be precisely these children who alienate, remain separate from, or are ineffective in tapping such potential resources. This self-perpetuation of adaptation is often couched in terms of "inner working models"; the child engages the environment within a framework of expectations and understandings, interpreting feedback in terms of these.

One anecdotal example concerns two children arriving at nursery school. Music was playing and children were "dancing." The first child approached a potential partner but was turned down; sulking, he went off into a corner, where he stayed for a long time. A second child arrived and by chance approached the same "partner." He too was turned down, but he went on to another child and both played happily. Both children had experiences confirming their expectations about the social world, the first that it is rebuffing and the second that it is responsive. In fact, the second child probably did not experience "rejection" at all, most likely wondering what was wrong with the unresponsive partner.

Such considerations yield hypotheses about change as well. Notable change probably occurs when there is a fundamental disruption of the child's basic expectations, most often in the context of changes in the quality of important relationships. Such fundamental change has been consistently linked to changes in parenting or the parenting context or to the presence of a new and transforming vital relationship. As three examples: those children who showed markedly improved adaptation between infancy and preschool significantly more often had mothers who formed a stable relationship with an adult partner in the intervening years (Erickson et al., 1985); those mothers who, though abused themselves as children, provided adequate care for their own children more often had an alternative caregiver or an extended therapy experience in childhood (Egeland, Jacobvitz, & Sroufe, 1988); and those institutionally reared girls showing adequate parenting as adults much more often had supportive spouses (Quinton, Rutter, & Liddle, 1984). Likewise, anecdotally, we observed a number of children improve their functioning under the care of our nursery school teachers.

Change is not easy, however, and often takes time, apparently becoming more difficult the longer a pattern has been in place. Certainly, stability increases over time. Moreover, it does not seem that change erases the past. There are many case examples. One involved a preschool child who flowered within the care of a particular teacher. One day she reported a dream in which her beloved teacher had hurled her against a wall. The teacher told her that she would never do that, whereupon the child amazingly asked her why not, and then, being told this was because the teacher liked her "so very much," the child asked the teacher to explain this as well. Another example is the 10-year-old at summer camp who maintained strong doubts about her likeability despite repeated evidence of her popularity. The preservation of early models also holds for those with secure histories. One child, whose father had recently been murdered, was moody and disengaged from adults in our middle childhood assessment, counter to all earlier assessments. However, by our teenage observation he was again the clear social star of the entire group and a confident, thoughtful young man. Basic expectations are slow to change. The shadows of earlier care can often still be seen in current adaptation. We demonstrated with group data that early experience predicts later behavior even beyond measures of current environmental support and that earlier adaptation may reappear following environmental changes or in special circumstances (e.g., particular kinds of stress; Sroufe et al., 1990). This is consistent with Suomi's observation (Novak, O'Neill, Beckley, & Suomi, 1992) that apparently rehabilitated monkeys (following early deprivation) reverted to very particular maladaptive behaviors when placed in test cages as adults, while in supportive environments these animals behaved unremarkably and had not shown these "signature stereotypies" for years.

Conclusion

Internalization is a critical developmental process. Basically, it refers to the adaptation to and incorporation of experience. From the level of brain physiology (Edelman, 1992; Schore, 1994) to the level of interpersonal and psychic functioning, that which is experienced becomes part of the self. In terms of the thesis stated here, not only parents' stated values and those behaviors that are praised and proscribed, but the practiced patterns of dyadic regulation are internalized by the child. Such internalization is both physiological and cognitive, influencing basic orientations (expectations) and affective responses to interpersonal situations, as well as more conscious beliefs and values, and influencing attitudes as well as behavioral style. Individual variations in the acceptance of feelings, comfort with emotional arousal (in social and nonsocial contexts), and, in general, the regulation of emotion are the result.

It is important to underscore that what is being recapitulated by the child are not specific behavioral features experienced with the caregiver, but the quality and patterning of the relationship, mediated by affect. Children with avoidant histories were not likely literally punched in the stomach when they had a stomach ache (and certainly they didn't punch their mothers in such a circumstance). Parents of secure children didn't get a teacher when their child was crying, nor did the children have direct experience nurturing the parent. But these children had repeated experiences of feeling vulnerable, the reactions of the other, and the emotional sequelae of these actions. They are thus familiar with an affective patterning in relationships, so now when they witness another being distressed and/or vulnerable they know the general kind of reaction that will recapture familiar emotional features of such an interchange. They are not constantly seeking to recapitulate these experiences or, in the case of the avoidant preschool child, to harm or exploit another. They are simply behaving in terms of their understanding and expectations regarding relationships with the aim of making experience meaningful.

Second, it is important to interpret carefully the fact that preschool children are having a profound effect on their own experience, be that isolating themselves from other children and alienating teachers or being emotionally engaged with both. This is what is commonly referred to as "child effects"; yet it is important to view these characteristics as developmentally constructed rather than as inherent in the child. Children are not born to be alienated or easily victimized. In particular, prospective longitudinal study reveals that those infants who are emotionally rebuffed by parents (a substantial portion of those who later show avoidant attachment) were generally robust and well organized in the very first months of life, whereas a few months later the toll of ongoing unavailability is manifest in the infant's more difficult behavior (Egeland & Sroufe, 1981). Moreover, the behaviors that alienate teachers and other children (defiance, aggression) are not even in the repertoire of the infant. It is not static characteristics of the child that are carried forward, but expectations concerning self, other, and relationships and patterns of emotional regulation, all deriving from patterns of regulation within the relationship system.

13 Summation

> Freud had hit upon a great truth about the human mind: It is from start to finish
> incapable of separating itself from its own experience and can only build upon
> that.
>
> Rosen (1989)

The study of early emotional life reveals much about the nature of development.
First and foremost, it becomes clear that development entails a particular kind
of growth or unfolding wherein what emerges derives in a logical, though complex way from what was present before as a precursor. The "emergent" is
qualitatively different from the precursor and at a new level of complexity; yet
the precursor serves as a prototype for the emergent, embodying an important
core essence of that which is to come.

The joy in peekaboo, for example, which involves among other things anticipation, coordination of a stored image with a present experience, and some
degree of person permanence, is qualitatively different from the newborn's sleep
smile or the 10-week-old's pleasure smile to familiar faces, but all three experiences involve the arousal (or tension) modulation core that is central in the
reaction.

Likewise, guilt is a qualitatively more sophisticated and differentiated reaction
than shame. Guilt involves a deviation from an internalized standard for behavior, entailing a threat to self-esteem and a desire for atonement. Compared with
shame it is a more specific reaction, based on a recognition of an unacceptable
behavior, which thus allows at least the possibility of reparative action. Shame
is a more global reaction, a pervasive sense of negative "being" (vs. the inappropriate "doing" in guilt). No specific, independent action can be taken by
the child to repair the damage of shame, which requires a more general re-
establishment of harmony in relationships. Yet both shame and guilt entail a
consciousness of self and a threat to its well-being.

Similarly, the fantasy play of the preschooler represents a dramatic transformation of early circular reactions, wherein the infant repeatedly kicks his or her
legs to make the bassinet rattle or a mobile turn or, later, drops toys repeatedly

235

from the high chair and is amused by the results. In fantasy play the repetitions of experience are often not literal copies of previous experience, but symbolic reworkings. Intrafamilial conflict may be represented by crashing toy cars, and in reenactments it is dolls that are diapered or scolded. Still, in both circular reactions and fantasy play a sense of mastery is gained through repetition, and the reward is in the doing.

Thus, although emergents are witnessed continually in development, it is never a case of something coming from nothing. The process is one in which an emergent derives from a prototype only to become the prototype for a subsequent emergent, as in the progression from the pleasant state associated with the newborn sleep smile to the pleasure smile of recognition to the joy of anticipation and/or incongruity in infant games. The recognition smile entails the arousal modulation of the sleep smile; the anticipatory smile or laugh embodies both the arousal modulation core and the cognitive recognition core.

The same features and processes that are seen in this review of the development of emotions also characterize the development of emotional regulation. Thus, the key progression in emotional regulation is from caregiver-orchestrated regulation to dyadic regulation to self-regulation. At each phase there are qualitative changes in the bases for regulation, and yet the emerging form bears a lawful relation to what was there before. For example, the advent of intentional infant signaling marks a dramatic increase in the precision and flexibility of regulation, allowing, among other things, regulation to be maintained or re-achieved even when the infant engages the environment at some distance from the caregiver. Yet the patterning and efficiency (or lack thereof) of the prior regulation is maintained in this more truly dyadic regulation. So too this dyadic regulation represents the foundation (prototype) for later caregiver-guided self-regulation and self-regulation proper. Although requiring both reading and response by the caregiver, the infant's active role in dyadic regulation sets the pattern for later autonomous efforts.

In addition to revealing the nature of development in its complexity, the study of emotional life also underscores the unity of development. This includes the close ties among the subdomains of emotional development (that of the emotions and of the emotional regulation capacity), ties between emotional development and other domains of development, harmony among levels of explanation of core processes, and links between the study of normative development and individual differences.

Thus, fundamental questions about the affects are: What is the changing basis for the emotions with development? Why does one emotion occur rather than another in response to a given event? In answering these questions one also gains insight into individual differences in emotional regulation. Different emotions emerge as the process for engendering tension progresses from CNS stimulation to cognitive effort to intentional action to a comparison of one's actions with internalized standards. Awareness, intentionality, and an increasingly active role for the self are underscored, as they are in the growth of emotional regulation. Likewise, the security of the context in which tension occurred was found to be instrumental in determining positive or negative emotion, and the developmental progression from external security (in the attachment relationship) to inner confidence is the key process in the development of effective self-regulation of emotion.

The reciprocal influence of emotional development and other aspects of development has been suggested throughout. As one important example, emotional development is very much the growth of awareness and the growth of self, while at the same time neither awareness nor the self can be well understood apart from emotional life. An understanding of both self-awareness and conscience makes the emotions of shame and guilt meaningful. But shame critically helps define the nature of self-awareness, and without the concept of guilt conscience has little meaning.

Also apparent is the harmony among different levels of describing the developmental process. This is especially clear in comparing recent descriptions of physiological regulation with those concerning growth of emotional regulation. As outlined earlier, self-regulation may be described as the progressive internalization of prior patterns of caregiver-orchestrated and more truly dyadic regulation of emotion. Similarly, those researchers who trace processes of state and arousal regulation in the CNS point to earlier regulation by the caregiver of physiological processes that infants "possess" but cannot regulate (e.g., Kraemer, Egbert, Schmidt, & McKinney, 1991; Schore, 1994) until, ultimately, such regulation is entrained in dynamic brain systems.

Finally, normative development and individual differences are seen as complementary parts of a whole in the study of emotional development. In fact, individual differences are best defined as deviations in normative processes. For example, fear reactions of infants in the face of threat are normal. They represent signals (to the infant and to the caregiver) that prompt proximity. Such episodes of threat and recovery actually promote the capacity for arousal modulation. But chronically fearful or anxious infants and young children are conceptualized in terms of poor tension modulation, related to an insecurity of context and a lack of dependable tension modulation within the caregiving relationship; and defensively uninvolved children are viewed as having been chronically rebuffed precisely when they signaled a need for tension modulation assistance. Children whose experience is based in criticism and those who are perpetually burdened by worry and guilt would be viewed as products of unreasonable standards, as well as inadequate guidance and support during the transition to self-regulation.

At the same time, the study of maladaptation serves to highlight critical normative issues. The anxiously attached infant lets one see the vital importance of dependable care in normal development, and the tantrum-prone toddler or the hyperdependent or depressed preschooler underscore the importance of accepting the child's movement toward autonomy, accompanied by appropriate guidance.

Understanding emotional life is complex. The emotions themselves are best understood in the context of development. And emotional development entails the myriad considerations outlined herein: the integration of emotional development with cognitive and social development, the convergent study of the twin aspects of emotional life, and joint, reciprocal consideration of normative development and individual differences.

References

Ahrens, R. (1954). Beitrag zur Entwicklung des Physiognomie-und Mimikerkennens, Teil I, II. *Zeitschrift fur Experimental und Angewandte Psychologie, 2,* 412–454, 599–633.

Ainsworth, M. D. S. (1967). *Infancy in Uganda: Infant care and the growth of love.* Baltimore: Johns Hopkins University Press.

Ainsworth, M. D. S. (1969). Object relations, dependency, and attachment: A theoretical review of the infant–mother relationship. *Child Development, 40,* 969–1025.

Ainsworth, M. D. S. (1970). *Manual for scoring maternal sensitivity.* Unpublished manuscript.

Ainsworth, M. D. S. (1973). The development of infant–mother attachment. In B. Caldwell & H. Ricciuti (Eds.), *Review of child development research* (Vol. 3, pp. 173–196). Chicago: University of Chicago Press.

Ainsworth, M. D. S., Bell, S., & Stayton, D. (1974). Infant–mother attachment and social development: Socialization as a product of reciprocal responsiveness to signals. In M. Richards (Ed.), *The integration of the child into the social world.* Cambridge University Press.

Ainsworth, M. B. S., Blehar, M., Waters, E., & Wall, S. (1978). *Patterns of attachment.* Hillsdale, NJ: Erlbaum.

Ainsworth, M. D. S., & Wittig, B. S. (1969). Attachment and exploratory behavior of one year olds in a strange situation. In B. M. Foss (Ed.), *Determinants of infant behavior* (Vol. 4, pp. 111–136). London: Methuen.

Ambrose, A. (1961). The development of the smiling response in early infancy. In B. Foss (Ed.), *Determinants of infant behavior* (Vol. 1, pp. 179–195). New York: Wiley.

Ambrose, A. (1963). The age of onset of ambivalence in early infancy: Indications from the study of laughing. *Journal of Child Psychology and Psychiatry, 4,* 167–181.

Amsterdam, B. (1972). Mirror self-image reactions before age two. *Developmental Psychobiology, 5,* 297–305.

Amsterdam, B., & Levitt, M. (1980). Consciousness of self and painful self-consciousness. *Psychoanalytic Study of the Child, 35,* 67–83.

Arend, R. (1983). *Infant attachment and patterns of adaptation in a barrier situation at age 3½ years.* Unpublished doctoral dissertation, University of Minnesota.

Arend, R., Gove, F., & Sroufe, L. A. (1979). Continuity of individual adaptation from infancy to kindergarten: A predictive study of ego-resiliency and curiosity in preschoolers. *Child Development, 50,* 950–959.

Arnold, M. (1960). *Emotion and personality* (Vol. 1 and 2). New York: Columbia University Press.

Baillargeon, R., & DeVos, J. (1991). Object permanence in young infants: Further evidence. *Child Development, 62,* 1227–1246.

Baldwin, J. M. (1897). Social and ethical interpretations in mental development. New York: Macmillan.

Ball, W., & Tronick, E. (1971). Infant responses to impending collision: Optical and real. *Science, 171,* 818–820.

Barrett, K., & Campos, J. (1987). Perspectives on emotional development: 2. A functionalist approach to emotions. In J. Osofsky (Ed.), *Handbook of infant development* (2nd ed., pp. 555–578). New York: Wiley.

Bates, J. (1989). Concepts and measures of temperament. In G. Kohnstamm, J. Bates, and M. Rothbart (Eds.), *Temperament in childhood* (pp. 3–26). New York: Wiley.

Bates, J., Maslin, C., & Frankel, K. (1985). Attachment security, mother–child interaction, and temperament as predictors of behavior problem ratings at age three years. In I. Bretherton & E. Waters (Eds.), *Growing points in attachment theory and research. Monographs of the Society for Research in Child Development, 50* (Whole No. 209), 167–193.

Beebe, B., & Lachman, F. M. (1988). Mother–infant mutual influence and precursors of psychic structure. In A. Goldberg (Ed.), *Progress in self-psychology* (Vol. 3, pp. 3–25). Hillsdale, NJ: Analytic Press.

Bell, S. (1970). The development of the concept of object as related to infant–mother attachment. *Child Development, 41,* 291–311.

Bell, S., & Ainsworth, M. D. S. (1972). Infant crying and maternal responsiveness. *Child Development, 43,* 1171–1190.

Belsky, J., & Isabella, R. (1988). Maternal, infant and social-contextual determinants of attachment security: A process analysis. In J. Belsky & T. Nezworski (Eds.), *Clinical implications of attachment* (pp. 41–94). Hillsdale, NJ: Erlbaum.

Berlyne, D. E. (1969). Laughter, humor and play. In G. Lindzey & E. Aronson (Eds.), *Handbook of social psychology* (2nd ed., Vol. 3, pp. 795–852). Reading, MA: Addison-Wesley.

Berlyne, D. E. (1971). *Aesthetics and psychology.* New York: Appleton-Century-Crofts.

Bertenthal, B., Campos, J., & Barrett, K. (1984). Self-produced locomotion: An organizer of emotional, cognitive, and social development in infancy. In R. Emde & R. Harmon (Eds.), *Continuities and discontinuities in development* (pp. 175–210). New York: Plenum.

Bertenthal, B. I., & Fischer, K. W. (1978). The development of self-recognition in the infant. *Developmental Psychology, 14,* 44–50.

Bettelheim, B. (1967). *The Empty Fortress.* New York: Free Press.

Birns, B., & Golden, M. (1972). Prediction of intellectual performance at three years from infant test and personality measures. *Merrill-Palmer Quarterly, 18,* 53–58.

Bischof, N. (1975). A systems approach towards the functional connections of fear and attachment, *Child Development. 46,* 801–817.

Blehar, M., Lieberman, A., & Ainsworth, M. (1977). Early face to face interaction and its relation to later infant–mother attachment. *Child Development, 48,* 182–194.

Block, J. (1987, April). *Longitudinal antecedents of ego-control and ego-resiliency in late adolescence.* Paper presented at the biennial meeting of the Society for Research in Child Development, Baltimore.

Block, J., & Gjerde, P. (1993, March). *Ego-resiliency through time.* Paper presented at the biennial meeting of the Society for Research in Child Development, New Orleans.

Block, J. H., & Block, J. (1980). The role of ego-control and ego-resiliency in the organization of behavior. In W. A. Collins (Ed.), *Minnesota symposia on child psychology* (Vol. 13, pp. 39–101). Hillsdale, NJ: Erlbaum.

Bloom, K. (1975, July). *Does the operant conditioning model have ecological validity for early social development?* Paper presented at the Meetings of the International Society for the Study of Behavioral Development. Guilford, England.

Bloom, K., & Esposito, A. (1975). Social conditioning and its proper control procedures. *Journal of Experimental Child Psychology, 19,* 209–222.

Boccia, M., & Campos, J. (1989). Maternal emotional signals, social referencing, and infants' reactions to strangers. In N. Eisenberg (Ed.), *Empathy and related emotional responses: New directions for child development* (pp. 25–49). San Francisco: Jossey-Bass.

Bohlin, G., Hagekull, B., Germer, M., Andersson, K., & Lindberg, L. (1990, April). *Early antecedents of attachment: Avoidant and resistant reunion behaviors as predicted by maternal interactive behavior and infant temperament.* Paper presented at the International Conference on Infant Studies, Toronto.

Bower, T. G. R., Broughton, J., & Moore, M. (1970). Infant responses to approaching objects. *Perception and Psychophysics, 9,* 193–196.

Bowlby, J. (1969/1982). *Attachment and loss* (Vol. 1), 2nd ed. New York: Basic.

Bowlby, J. (1973). *Attachment and loss* (Vol. 2). New York: Basic.

Brackbill, Y. (1958). Extinction of the smiling response in infants as a function of reinforcement schedule. *Child Development, 29,* 115–124.

Brackbill, Y. (1975). Psychophysiological measures of pharmacological toxicity in infants: Perinatal and postnatal effects. In P. L. Morselli, S. Garattini, & F. Sereni (Eds.), *Basic therapeutic aspects of perinatal pharmacology* (pp. 21–28). New York: Raven.

Brazelton, T. B. (1969). *Infants and Mothers.* New York: Delacorte.

Brazelton, T. B., & Cramer, B. (1990). *The earliest relationship.* Reading, MA: Addison-Wesley.

Brazelton, T. B., Koslowski, B., & Main, M. (1974). The origins of reciprocity: The early mother-infant interaction. In M. Lewis & L. Rosenblum (Eds.), *The effect of the infant on its caretaker* (pp. 49–76). New York: Wiley.

Breger, L. (1974). *From instinct to identity.* Englewood Cliffs, NJ: Prentice-Hall.

Bretherton, I., & Ainsworth, M. D. S. (1974). Responses of one-year-olds to a stranger in a strange situation. In M. Lewis & L. Rosenblum (Eds.), *The origins of fear* (pp. 131–164). New York: Wiley.

Bretherton, I., & Bates, E. (1985). The development of representation from 10 to 28 months: Differential stability of language and symbolic play. In R. Emde & R. Harmon (Eds.), *Continuities and discontinuities in development* (pp. 171–199). New York: Plenum.

Bridges, K. (1932). Emotional development in early infancy. *Child Development, 3,* 324–341.

Bridges, L., & Grolnick, W. (1995). The development of emotional self-regulation in infancy and early childhood. In N. Eisenberg (Ed.), *Social Development: Review of Child Development Research,* (Vol. 15, pp. 185–211). Thousand Oaks, CA: Sage.

Broberg, A., Lamb, M., & Hwang, P. (1990). Inhibition: Its stability and correlates in sixteen- to forty-month-old children. *Child Development, 61,* 1153–1163.

Brody, S., & Axelrod, S. (1970). *Anxiety and ego formation in infancy.* New York: International Universities Press.

Bronson, G., & Pankey, W. (1977). On the distinction between fear and wariness. *Child Development, 48,* 1167–1183.

Bronson, G. W. (1972). Infants' reactions to unfamiliar persons and novel objects. *Monographs of the Society for Research in Child Development, 32* (3, Serial No. 148).

Bronson, W. (1981). *Toddlers' behavior with agemates: Issues of interaction, cognition, and affect.* Norwood, NJ: Ablex.

Brownell, C., & Brown, E. (1985, April). *Age differences in possession negotiations during the second year.* Paper presented at the biennial meeting of the Society for Research in Child Development, Toronto.

Bruner, J. (1975). The ontogenesis of speech acts. *Journal of Child Language, 2,* 1–19.

Buhler, C. (1930). *The first year of life.* New York: Day.

Butterworth, G. E. (1991). The ontogeny and phylogeny of joint visual attention. In A. Whiten (Ed.), *Natural theories of mind* (pp. 223–232). Oxford: Basil Blackwell.

Campos, J. J., Barrett, K. C., Lamb, M. E., Goldsmith, H. H., & Stenberg, C. (1983). Socioemotional development. In P. H. Mussen (Ed.), *Handbook of child psychology* (4th ed., pp. 783–815). New York: Wiley.

Campos, J., Campos, R., & Barrett, K. (1989). Emergent themes in the study of emotional development and emotional regulation. *Developmental Psychology, 25,* 394–402.

Campos, J., Emde, R., & Gaensbauer, T. (1975). Cardiac and behavioral interrelationships in the reactions of infants to strangers. *Developmental Psychology, 11,* 589–601.

Camras, L., Holland, E., & Patterson, M. (1993). Facial expression. In M. Lewis & J. Haviland (Eds.), *Handbook of emotions* (pp. 199–208).

Cannon, W. (1927). The James–Lange theory of emotions: A critical examination and alternative theory. *American Journal of Psychology, 39,* 106–124.

Carlson, E. A., Jacobvitz, D., & Sroufe, L. A. (1995). A developmental investigation of inattentiveness and hyperactivity. *Child Development, 66,* 37–54.

Carlson, V., Cicchetti, D., Barrett, D., & Braunwald, K. (1989). Disorganized/disoriented attachment relationships in maltreated infants. *Developmental Psychology, 25,* 525–531.

Carr, S., Dabbs, J., & Carr, T. (1975). Mother–infant attachment: The importance of the mother's visual field. *Child Development, 46,* 331–338.

Chance, M. R. A. (1962). An interpretation of some agonistic postures: The role of "cut-off" acts and postures. *Symposia of the Zoological Society of London, 8,* 71–89.

Changeux, J. P., & Dehaene, S. (1989). Neuronal models of cognitive function. *Cognition, 33,* 63–109.

Charlesworth, W. (1969). The role of surprise in cognitive development. In D. Elkind & J. Flavell (Eds.), *Studies in cognitive development* (pp. 257–314). London: Oxford University Press.

Charlesworth, W. R., & Kreutzer, M. A. (1973). Facial expressions of infants and children. In P. Ekman (Ed.), *Darwin and facial expression* (pp. 91–168). New York: Academic.

Chazan, S. (1981). Development of object permanence as a correlate of dimensions of maternal care. *Developmental Psychology, 17,* 79–81.

Chevalier-Skolnikoff, S. (1973). Facial expression of emotion in nonhuman primates. In P. Ekman (Ed.), *Darwin and facial expression* (pp. 11–90). New York: Academic.

Chugani, H. T. (1994). Development of regional brain glucose metabolism in relation to behavior and plasticity. In G. Dawson & K. Fischer (Eds.), *Human behavior and the developing brain* (pp. 153–175). New York: Guilford.

Cicchetti, D., & Beeghly, M. (1990). *Down syndrome: A developmental perspective.* Cambridge University Press.

Cicchetti, D., & Hesse, P. (1983). Affect and intellect: Piaget's contributions to the study of infant emotional development. In R. Plutchik & H. Kellerman (Eds.), *Emotion: Theory, research and experience*: Vol. 2, *Emotion in early development* (pp. 115–170). New York: Academic.

Cicchetti, D., & Sroufe, L. A. (1976). The relationship between affective and cognitive development in Down's syndrome infants. *Child Development, 47,* 920–929.

Cicchetti, D., & Sroufe, L. A. (1978). An organizational view of affect: Illustration from the study of Down's syndrome infants. In M. Lewis & L. Rosenblum (Eds.), The development of affect (pp. 309–350). New York: Plenum.

Clemente, C., Purpura, D., & Mayer, F. (1972). *Maturation of brain mechanisms related to sleep behavior.* New York: Academic.

Clifford, C. (1984). A genetic and environmental analysis of a twin family study of alcohol use, anxiety, and depression. *Genetic Epidemiology, 1,* 63–79.

Cole, P., Barrett, K., & Zahn-Waxler, C. (1992). Emotion displays in two-year-olds during mishaps. *Child Development, 63,* 314–324.

Collins, P. F., & Depue, R. A. (1992). A neurobehavioral systems approach to developmental psychopathology: Implications for disorders of affect. In D. Cicchetti (Ed.), *Developmental perspectives on depression. Rochester Symposium on Developmental Psychopathology* (Vol. 4, pp. 29–101). Rochester, NY: University of Rochester Press.

Columbo, J. (1982). The critical period concept: Research, methodology, and theoretical issues. *Psychological Bulletin, 92,* 260–275.

Condon, W. S., & Sander, L. W. (1974). Neonate movement is synchronized with adult speech: Interactional participation and language acquisition. *Science, 183,* 99–101.

Crockenberg, S. (1981). Infant irritability, mother responsiveness, and social support influences on the security of infant–mother attachment. *Child Development, 52,* 857–865.

Darwin, C. (1859). *The origin of species.* London: Murray.

Darwin, C. (1872/1965). *Expression of emotions in man and animals.* London: Murray.

Dienstbier, R. (1984). The role of emotion in moral socialization. In C. Izard, J. Kagan, & R. Zajonc (Eds.), *Emotion, cognition, and behavior* (pp. 484–513). Cambridge University Press.

Dodge, K., & Somberg, D. (1987). Hostile attributional biases among aggressive boys are exacerbated under conditions of threats to the self. *Child Development, 58,* 213–224.

Doyle, A., Bowker, A., Hayvren, M., Sherman, L., Serbin, L., & Gold, D. (1985). Developmental changes in social and solitary pretend play during middle childhood. *Research Bulletins* (Vol. 12, pp. 1–42). Centre for Research in Human Development, Concordia University.

Dunn, J., & Munn, P. (1985). Becoming a family member: Family conflict and the development of social understanding in the second year. *Child Development, 56,* 480–492.

Edelman, G. (1987). *Neurodarwinism.* New York: Basic.

Edelman, G. (1992). *Bright air, brilliant fire.* New York: Basic.

Eder, R., & Mangelsdorf, S. (in press). The emotional basis of early personality development: Implications for the emergent self-concept. In S. Briggs, R. Hogan, & W. Jones (Eds.), *Handbook of personality psychology.* Orlando, FL: Academic.

Egeland, B., & Farber, E. (1984). Infant–mother attachment: Factors related to its development and changes over time. *Child Development, 55,* 753–771.

Egeland, B., Jacobvitz, D., & Sroufe, L. A. (1988). Breaking the cycle of abuse: Relationship predictions. *Child Development, 59,* 1080–1088.

Egeland, B., Kalkoske, M., Gottesman, N., & Erickson, M. (1990). Preschool behavior problems: Stability and factors accounting for change. *Journal of Child Psychology and Psychiatry, 31*, 891–909.

Egeland, B., Pianta, R., & O'Brien, M. (1993). Maternal intrusiveness in infancy and child maladaptation in the early school years. *Development and Psychopathology, 81*, 359–370.

Egeland, B., & Sroufe, L. A. (1981). Developmental sequelae of maltreatment in infancy. In D. Cicchetti & R. Rizley (Eds.), *Development approaches to child maltreatment: New directions for child development* (pp. 77–91). San Francisco: Jossey-Bass.

Eisenberg, N. (1989). *Empathy and related emotional responses: New directions for child development.* San Francisco: Jossey-Bass.

Ekman, P., & Friesen, W. V. (1971). Constants across cultures in the face and emotion. *Journal of Personality & Social Psychology, 17*, 124–129.

Ekman, P., & Friesen, W. (1975). *Unmasking the face.* Englewood Cliffs, NJ: Prentice-Hall.

Ekman, P., & Friesen, W. (1976). Measuring facial movement. *Journal of Environmental Psychology and Nonverbal Behavior, 1* (1), 56–75.

Ekman, P., & Friesen, W. (1990). The Duchenne's smile: Emotion expression and brain physiology. *Journal of Personality and Social Psychology, 58* (Pt. 2), 342–353.

Ekman, P., Friesen, W., & Simons, R. (1985). Is the startle reaction an emotion? *Journal of Personality and Social Psychology, 49*, 1416–1426.

Ekman, P., & Oster, H. (1979). Facial expression of emotions. *Annual Review of Psychology, 30*, 527–554.

Elicker, J., Englund, M., & Sroufe, L. A. (1992). Predicting peer competence and peer relationships in childhood from early parent–child relationships. In R. Parke & G. Ladd (Eds.), *Family–peer relationships: Modes of linkage* (pp. 77–106). Hillsdale, NJ: Erlbaum.

Emde, R. (1980). Toward a psychoanalytic theory of affect. Part 1. The organizational model and its propositions. In S. Greenspan & G. Pollock (Eds.), *The course of life: Psychoanalytic contributions toward understanding personality and development* (pp. 63–83). Adelphi, MD: Mental Health Study Center, NIMH.

Emde, R. (1992). Social referencing research: Uncertainty, self, and the search for meaning. In S. Feinman (Ed.), *Social referencing and the social construction of reality* (pp. 79–94). New York: Plenum.

Emde, R., Biringen, Z., Clyman, R., & Oppenheim, D. (1991). The moral self of infancy: Affective core and procedural knowledge. *Developmental Review, 11*, 251–270.

Emde, R., & Buchsbaum, H. (1990). "Didn't you hear my mommy?" Autonomy with connectedness in moral self-emergence. In D. Cicchetti & M. Beeghly (Eds.), *The self in transition* (pp. 35–60). Chicago: University of Chicago Press.

Emde, R. N., Campos, J. J., Reich, J., & Gaensbauer, T. S. (1978). Infant smiling at five and nine months: Analysis of heart rate and movement. *Infant Behavior and Development, 1*, 26–35.

Emde, R., Gaensbauer, T., & Harmon, R. (1976). Emotional expression in infancy: A biobehavioral study. *Psychological Issues Monograph Series, 10* (No. 37), 1–198.

Emde, R. N., Katz, E. L., & Thorpe, J. K. (1978). Emotional expression in infancy: Early deviations in Down syndrome. In M. Lewis & L. A. Rosenblum (Eds.), *The development of affect* (pp. 125–148). London: Plenum.

Emde, R., & Koenig, K. L. (1969). Neonatal smiling and rapid eye movement states. *American Academy of Child Psychiatry, 8*, 57–67.

Emde, R. N., McCartney, R. D., & Harmon, R. J. (1971). Neonatal smiling in REM states, Part 4. Premature study. *Child Development, 42,* 1657–1661.

Engel, G. (1971). Attachment behavior, object relations and the dynamic-economic points of view: Critical review of Bowlby's attachment and loss. *International Journal of Psycho-Analysis, 52,* 183–196.

Erickson, M., Egeland, B., & Sroufe, L. A. (1985). The relationship between quality of attachment and behavior problems in preschool in a high risk sample. In I. Bretherton & E. Waters (Eds.), *Growing points in attachment theory and research. Monographs of the Society for Research in Child Development* (Whole No. 209, 147–186).

Erikson, E. (1959). Identity and the life cycle: Selected papers. *Psychological Issues, 1,* 5–165.

Erikson, E. (1963). *Childhood and society* (2nd ed.). New York: Norton.

Escalona, S. (1968). *The roots of individuality.* Chicago: Aldine.

Feldman, S., & Ingham, M. (1975). Attachment behavior: A validation study in two age groups. *Child Development, 46,* 319–330.

Fenichel, O. (1945). *Psychoanalytic theory of neurosis.* New York: Norton.

Field, T. (1985). Attachment as psychobiological attunement: Being on the same wavelength. In M. Reite & T. Field (Eds.), *The psychobiology of attachment and separation* (pp. 415–454). Orlando, FL: Academic.

Field, T., & Fogel, A. (1982). *Emotion and early interaction.* Hillsdale, NJ: Erlbaum.

Fiske, S. (1982). Schema triggered affect: Applications to social perception. In M. Clark & S. Fiske (Eds.), *Affect and cognition: The 17th Annual Carnegie Symposium on Cognition* (pp. 55–78). Hillsdale, NJ: Erlbaum.

Fogel, A. (1982). Affect dynamics in early infancy: Affective tolerance. In T. Field & A. Fogel (Eds.), *Emotion and early interaction.* Hillsdale, NJ: Erlbaum.

Fogel, A. (1993). *Developing through relationships: Origins of communication, self, and culture.* Chicago, IL: University of Chicago Press.

Fogel, A., & Thelen, E. (1987). Development of early expressive and communicative action: Reinterpreting the evidence from a dynamic systems perspective. *Developmental Psychology, 23,* 747–761.

Fox, N. A., Kimmerly, N. L., & Schafer, W. D. (1991). Attachment to mother/attachment to father: A meta-analysis. *Developmental Psychology, 62,* 210–225.

Freedman, D. (1965). An ethological approach to the genetical study of human behavior. In S. Vandenberg (Ed.), *Methods and goals in human behavior genetics* (pp. 141–162). New York: Academic.

Freud, A., & Dann, S. (1951). An experiment in group upbringing. *Psychoanalytic Study of the Child, 6,* 127–168.

Frijda, N. H. (1988). The laws of emotion. *American Psychologist, 43,* 349–358.

Funkenstein, D. H., King, S. H., & Drolette, M. E. (1957). *Mastery of stress.* Cambridge, MA: Harvard University Press.

Gallup, G. G. (1977). Self-recognition in primates: A comparative approach to the bidirectional properties of consciousness. *American Psychologist, 32,* 329–338.

Garber, J., Cohen, E., Bacon, P., Egeland, B., & Sroufe, L. A. (1985, April). *Depression in preschoolers: Reliability and validity of a behavioral observation measure.* Paper presented at the meeting of the Society for Research in Child Development, Toronto.

Gellhorn, E. (1968). *Biological foundations of emotion.* Glenview, IL: Scott, Foresman.

Gewirtz, J. L. (1965). The course of infant smiling in four child-rearing environments in Israel. In B. M. Foss (Ed.), *Determinants of infant behavior* (Vol. 3, pp. 205–248). London: Methuen.

Gianino, A., & Tronick, E. Z. (1988). The mutual regulation model: The infants' self and interactive regulation and coping and defensive capacities. In T. M. Field, P. M. McCabe, & N. Schneiderman (Eds.), *Stress and coping across development* (pp. 47–68). Hillsdale, NJ: Erlbaum.

Glick, J. (1992). Werner's relevance for contemporary developmental psychology. *Developmental Psychology, 28,* 558–565.

Gottlieb, G. (1991). Experiential canalization of behavioral development: Theory. *Developmental Psychology, 27,* 4–13.

Goodenough, F. (1934). *Developmental psychology: An introduction to the study of human behavior* (2nd ed.). New York: Appleton-Century.

Gould, S. J. (1989). *Wonderful life: The Burgess shale and the nature of history.* New York: Norton.

Gove, L. (1983). *Patterns and organizations of behavior and affective expression during the second year of life.* Unpublished Ph.D. dissertation, University of Minnesota, Minneapolis, MN.

Graham, F. K., & Clifton, R. K. (1966). Heart-rate change as a component of the orienting response. *Psychological Bulletin, 65,* 305–320.

Greenough, W. T., & Black, J. E. (1992). Induction of brain structure by experience: Substates for cognitive development. In M. R. Gunnar & C. A. Nelson (Eds.), *Minnesota Symposia on Child Psychology: Vol. 24, Developmental behavioral neuroscience* (pp. 155–200). Hillsdale, NJ: Erlbaum.

Grossmann, K., Grossmann, K. E., Spanger, G., Suess, G., & Unzer, L. (1985). Maternal sensitivity and newborn orienting responses as related to quality of attachment in northern Germany. In I. Bretherton & E. Waters (Eds.), *Growing points in attachment theory and research. Monographs of the Society for Research in Child Development* (Whole No. 209, pp. 233–256).

Gunnar, M. (1991). The psychobiology of infant temperament. In J. Columbo & J. Fagan (Eds.), *Individual differences in infancy: Reliability, stability, and prediction* (pp. 387–409). Hillsdale, NJ: Erlbaum.

Gunnar, M. R., Leighton, K., & Peleaux, R. (1984). Effects of temporal predictability on the reactions of one-year-olds to potentially frightening toys. *Developmental Psychology, 120,* 449–458.

Gunnar, M., Mangelsdorf, S., Larson, M., & Hertsgaard, L. (1989). Attachment, temperament, and adrenocortical activity in infancy: A study of psychoendocrine regulation. *Developmental Psychology, 25,* 355–363.

Gunnar, M., & Stone, C. (1984). The effects of positive maternal affect on infant responses to pleasant, ambiguous, & fear-provoking toys. *Child Development, 55,* 1231–1236.

Hamburg, D. (1963). Emotions in the perspective of human evolution, In P. H. Knapp (Ed.), *Expression of emotions in man* (pp. 300–317). New York: International Universities Press.

Harlow, H. F. (1958). The nature of love. *American Psychologist, 13,* 673–685.

Harlow, H. F., & Harlow, M. K. (1966). Learning to love. *American Scientist, 54,* 244–272.

Harmon, R. J., & Emde, R. N. (1972). Spontaneous REM behaviors in a microcephalic infant. *Perceptual and Motor Skills, 34,* 827–833.

Hartup, W. (1963). Dependence and independence. In H. Stevenson (Ed.), *Child psychology: The 62nd yearbook of the National Society for the Study of Education* (pp. 333–363). Chicago: University of Chicago Press.

Haviland, J. (1975). Looking smart: The relationship between affect and intelligence in infancy. In M. Lewis (Ed.), *Origins of infant intelligence* (pp. 353–378). New York: Plenum.

Hayes, A. (1984). Interaction, engagement, and the origins of communication: Some constructive concerns. In L. Feagans, C. Garney, & R. Golinkoff (Eds.), *The origins and growth of communications* (pp. 136–161). Norwood, NJ: Ablex.

Hebb, D. (1946). On the nature of fear. *Psychological Review, 53,* 259–276.

Hebb. D. (1949). *The organization of behavior.* New York: Wiley.

Heinicke, C., & Westheimer, I. (1966). *Brief separations.* New York: International Universities Press.

Henderson, B., & Moore, S. (1980). Children's responses to objects differing in novelty in relation to level of curiosity and adult behavior. *Child Development, 51,* 457–465.

Hiatt, S., Campos, J., & Emde, R. (1979). Facial patterning and infant emotional expression: Happiness, surprise, and fear. *Child Development, 50,* 1020–1035.

Hiester, M. K. (1993). Generational boundary dissolution between mothers and children in early childhood and early adolescence: A longitudinal study. Unpublished doctoral dissertation, University of Minnesota.

Hofer, M. A. (1990). Early symbiotic processes: Hard evidence from a soft place. In R. A. Glick & S. Bone (Eds.), *Pleasure beyond the pleasure principle* (pp. 55–78). New Haven, CT: Yale University Press.

Hoffman, M. (1979). Development of moral thought, feeling, and behavior. *American Psychologist, 34,* 958–966.

Hoffman, M. (1985). Affect, cognition, and motivation. In R. Sorrento & E. T. Higgins (Eds.), *Handbook of motivation and cognition* (pp. 244–280). New York: Guilford.

Hornik, R., Risenhoover, N., & Gunnar, M. (1987). The effects of maternal positive, neutral, and negative affective communication on infant responses to new toys. *Child Development, 58,* 937–944.

Horowitz, M. J. (1987). *States of mind: Configurational analysis of individual psychology.* New York: Plenum Medical Book Company.

Huebner, R., & Izard, I. (1988). Mother's responses to infants' facial expressions of sadness, anger, and physical distress. *Motivation and Emotion, 12,* 185–196.

Isaacson, R. L. (1982). *The limbic system.* New York: Plenum.

Isabella, R. (1993). Origins of attachment: Maternal interactive behavior across the first year. *Child Development, 64,* 605–621.

Isabella, R. A., & Belsky, J. (1991). Interactional synchrony and the origins of infant–mother attachment: A replication study. *Child Development, 62,* 373–384.

Izard, C. (1977). *Human emotions.* New York: Plenum.

Izard, C. (1978). On the ontogenesis of emotions and emotion-cognition relationships in infancy. In M. Lewis & L. Rosenblum (Eds.), *The development of affect* (pp. 389–413). New York: Plenum.

Izard, C. (1990). Facial expressions and the regulation of emotion. *Journal of Personality and Social Psychology, 58,* 487–498.

Izard, C. E. (1991). *The psychology of emotions.* New York: Plenum Press.

Izard, C. E., Hembree, E. A., & Huebner, R. R. (1987). Infants' emotion expressions to acute pain: Developmental change and stability of individual differences. *Developmental Psychology, 23,* 105–113.

Izard, C., & Malatesta, C. (1987). Perspectives on emotional development: Part 1. Differential emotions theory of early emotional development. In J. Osofsky (Ed.), *Handbook of infant development* (2nd ed., pp. 494–554). New York: Wiley Interscience.

Jackson, E., Campos, J., & Fischer, K. (1978). The question of decalage between object permanence and person permanence. *Developmental Psychology, 14,* 1–10.

Jacobson, T., Edelstein, W., & Hofmann, V. (1994). A longitudinal study of the relationship between representations of attachment in childhood and cognitive functioning in childhood and adolescence. *Developmental Psychology, 30,* 112–124.

Jacobvitz, E., & Sroufe, L. A. (1987). The early caregiver–child relationship and attention deficit disorder with hyperactivity in kindergarten. *Child Development, 58,* 1488–1495.

James, W. (1890). *The principles of psychology.* New York: Holt.

Jones, S. S., Collins, K., & Hong, H.-W. (1991). An audience effect on smile production in 10-month-old infants. *Psychological Science, 2,* 45–49.

Kagan, J. (1967). On the need for relativism. *American Psychologist, 22,* 131–142.

Kagan, J. (1971). *Change and continuity in infancy.* New York: Wiley.

Kagan, J., Keasley, R. B., & Zelazo, P. R. (1978). *Infancy: Its place in human development.* Cambridge, MA: Harvard University Press.

Kagan, J., Reznick, J., & Gibbons, J. (1989). Inhibited and uninhibited types of children. *Child Development, 60,* 838–845.

Karmiloff-Smith, A. (1993). NeoPiagetians: A theoretical misnomer? *SRCD Newsletter* (Spring). Chicago: Society for Research in Child Development.

Kellerman, H. (1983). An epigenetic theory of emotions in early development. In R. Plutchik & H. Kellerman (Eds.), *Emotion: Theory, research, and experience* (pp. 315–349). New York: Academic.

Kelley, A. E., & Stinus, L. (1984). Neuroanatomical and neurochemical substrates of affective behavior. In N. A. Fox & R. J. Davidson (Eds.), *The psychobiology of affective development* (pp. 1–75). Hillsdale, NJ: Erlbaum.

Kestenbaum, R., Farber, E., & Sroufe, L. A. (1989). Individual differences in empathy among preschoolers: Concurrent and predictive validity. In N. Eisenberg (Ed.), *Empathy and related emotional responses: New directions for child development* (pp. 51–56). San Francisco: Jossey-Bass.

Kierkegaard, S. (1938). *Purity of heart is to will one thing* (Douglas V. Steer, Trans.). New York: Harper & Row.

Kiser, L., Bates, J., Maslin, C., & Bayles, K. (1986). Mother–infant play at six months as a predictor of attachment security at thirteen months. *Journal of the American Academy of Child Psychiatry, 25,* 68–75.

Kitchener, R. (1983). Developmental explanations. *Review of Metaphysics, 36,* 791–817.

Klaus, M., & Kennell, J. (1976). *Maternal–infant bonding.* St. Louis, MO: Mosby.

Kochanska, G. (1991). Socialization and temperament in the development of guilt and conscience. *Child Development, 62,* 1379–1392.

Kochanska, G. (1993). Toward a synthesis of parental socialization and child temperament in early development of conscience. *Child Development, 64,* 325–347.

Kopp, C. (1989). Regulation of distress and negative emotions: A developmental view. *Developmental Psychology, 25,* 343–354.

Kopp, C., Krakow, J., & Vaughn, B. (1983). The antecedents of self-regulation in young handicapped children. In M. Perlmutter (Ed.), *Minnesota Symposia on Child Psychology* (Vol. 17, pp. 93–128). Hillsdale, NJ: Erlbaum.

Korner, A. (1969). Neonatal startles, smiles, erections and reflex sucks as related to state, sex, and individuality. *Child Development, 40,* 1039–1053.

Korner, A. (1971). Individual differences at birth: Implications for early experience and later development. *American Journal of Orthopsychiatry, 41,* 608–619.

Korner, A., Brown, B., Dimiceli, S., Forest, T., Stevenson, D., Lane, N., Constantinou,

J., & Thom, V. (1989). Stable individual differences in developmentally changing preterm infants: A replicated study. *Child Development, 60,* 502–513.

Korner, A., Hutchinson, C., Kopershi, J., Kraemer, J., & Schneider, P. (1981). Stability of individual differences of neonatal motor and crying pattern. *Child Development, 52,* 83–90.

Korner, A. F., Brown, B. W., Dimiceli, S., Forrest, T., Stevenson, D. K., Lane, N. M., Constantinou, J., & Thom, V. A. (1989). Stable individual differences in developmentally changing preterm infants: A replicated study. *Child Development, 60,* 502–513.

Kraemer, G., Ebert, M., Schmidt, D., & McKinney, W. (1991). Strangers in a strange land: A psychobiological study of infant monkeys before and after separation from real or inanimate mothers. *Child Development, 62,* 548–566.

Kraemer, G. W. (1992). A psychobiological theory of attachment. *Behavioral and Brain Sciences, 15,* 493–541.

Kuczynski, L., & Kochanska, G. (1990). Children's noncompliance from toddlerhood to age five. *Developmental Psychology, 26,* 398–408.

Kuo, Z.-Y. (1967). *The dynamics of behavior development: An epigenetic view.* New York: Random House.

Lamb, M. E. (1981). The development of social expectations in the first year of life. In M. E. Lamb & L. R. Sherwood (Eds.), *Infant social cognition: Empirical and theoretical consequences* (pp. 155–175). Hillsdale, NJ: Erlbaum.

Lazarus, R. (1966). *Psychological stress and the coping process.* New York: McGraw-Hill.

Lazarus, R. (1991). *Emotion and adaptation.* New York: Oxford University Press.

Lenneberg, E. (1967). *Biological foundations of language.* New York: Wiley.

Levenson, R. (1988). Emotion and the autonomic nervous system: A prospectus for research on autonomic specificity. In H. Wagner (Ed.), *Social psychophysiology and emotion: Theory and clinical applications* (pp. 17–42). London: Wiley.

Lewis, M. (1992). The self in self-conscious emotions: Commentary on Stipek et al. *Monographs of the Society for Research in Child Development, 57* (Serial No. 226), 85–95.

Lewis, M., Alessandri, S., & Sullivan, M. (1992). Differences in shame and pride as a function of children's gender and task difficulty. *Child Development, 63,* 630–638.

Lewis, M., & Brooks-Gunn, J. (1979). *Social cognition and the acquisition of self.* New York: Plenum.

Lewis, M., & Goldberg, S. (1969). Perceptual-cognitive development in infancy: A generalized expectancy model as a function of mother–infant interaction. *Merrill-Palmer Quarterly, 15,* 81–100.

Lewis, M., & Michalson, L. (1983). *Children's emotions and moods: Developmental theory and measurements.* New York: Plenum.

Lewis, M., & Rosenblum, L. (Eds.). (1974). *The origins of fear: The origins of behavior, Vol. 2.* New York: Wiley.

Lichtenberg, J. D. (1989). *Psychoanalysis and motivation.* Hillsdale, NJ: Analytic Press.

Lieberman, A., Weston, D., & Pawl, J. (1991). Preventive intervention and outcome with anxiously attached dyads. *Child Development, 62,* 199–209.

Loevinger, J. (1976). *Ego development: Conceptions and theories.* San Francisco: Jossey-Bass.

Londerville, S., & Main, M. (1981). Security of attachment, compliance, and maternal training methods in the second year of life. *Developmental Psychology, 17,* 289–299.

Luria, A. R. (1980). *Higher cortical functions in man* (2nd ed.). New York: Basic.

Maccoby, E. (1980). *Social development.* New York: Harcourt, Brace, Jovanovich.

Maccoby, E., & Martin, J. (1983). Socialization in the context of the family. In E. M. Hetherington (Ed.), *Handbook of child psychology: Socialization, personality, and social development* (Vol. 4, pp. 1–101). New York: Wiley.

MacLean, P. D. (1973). *A triune concept of the brain and behavior.* Toronto: University of Toronto Press.

MacLean, P. D. (1993). Cerebral evolution of emotion. In M. Lewis & J. M. Haviland (Eds.), *Handbook of emotions* (pp. 67–86). New York: Guilford.

Magnussun, D. (1988). *Individual development from an interactional perspective.* Hillsdale, NJ: Erlbaum.

Magnusson, D., & Torestad, B. (1993). A holistic view of personality: A model revisited. *Annual Review of Psychology, 44,* 427–452.

Mahler, M., Pine, F., & Bergman, A. (1975). *The psychological birth of the human infant.* New York: Basic.

Main, M. (1977). Analysis of a peculiar form of reunion behavior seen in some daycare children: It's history and sequelae in children who are home-reared. In R. Webb (Ed.), *Social development in day care* (pp. 33–78). Baltimore: Johns Hopkins University Press.

Main, M., & Hesse, E. (1990). Parents' unresolved traumatic experiences are related to infant disorganized attachment status: Is frightened and/or frightening parental behavior the linking mechanism? In M. Greenberg, D. Cicchetti, & E. Cummings (Eds.), *Attachment in the preschool years* (pp. 161–182). Chicago: University of Chicago Press.

Main, M., & Weston, D. (1981). The quality of the toddler's relationship to mother and to father as related to conflict behavior and readiness to establish new relationships. *Child Development, 52,* 932–940.

Malatesta-Magai, C. (1991). Emotional socialization: Its role in personality and developmental psychopathology. In D. Cicchetti & S. Toth (Eds.), *Internalizing and externalizing expressions of dysfunction. Rochester Symposium on Developmental Psychopathology* (Vol. 2, pp. 203–224). Hillsdale, NJ: Erlbaum.

Mandler, G. (1975). *Mind and emotion.* New York: Wiley.

Mandler, G. (1984). *Mind and body: Psychology of emotion and stress.* New York: Norton.

Mangelsdorf, S., Gunnar, M., Kestenbaum, R., Lang, S., & Andreas, D. (1990). Infant proneness-to-distress temperament, maternal personality, and mother–infant attachment: Associations and goodness of fit. *Child Development, 61,* 820–831.

Mangelsdorf, S., Watkins, S., & Lehn, L. (1991, April). *The role of control in the infant's appraisal of strangers.* Paper present at the biennial meeting of the Society for Research in Child Development, Seattle.

Mans, L., Cicchetti, D., & Sroufe, L. A. (1978). Mirror reactions of Down syndrome infants and toddlers: Cognitive underpinnings of self-recognition. *Child Development, 49,* 1247–1250.

Masters, J., & Wellman, H. (1974). Human infant attachment: A procedural critique. *Psychological Bulletin, 81,* 218–237.

Matas, L., Arend, R., & Sroufe, L. A. (1978). Continuity of adaptation in the second year: The relationship between quality of attachment and later competence. *Child Development, 49,* 547–556.

Matheny, A. (1989). Children's behavioral inhibitions over age and across situations: Genetic similarity for a trait change. *Journal of Personality, 57,* 215–235.

Matsumoto, D. (1987). The role of facial response in the experience of emotion: More methodological problems and a meta-analysis. *Journal of Personality and Social Psychology, 52*, 769–774.

Mayes, L., & Zigler, E. (1992). An observational study of the affective concomitants of mastery in infants. *Journal of Child Psychology and Psychiatry and Allied Disciplines, 33*, 659–667.

McCall, R. (1972). Smiling and vocalization in infants as indices of perceptual-cognitive processes. *Merrill-Palmer Quarterly, 18*, 341–348.

McCall, R., & McGhee, P. (1977). The discrepancy hypothesis of attention and affect in infants. In I. Uzgiris & F. Weizman (Eds.), *The structuring of experience* (pp. 179–210). New York: Plenum.

Meili, R. (1955). Angstentsehung bei Kleinkindern. *Schweizerische Zeitschrift fur Psychologie und ihre Anwndungen, 14*, 195–212.

Motti, F., Cicchetti, D., & Sroufe, L. A. (1983). From infant affect expression to symbolic play: The coherence of development in Down syndrome infants. *Child Development, 54*, 1168–1175.

Murphy, L. (1962). *The widening of childhood: Paths toward mastery.* New York: Basic.

Murphy, L., & Moriarty, A. (1976). *Vulnerability, coping, and growth.* New Haven, CT: Yale University Press.

Nelson, C. A. (1994). The neural bases of infant temperament. In J. E. Bates & T. D. Wachs (Eds.), *Temperament: Individual differences at the interface of biology and behavior* (pp. 47–82). Washington, D.C.: APA Press.

Nelson, C. A. (in press). The ontogeny of human memory: A cognitive neuroscience perspective. *Developmental Psychology.*

Nelson, K., & Gruendel, J. (1981). Generalized event representation: Basic building blocks of cognitive development. In A. Brown & M. Lamb (Eds.), *Advances in developmental psychology* (Vol. 1, pp. 131–158). Hillsdale, NJ: Erlbaum.

Nezworski, M. T. (1983). *Continuity in adaptation into the fourth year: Individual differences in curiosity and exploratory behavior of preschool children.* Unpublished doctoral dissertation, University of Minnesota, Minneapolis.

Novak, M., O'Neill, P., Beckley, S., & Suomi, S. (1992). Naturalistic environments for captive primates. In E. Gibbons, E. Wyers, & E. Waters (Eds.), *Naturalistic habitats in captivity.* New York: Academic.

Osofsky, J. D., & Danzger, B. (1974). Relationships between neonatal characteristics and mother–infant interaction. *Developmental Psychology, 10*, 124–130.

Oster, H., & Ekman, P. (1978). Facial behavior in child development. In A. Collins (Ed.), *Minnesota Symposia on Child Development* (Vol. 11, pp. 231–276). Hillsdale, NJ: Erlbaum.

Oster, H., Hegley, D., & Nagel, L. (1992). Adult judgments and fine-grained analyses of infant facial expressions: Testing the validity of *a priori* coding formulas. *Developmental Psychology, 28*, 1115–1131.

Overton, W. F., & Reese, H. W. (1972). Models of development: Methodological implications. In J. R. Nesselroade and H. W. Reese (Eds.), *Life-span developmental psychology: Methodological issues* (pp. 65–86). New York: Academic.

Oyama, S. (1985). *The ontogeny of information.* Cambridge University Press.

Pancake, V. R. (1988). *Quality of attachment in infancy as a predictor of hostility and emotional distance in preschool peer relationships.* Unpublished doctoral dissertation, University of Minnesota, Minneapolis.

Papousek, H. (1977). The development of learning ability in infancy. In G. Nissen (Ed.), *Intelligence, learning, and learning disturbances* (pp. 131–162). New York: Springer-Verlag.

Papousek, H., & Papousek, M. (1977). Mothering and the cognitive headstart:

Psychobiological consideration. In H. R. Schaffer (Ed.), *Studies in mother–infant interactions* (pp. 215–245). London: Academic.

Papousek, M., Papousek, H., & Bornstein, M. (1985). The naturalistic vocal environment of young infants: On the significance of homogeneity and variability in parental speech. In T. Field & N. Fox (Eds.), *Social perception in infants* (pp. 82–105). New York: Academic.

Papousek, M., Papousek, H., & Harris, B. J. (1986). The emergence of play in parent–infant interactions. In D. Gorlitz & J. F. Wohlwill (Eds.), *Curiosity, imagination, and play: On the development of spontaneous cognitive and motivational processes* (pp. 214–246). Hillsale, NJ: Erlbaum.

Paradise, E., & Curcio, F. (1974). The relationship of cognitive and affective behaviors to fear of strangers in male infants. *Developmental Psychology, 10,* 476–483.

Parker, J., & Asher, S. (1987). Peer relations and later social adjustment. *Psychological Bulletin, 102,* 357–389.

Parmelee, A. (1972). Development of states in infants. In C. Clemente, D. Purpura, & F. Mayer (Eds.), *Maturation of brain mechanisms related to sleep behavior* (pp. 86–114). New York: Academic.

Parritz, R. (1989). *An examination of toddler coping in three challenging situations.* Unpublished doctoral dissertation, University of Minnesota.

Parrott, W. G., & Gleitman, H. (1989). Infants' expectations in play: The joy of peek-a-boo. *Cognition and Emotion, 3,* 291–311.

Pettit, G., & Bates, J. (1989). Family interaction patterns and children's behavior problems from infancy to 4 years. *Developmental Psychology, 25,* 413–420.

Pianta, R., Egeland, B., & Sroufe, L. A. (1989). Continuity and discontinuity in maternal sensitivity at 6, 24, and 42 months in a high-risk sample. *Child Development, 60,* 481–487.

Piaget, J. (1952). *The origins of intelligence in children.* New York: Routledge & Kagan Paul.

Piaget, J. (1962). *Play, dreams and imitation in childhood.* New York: Norton.

Piaget, J., & Inhelder, B. (1969). *The psychology of the child.* New York: Basic.

Plomin, R. (1990). *Nature and nurture: An introduction to human behavioral genetics.* Pacific Grove, CA: Brooks/Cole.

Plutchik, R. (1980). *Emotion: A psychoevolutionary synthesis.* New York: Harper & Row.

Plutchik, R. (1983). Emotions in early development: A psychoevolutionary approach. In R. Plutchik & H. Kellerman (Eds.), *Emotions: Theory, research, and experience* (pp. 221–257). New York: Academic.

Power, T., & Chapieski, M. (1986). Childrearing and impulse control in toddlers: A naturalistic investigation. *Developmental Psychology, 22,* 271–275.

Power, T., & Manire, S. (1992). Child rearing and internalization: A developmental perspective. In J. Janssens & J. Gerris (Eds.), *Child rearing: Influence on prosocial and moral development* (pp. 101–123). The Netherlands: Swets & Zeitlinger.

Prechtl, H. (1979). Qualitative changes of spontaneous movement in fetus and preterm infant are a marker of neurological dysfunction. *Early Human Development, 3,* 151–158.

Quinton, D., Rutter, M., & Liddle, C. (1984). Institutional rearing, parenting difficulties, and marital support. *Psychological Medicine, 14,* 107–124.

Rheingold, H. (1983). *Two-year-olds chart an optimistic future.* Paper presented at the Harvard Medical School Conference on Affective Development in Infancy, Boston.

Rheingold, H., & Eckerman, C. O. (1971). Departures from the mother. In H. R. Schaffer (Ed.), *The origins of human social relations* (pp. 186–223). New York: Academic.

Rheingold, H., & Eckerman, C. O. (1973). Fear of the stranger: A critical examination. In H. W. Reese (Ed.), *Advances in child development and behavior* (pp. 186–223). New York: Academic.

Robertson, J., & Robertson, J. (1971). Young children in brief separation: A fresh look. *Psychoanalytic Study of the Child, 26*, 264–315.

Robson, K. S. (1967). The role of eye-to-eye contact in maternal–infant attachment. *Journal of Child Psychology and Psychiatry, 8*, 13–25.

Rode, S., Chang, P., Fisch, R., & Sroufe, L. A. (1981). Attachment patterns of infants separated at birth. *Developmental Psychology, 17*, 188–191.

Rosen, N. (1989). *John and Anzia: An American romance.* New York: Dutton.

Rosenberg, D. (1984). *The quality and content of preschool fantasy play: Correlates in concurrent social-personality function and early mother–child attachment relationships.* Unpublished doctoral dissertation, University of Minnesota.

Rosenblum, L. A. (1987). Influences of environmental demand on maternal behavior and infant development. In N. A. Krasnegor, E. M. Blass, M. A. Hofer, & W. P. Smotherman (Eds.), *Perinatal development: A psychobiological perspective* (pp. 377–395). Orlando, FL: Academic.

Rothbart, M. (1989). Temperament in childhood: A framework. In G. Kohnstamm, J. Bates, and M. Rothbart (Eds.), *Temperament in childhood* (pp. 59–73). New York: Wiley.

Rothbart, M. K. (1973). Laughter in young children. *Psychological Bulletin, 80*, 247–256.

Rovee-Collier, C. (1989). The joy of kicking: Memories, motives, and mobiles. In P. Solomon, G. Goethals, C. Kelley, & B. Stephens (Eds.), *Memory: Interdisciplinary approaches* (pp. 151–180). New York: Springer-Verlag.

Salzen, E. A. (1963). Visual stimuli eliciting the smiling response in the human infant. *Journal of Genetic Psychology, 102*, 51–54.

Sameroff, A. J. (1983). Developmental systems: Context and evolution. In P. H. Mussen (Ed.), *Handbook of Child Psychology: Vol. 1. History, theory, and methods* (4th ed., pp. 237–294). New York: Wiley.

Sameroff, A. J., & Cavanaugh, P. J. (1979). Learning in infancy: A developmental perspective. In J. Osofsky (Ed.), *The handbook of infant development* (pp. 344-392). New York: Wiley.

Sander, L. (1975). Infant and caretaking environment. In E. J. Anthony (Ed.), *Explorations in child psychiatry* (pp. 129–165). New York: Plenum.

Sander, L. (1976). Epilogue. In E. Rexford, L. Sander, & T. Shapiro (Eds.), *Infant Psychiatry* (pp. 286–292). New Haven, CN: Yale University Press.

Sander, L. (in press). Recognition process: Organization and specificity in early development. In J. Osofsky (Ed.), *The handbook of infant development.* New York: Wiley.

Santostefano, S. (1978). *A biodevelopmental approach to clinical child psychology.* New York: Wiley.

Scarr, S., & Salapatek, P. (1970). Patterns of fear development during infancy. *Merrill-Palmer Quarterly, 16*, 53–90.

Schacter, S. (1966). The interaction of cognitive and physiological determinants of emotional state. In C. Spielberger (Ed.), *Anxiety and Behavior* (pp. 193–224). New York: Academic.

Schaffer, H., & Callender, M. (1959). Psychological effects of hospitalization in infancy. *Pediatrics, 24*, 528–539.

Schaffer, H., Greenwood, A., & Parry, M. (1972). The onset of wariness. *Child Development, 43*, 165–175.

Schaffer, H. R. (1974). Cognitive components of the infant's response to strangeness. In M. Lewis & L. A. Rosenblum (Eds.), *The origins of fear: The origins of behavior* (Vol. 2, pp. 11–24). New York: Wiley.

Schaffer, H. R., & Emerson, P. E. (1964). The development of social attachments in infancy. *Monographs of the Society for Research in Child Development, 29* (Serial No. 94).

Schore, A. N. (1994). *Affect regulation and the origin of the self: The neurobiology of emotional development.* Hillsdale, NJ: Erlbaum.

Schwartz, A., Campos, J., & Baisel, E. (1973). The visual cliff: Cardiac and behavioral correlates on the deep and shallow sides at five and nine months of age. *Journal of Experimental Child Psychology, 15,* 85–99.

Sears, R., Maccoby, E., & Levin, H. (1957). *Patterns of child rearing.* Evanston, IL: Row, Peterson.

Shultz, T. R., & Zigler, E. (1970). Emotional concomitants of visual mastery in infants: The effects of stimulus movement on smiling and vocalizing. *Journal of Experimental Child Psychology, 10,* 390–402.

Singer, L., Brodzinsky, D., Ramsay, D., Steir, M., & Waters, E. (1985). Mother–infant attachment in adoptive families. *Child Development, 56,* 1543–1551.

Skarin, K. (1977). Cognitive and contextual determinants of stranger fear in 6 and 11 month old infants. *Child Development, 48,* 537–544.

Sokolov, E. N. (1963). *Perception and the conditioned reflex.* New York: Macmillan.

Sorce, J., & Emde, R. (1981). Mother's presence is not enough: The effect of emotional availability on infant exploration and play. *Developmental Psychology, 17,* 737–745.

Sorce, J. F., Emde, R. N., Campos, J. J., & Klinnert, M. D. (1985). Maternal emotional signaling: Its effect on the visual cliff behavior of one-year-olds. *Developmental Psychology, 21,* 195–200.

Spiker, D. (1990). Early intervention from a developmental perspective. In D. Cicchetti & M. Beeghly (Eds.), *Children with Down syndrome* (pp. 424–448). Cambridge University Press.

Spiker, D., Ferguson, J., & Brooks-Gunn, J. (1993). Enhancing maternal interactive behavior and child social competence in low birth weight, premature infants. *Child Development, 64,* 754–768.

Spitz, R. (1957). *No and yes.* New York: International Universities Press.

Spitz, R. (1965). *The first year of life.* New York: International Universities Press.

Spitz, R. A., Emde, R. N., & Metcalf, D. R. (1970). Further prototypes of ego formation: A working paper from a research project on early development. *Psychoanalytic Study of the Child, 25,* 417–441.

Sroufe, J. (1991). Assessment of parent–adolescent relationships: Implications for adolescent development. *Journal of Family Psychology, 5,* 21–45.

Sroufe, L. A. (1977). Wariness of strangers and the study of infant development. *Child Development, 48,* 731–746.

Sroufe, L. A. (1979a). Socioemotional development. In J. Osofsky (Ed.), *Handbook of infant development* (pp. 462–516). New York: Wiley.

Sroufe, L. A. (1979b). The coherence of individual development. *American Psychologist, 34,* 834–841.

Sroufe, L. A. (1982). The organization of emotional development. *Psychoanalytic Inquiry, 1,* 575–599.

Sroufe, L. A. (1983). Infant–caregiver attachment and patterns of adaptation and competence in the preschool. In M. Perlmutter (Ed.), *Minnesota Symposia in Child Psychology* (Vol. 16, pp. 41–83). Hillsdale, NJ: Erlbaum.

Sroufe, L. A. (1984). The organization of emotional development. In K. Scherer & P. Ekman (Eds.), *Approaches to emotion* (pp. 109–128). Hillsdale, NJ: Erlbaum.

Sroufe, L. A. (1985). Attachment classification from the perspective of infant–caregiver relationships and infant temperament. *Child Development, 56,* 1–14.

Sroufe, L. A. (1988). The role of infant–caregiver attachment in development. In J. Belsky & T. Nezworski (Eds.), *Clinical implications of attachment* (pp. 18–38). Hillsdale, NJ: Erlbaum.

Sroufe, L. A. (1989). Pathways to adaptation and maladaptation: Psychopathology as developmental deviation. In D. Cicchetti (Ed.), *Rochester Symposia on Developmental Psychopathology* (Vol. 1, pp. 13–14). Hillsdale, NJ: Erlbaum.

Sroufe, L. A. (1990). An organizational perspective on the self. In D. Cicchetti & M. Beeghly (Eds.), *Transitions from infancy to childhood: The self* (pp. 281–307). Chicago: University of Chicago Press.

Sroufe, L. A. (1991). Considering normal and abnormal together: The essense of developmental psychopathology. *Development and psychopathology, 2,* 335–347.

Sroufe, L. A., Carlson, E., & Shulman, S. (1993). Individuals in relationships: Development from infancy through adolescence. In D. C. Funder, R. D. Parke, C. Tomlinson-Keasey, & K. Widaman (Eds.), *Studying lives through time: Personality and development* (pp. 315–342). Washington, D.C.: American Psychological Association.

Sroufe, L. A., Cooper, R., & DeHart, G. (in press). *Child Development: Its nature and course* (3rd ed.). New York: McGraw-Hill.

Sroufe, L. A., Egeland, B., & Kreutzer, T. (1990). The fate of early experience following developmental change: Longitudinal approaches to individual adaptation in childhood. *Child Development, 61,* 1363–1373.

Sroufe, L. A., & Fleeson, J. (1986). Attachment and the construction of relationships. In W. Hartup & Z. Rubin (Eds.), *Relationships and development* (pp. 51–71). Hillsdale, NJ: Erlbaum.

Sroufe, L. A., & Fleeson, J. (1988). The coherence of family relationships. In R. A. Hinde & J. Stevenson-Hinde (Eds.), *Relationships within families: Mutual influences* (pp. 27–47). Oxford University Press.

Sroufe, L. A., Fox, N., & Pancake, V. (1983). Attachment and dependency in developmental perspective. *Child Development, 54,* 1615–1627.

Sroufe, L. A., Schork, E., Motti, F., Lawroski, N., & LaFrenier, P. (1984). The role of affect in social competence. In C. Izard, J. Kagan, & R. Zajonc (Eds.), *Emotions, cognition, and behavior* (pp. 289–319). Oxford University Press.

Sroufe, L. A., & Waters, E. (1976). The ontogenesis of smiling and laughter: A perspective on the organization of development in infancy. *Psychological Review, 83,* 173–189.

Sroufe, L. A., & Waters, E. (1977a). Attachment as an organizational construct. *Child Development, 48,* 1184–1199.

Sroufe, L. A., & Waters, E. (1977b). Heart rate as a convergent measure in clinical and developmental research. *Merrill-Palmer Quarterly, 23,* 3–27.

Sroufe, L. A., Waters, E., & Matas, L. (1974). Contextual determinants of infant affective response. In M. Lewis & L. Rosenblum (Eds.), *The origins of behavior: Vol. 2, Fear* (pp. 49–72). New York: Wiley.

Sroufe, L. A., & Wunsch, J. P. (1972). The development of laughter in the first year of life. *Child Development, 43,* 1326–1344.

Stechler, G., & Carpenter, G. (1967). A viewpoint on early affective development. In J. Hellmuth (Ed.), *The exceptional infant* (Vol. 1, pp. 163–190). Seattle: Special Child Publications.

Stechler, G., & Latz, E. (1966). Some observations on attention and arousal in the human infant. *Journal of the American Academy of Child Psychiatry, 5,* 517–525.

Stern, D. (1974). The goal and structure of mother–infant play. *Journal of the American Academy of Child Psychiatry, 13,* 402–421.

Stern, D. (1985). *The interpersonal world of the infant: A view from psychoanalysis and developmental psychology.* New York: Basic.

Stern, D. N. (1990). Joy and satisfaction in infancy. In R. A. Glick & S. Bone (Eds.), *Pleasure beyond the pleasure principle* (pp. 13–25). New Haven, CN: Yale University Press.

Stipek, D., Recchia, S., & McClintic, S. (1992). Self-evaluation in young children. *Monographs of the Society for Research in Child Development, 57* (Serial No. 226).

Stirnimann, F. (1940). *Psychologie des neugebornen Kindes.* Munich: Kindler Verlag.

Suess, G., Grossmann, K. E., & Sroufe, L. A. (1992). Effects of infant attachment to mother and father on quality of adaptation in preschool: From dyadic to individual organization of the self. *International Journal of Behavioral Development, 15,* 43–66.

Takahashi, M. (1973). Smiling responses in newborn infants: Relations to arousal level, spontaneous movements, and the tactile stimulus. *Japanese Journal of Psychology, 44,* 46–50.

Tennes, K., Emde, R., Kisley, A., & Metcalf, D. (1972). The stimulus barrier in early infancy: An exploration of some of the formulations of John Benjamin. In R. Holt & E. Peterfreund (Eds.), *Psychoanalysis and contemporary science* (pp. 206–234). New York: Macmillan.

Termine, N. T., & Izard, C. E. (1988). Infants' responses to their mothers' expressions of joy and sadness. *Developmental Psychology, 24,* 223–229.

Thelen, E. (1989). Self-organization in developmental processes: Can a systems approach work? In M. Gunnar & Thelen (Eds.), *Systems and development. Minnesota Symposia in Child Psychology* (Vol. 22, pp. 77–117). Hillsdale, NJ: Erlbaum.

Thompson, R. A. (1990). Emotion and self-regulation. *Nebraska Symposium on Motivation* (pp. 367–467).

Tinbergen, N. (1951). *The study of instinct.* London: Oxford University Press.

Tomkins, S. (1962). *Affect, imagery, and consciousness* (Vol. 1). New York: Springer.

Tomkins, S. (1963). *Affect, imagery, and consciousness: Vol. 2. The negative affects.* New York: Springer.

Tomkins, S. (1981). The quest for primary motives: Biography and autobiography of an idea. *Journal of Personality and Social Psychology, 41,* 306–329.

Tracy, R., Lamb, M., & Ainsworth, M. D. S. (1976). Infant approach behavior as related to attachment. *Child Development, 47,* 571–578.

Trevarthen, C. (1990). Growth and education of the hemispheres. In C. Trevarthen (Ed.), *Brain circuits and functions of the mind* (pp. 334–363). Cambridge University Press.

Tronick, E. (1989). Emotions and emotional communication in infants. *American Psychologist, 44,* 112–119.

Tronick, E., Als, H., Adamson, L., Wise, S., & Brazelton, T. B. (1978). The infant's response to entrapment between contradictory messages in face-to-face interaction. *Journal of the American Academy of Child Psychiatry, 17,* 1–13.

Troy, M., & Sroufe, L. A. (1987). Victimization among preschoolers: Role of attachment relationship history. *Journal of the American Academy of Child and Adolescent Psychiatry, 26,* 166–172.

Tucker, D. M. (1992). Developing emotions and cortical networks. In M. R. Gunnar & C. A. Nelson (Eds.), *Minnesota Symposia on Child Psychology: Vol. 24, Developmental behavioral neuroscience* (pp. 75–128). Hillsdale NJ: Erlbaum.

Turkewitz, G. (1987). Psychobiology and developmental psychology: The influence of T. C. Schneirla on human developmental psychology. *Developmental Psychobiology, 20,* 369–375.

Urban, J., Carlson, E., Egeland, B., & Sroufe, L. A. (1991). Patterns of individual adaptation across childhood. *Development and Psychopathology, 3,* 445–460.

van den Boom, D. (in press). Two-year outcome of an experimental manipulation of sensitive responsiveness among lower class mothers with irritable infants. *Child Development.*

van Hooff, J. A. R. A. M. (1972). A comparative approach to the phylogeny of laughter and smiling. In R. Hinde (Ed.), *Non-verbal communication* (pp. 207–241). Cambridge University Press.

van Lieshout, C. (1975). Young children's reactions to barriers placed by their mothers. *Child Development, 46,* 879–886.

Vaughn, B. (1977). *The development of greeting behavior in infants from 6 to 12 months of age.* Unpublished doctoral dissertation, University of Minnesota.

Vaughn, B., Egeland, B., Waters, E., & Sroufe, L. A. (1979). Individual differences in infant–mother attachment at 12 and 18 months: Stability and change in families under stress. *Child Development, 50,* 971–975.

Vaughn, B., Lefever, G., Seifer, R., & Barglow, P. (1989). Attachment behavior, attachment security, and temperament during infancy. *Child Development, 60,* 728–737.

Vaughn, B., & Sroufe, L. A. (1979). The temporal relationship between infant HR acceleration and crying in an aversive situation. *Child Development, 50,* 565–567.

Vaughn, B., Stevenson-Hinde, J., Waters, E., Kotsaftis, A., Lefever, G., Shouldice, A., Trudel, M., & Belsky, J. (1992). Attachment security and temperament in infancy and early childhood: Some conceptual clarifications. *Developmental Psychology, 28,* 463–473.

Vine, I. (1973). The role of facial visual signalling in early social development. In M. von Cranach & I. Vine (Eds.), *Social communication and movement: Studies of men and chimpanzees* (pp. 195–297). London: Academic.

Vygotsky, L. (1962). *Thought and language.* Cambridge, MA: MIT Press.

Vygotsky, L. (1978). *Mind and society.* Cambridge, MA: Harvard University Press.

Waddington, C. (1957). *The strategy of the genes.* London: Allen & Unwin.

Wahler, R. (1967). Infant social attachments: A reinforcement theory interpretation and investigation. *Child Development, 38,* 1074–1088.

Waldrop, W. M. (1992). *Complexity.* New York: Simon & Schuster.

Ward, M., Carlson, E., Altman, S., Levine, L., Greenberg, R., & Kessler, D. (1990, April). *Predicting infant–mother attachment from adolescents' prenatal working models of relationships.* Paper presented at the International Conference on Infant Studies, Montreal.

Waters, E. (1978). The stability of individual differences in infant–mother attachment. *Child Development, 49,* 483–494.

Waters, E., Kondo-Ikemura, K., & Richters, J. (1990). Learning to love: Milestones and mechanisms in attachment, identity and identification. In M. Gunnar & L. A. Sroufe (Eds.), *Minnesota Symposia in Child Psychology: Vol. 23. Self-processes in development.* Hillsdale, NJ: Erlbaum.

Waters, E., Matas, L., & Sroufe, L. A. (1975). Infants' reactions to an approaching stranger: Description, validation and functional significance of wariness. *Child Development, 46,* 348–365.

Waters, E., & Sroufe, L. A. (1983). A developmental perspective on competence. *Developmental Review, 3,* 79–97.

Waters, E., Wippman, J., & Sroufe, L. A. (1979). Attachment, positive affect, and competence in the peer group: Two studies in construct validation. *Child Development, 50,* 821–829.

Watson, J. B. (1924/1970). *Behaviorism.* New York: Norton.

Watson, J. S. (1972). Smiling, cooing, and "the game." *Merrill-Palmer Quarterly, 18,* 323–340.

Weinraub, M., & Lewis, M. (1977). The determinants of children's responses to separation. *Monographs of the Society for Research in Child Development, 42* (Serial No. 172).

Wenar, C. (1976). Executive competence in toddlers: A prospective, observational study. *Genetic Psychology Monographs, 93,* 189–285.

Werner, H., & Kaplan, B. (1963). *Symbol formation: An organismic-developmental approach to language and the expression of thought.* New York: Wiley.

Wertsch, J. (1979). From social interaction to higher psychological processes: A clarification of Vygotsky's theory. *Human Development, 22,* 1–22.

White, R. (1959). Motivation reconsidered: The concept of competence. *Psychological Review, 66,* 297–333.

Wolf, D. (1982). Understanding others: A longitudinal case study of the concept of independent agency. In G. Furman (Ed.), *Action and thought* (pp. 297–327). New York: Academic.

Wolf, D. (1990). Being of several minds: Voices and versions of the self in early childhood. In D. Cicchetti & M. Beeghly (Eds.), *The self in transition* (pp. 183–212). Chicago: University of Chicago Press.

Wolff, P. (1963). Observations on the early development of smiling. In B. M. Foss (Ed.), *Determinants of infant behavior* (Vol. 2). London: Methuen.

Wolff, P. (1969). Crying and vocalization in early infancy. In B. M. Foss (Ed.), *Determinants of infant behavior* (Vol. 4, pp. 81–110). New York: Wiley.

Yarrow, L., Rubenstein, J., & Pederson, F. (1975). *Infant and environment.* New York: Halsted.

Yonas, A. (1981). Infants' responses to optical information for collision. In R. Aslin & L. Pettersen (Eds.), *Development of perception: Psychobiological perspectives* (Vol. 2, pp. 313–334). New York: Academic.

Yonas, A., Cleaves, W., & Petterson, L. (1978). Development of sensitivity to pictorial depth. *Science, 200,* 77–79.

Younger, B. A., & Cohen, L. B. (1985). How infants form categories. In G. Bower (Ed.), *The psychology of learning and motivation: Advances in research and theory* (pp. 112–143). New York: Academic.

Zahn-Waxler, C., Radke-Yarrow, M., & King, R. (1979). Childrearing and children's prosocial initiations toward victims of distress. *Child Development, 50,* 319–330.

Zahn-Waxler, C., Radke-Yarrow, M., Wagner, E., & Chapman, M. (1992). Development of concern for others. *Developmental Psychology, 28,* 126–136.

Zajonc, R. (1984). On the primacy of affect. *American Psychologist, 39,* 117–123.

Zaslow, R. W., & Breger, L. (1969). A theory and treatment of autism. In L. Breger (Ed.), *Clinical-cognitive psychology models and integrations* (pp. 98–134). Englewood Cliffs, NJ: Prentice-Hall.

Zelazo, P. R. (1971). Smiling to social stimuli: Eliciting and conditioning effects. *Developmental Psychology, 4,* 32–42.

Zelazo, P. R. (1972). Smiling and vocalizing: A cognitive emphasis. *Merrill-Palmer Quarterly, 18,* 349–365.

Zelazo, P. R., & Komer, M. J. (1971). Infant smiling to nonsocial stimuli and the recognition hypothesis. *Child Development, 42,* 1327–1339.

Index